Also by Anthony G. Picciano

Online Education: Foundations, Planning, and Pedagogy

Online education policy and practice: The past, present, and future of the digital university.

Educational Leadership and Planning for Technology

Data-Driven Decision Making for Effective School Leadership

Distance Learning: Making Connections across Virtual Space and Time

Educational Research Primer

Computers in the Schools: A Guide to Planning and Administration

The Great American Education-Industrial Complex: Ideology, Technology and Profits with Joel Spring.

Blended Learning Research Perspectives; Volumes 1, 2, and 3 with Charles Dziuban, Charles Graham, and Patsy Moskal.

The community college in the post-recession reform era: Aims and outcomes of a decade of experimentation with Chet Jordan.

CUNY's first fifty years: Triumphs and ordeals of a people's university with Chet Jordan.

The Bathtub Wasn't in the Kitchen Anymore (Novel by Gerade DeMichele)

For further information please visit anthonypicciano.com

THE COMPUTER
WASN'T IN THE BASEMENT
ANYMORE

My Fifty + Years in Education Technology (1970-2021)

ANTHONY G. PICCIANO

EDITED BY ELAINE BOWDEN

To students and colleagues who blessed my fifty years of learning, teaching, and administering!

"The computer is the most extraordinary of man's technological clothing; it's an extension of our central nervous system. Beside it, the wheel is a mere hula-hoop."

- Marshall McLuhan

INTRODUCTION

O n and off from 2015 through 2019, I wrote a coming-of-age novel and memoir entitled, *Our Bathtub Wasn't in the Kitchen Anymore.* This book, that took place in the South Bronx, spanned the 1950s and 1960s and followed one life's journey from toddler to adulthood. The protagonist's adventures were based on my experiences as I navigated friendships, education, and the twists and turns of growing up in a small Italian neighborhood. *Our Bathtub...* also explored the stories of families, some having lived in our enclave for generations before being forced to abandon the neighborhood as it underwent societal upheaval. The only bathtub in our apartment, as was true for the many families that lived in the old neighborhoods of the South Bronx, was in the kitchen. When we were forced to move, my parents bought a small, attached home in the North Bronx that had two bathrooms, one of which had all of the modern conveniences including a bathtub and shower. That move and the nature of our bath facilities were symbols of my journey through the first twenty years of my life, as I experienced new friends, places, and institutions. As my values changed, I came to realize that there is a time and place for everything and that one, hopefully, adapts and grows.

In April 2020, when my novel was published, I sent copies to several colleagues of mine including Charles Graham, a professor at Brigham Young University. Charles and I had co-authored three academic books together and we had become good friends. Charles' background growing up in Utah in a devout Mormon family, was quite different from mine, as I had grown up among Italian Catholics in the South Bronx. He read the novel and sent me this email:

"I found myself wishing that you hadn't ended where you did. Because the Vietnam War seemed to be such an important part of your learning and struggle with the truth around you...I was also hoping to find out how you chose to move into educational technology and ultimately online/blended learning and become a player in that domain. *Volume 2: The Computer Wasn't in the Library Anymore*." (Graham., May 20, 2020)

So here it is, Charles.

After I graduated Cardinal Spellman High School in 1965, I enrolled as a night student at Hunter College in the Bronx where I eventually majored in political science and minored in history. For two years, I worked during the day at Federation Bank & Trust Company until 1967. I decided to attend college full-time and took on a number of new jobs including ironworker in the summers and piece work in my father's warehouse (4 cents apiece wrapping brass plaques and other merchandize in small packages). At the college, I worked in the library, in the SEEK (Search for Education, Elevation and Knowledge) Program as a tutor, in the business office, and in the computer center. The ironworker pay was excellent, but it was dangerous and hard working on open thirty-story buildings. Piece work was the most boring job I ever had and I couldn't wait to get away from it. I enjoyed working in the library as I came to understand a lot about how to conduct research while in the stacks. It also cemented my lifelong love of reading. Working as a tutor gave me a genuine appreciation for the failures of our society in educating black and Latino/Latina students. The SEEK program gave them a chance at a college education and also gave them the advisement, counseling and tutoring services they needed to succeed. In the business office I met a number of good people, including Gerald Mermelstein, Dan Laura, and Tom Moore, who helped me advance very early on in my career.

It was my work at Federation Bank & Trust Company, when I was still a part-time student, that introduced me to computer technology. I was a teller in June of 1966, when I was called to the Personnel Office and asked if I would be part of group helping the bank convert to a new IBM computer system. Banks were among the first commercial users of computing technology and at the time, there was no such thing as a major in computer science. I agreed to join the group and while training at IBM, I learned a lot about digital technology. There was hardware (central processing unit, input devices, output devices, and storage devices) and software (the programs of instructions that directed the hardware). I also learned about database file systems and organization. I wrote a couple of small programs, but I was in no way a programmer. I did, however, easily understand all of the concepts being introduced to me. Later on, when I was working in the college business office as a student aide, one of my supervisors recommended that I work part-time at the new computer center just being organized. The computer center was a small operation with four full-time people (director, programmer, operations supervisor, and data entry supervisor). I enjoyed the work and learned a good deal in a relatively short period of time, including the basics of computer programming.

My first fulltime university position was as a laboratory technician in the computer center of Herbert Lehman College, a recently founded institution of higher learning in the Bronx that was formerly Hunter College's Bronx Campus. My appointment started on January 1, 1970 and that day was the beginning of fifty plus years at six public colleges in the City University and State University of New York. I went on to hold positions as computer programmer, director, dean and senior vice president as well as adjunct instructor, professor and executive officer of a PhD program in urban education. In each of these positions, education technology played a part in much of what I did. In many ways, it helped shaped me professionally as I came to learn the importance of change and the ability to adjust to new situations and face new challenges. The adage 'the more something changes, the more it remains the same" is partly true; you change while a part of you remains. As I write this in the early part of 2020, I am a professor at Hunter College teaching in the graduate programs in the school of education, where a few months ago all of the courses were abruptly moved to fully online delivery, as New York City and the rest of the world began to battle the scourge which was the coronavirus pandemic as it infected tens of millions of people and killed millions.

Between 1970 and 2021, I worked within all types of digital environments from plug board computers to large mainframes, to emerging PCs, to the Internet, and to the latest iPhones and handheld devices. I have come to see that these fifty plus years weren't just about technology but about how events in the larger institutions with which I was affiliated as well as the broader society were integrated into a complex web of interactions that shaped and molded everything. They drove each other and I wanted to understand them all.

My purpose in writing *The Computer Wasn't in the Basement Anymore..* is to share my insights, gained from my experience of fifty plus years, all of which involved some aspect of education technology, and included administrative, instructional and research activities. The title reflects how computer technology, once relegated to out of the way places such as basements, has blossomed with the ubiquity of the Internet, social networking, and smartphones. Computers are now everywhere in every room of every home, office, restaurant, industry, store, school, college, and in our pockets. This book, unlike *Our Bathtub Wasn't in the Kitchen Anymore*, is a true recounting of my part of the story. The names haven't been changed to protect the innocent.

CONTENTS

PART I

Herbert H. Lehman College
The Bronx, New York
1970-1975

1

I n 1968, Hunter College in the Bronx was separated from Hunter College and renamed Herbert H. Lehman College, giving the borough its first independent public senior college. The campus was built in 1937 on thirty acres of land next to the Jerome Park Reservoir in the North Bronx and had served as a naval training ground for WAVES (Women Accepted for Voluntary Emergency Services) during World War II. The first meeting of the United Nations Security Council was held in its gymnasium in 1946. Under the leadership of Lehman's first president, Leonard Lief, the college retained most of the academic programs it had inherited from Hunter College. Faculty were given the option of remaining at Hunter College or switching to Lehman while retaining all seniority rights. Many of the Hunter faculty decided to be a part of the new college. By 1970, when I joined the staff, Lehman College had an overall enrollment approaching 12,000 students (headcount) in undergraduate and graduate master's programs.

The Lehman College computer center was located in a temporary building made of prefabricated metal that overlooked the reservoir. The "Quonset-hut" was a one-story structure that housed the business office, admissions, the graduate registrar's office, the SEEK administrative offices, and the computer center. Bob Attianese, who had been a programmer, became the acting director of the computer center when Steve Mitchell, the first director, resigned in 1969. Anita Better was the manager of the data entry staff, and I was put in charge of computer operations which entailed managing drawers and drawers of card files. There was also a staff of six part-timers, all of whom operated either keypunch machines or unit-record equipment (sorter, collator, and interpreter) designed to manage card files in the early days of data processing. There were two computers in the center. An IBM 407 Accounting Machine, which was first introduced in 1949, and was <u>one of the mainstays of</u> the <u>IBM</u> long line of <u>tabulating machines</u> dating back to the days of <u>Herman Hollerith</u>, who designed the coding scheme for the first 80-column/12-row card. The 407 was programmed using a plug-board control panel that looked like a miniature telephone switchboard. It had a very limited number of functions. It could read cards, print the information that was on the cards, and do basic arithmetic operations (add, subtract, multiply, and divide). By 1970, it was being used mostly for simple printing applications. In 1968, Lehman College purchased an IBM 1130 computer configuration which included a card reader/card punch, a printer, 32,000 bytes of magnetic core memory, and three disk drives, each capable of storing one million bytes of data on a removable, 14-inch, oxide-coated aluminum disk. The software consisted of a disk operating system, an assembler, and a Fortran (Formula Translation) compiler. All of the applications at the center in 1970 were written in Fortran, an algebra-like programming language orig- inally designed for science and mathematics problem-solving. The college offered one computer course in the mathematics department where students learned Fortran programming. A small keypunch laboratory was available where students could keypunch their programs on cards and submit them to be run on the IBM 1130 on a fixed schedule usually four times per day. Any data needed by the student program also had to be included in the card deck the students submitted. The limited disk space made it impossible to allow the students to store programs on the computer.

The computer center reported to the Dean of Administration, Wilbur Edel. He was a first-rate administrator, who while dubious of the financial investment in computer technology, supported the center's initiatives. He wrote a short article in 1968, entitled, *Beware the Computer Trap,* in which he suggested that it was unlikely that significant savings would accrue from an investment in computer technology. This position was clearly counter to popular sales pitches from IBM and other manufacturers claiming that computers would pay for themselves in the long run by making operations more efficient. Edel was quite clear that the priorities of the center were to develop administrative applications, especially student record keeping systems. Student enrollment was growing at a rate of about ten percent per year, mostly due to the new open admissions policy that CUNY adopted in 1969 guarantying admission to every high school graduate in New York City. This policy was one of the results of student protests and strikes in spring 1969. (Sheila Gordon did an extensive analysis of open admissions at CUNY in her dissertation, *The Transformation of the City University of New York, 1945-1970*. Picciano and Jordan also have a chapter devoted to open admissions in, *CUNY's First Fifty Years: Triumphs and Ordeals of a People's University*.) The implementation of this policy was to commence in September 1970. I understood our priorities as laid out by Edel but I was also hoping that the center could do more to advance academic computing. The fact of the matter, however, was that there were few faculty who expressed any support for this. With the exception of one professor in the physics department, one professor in teacher education, and the one adjunct lecturer who taught computer programming in the mathematics department, there weren't any faculty using the center.

During the spring 1970, college campuses around the country became the scenes of protests, sit-ins and demonstrations against the Vietnam War. I was sympathetic but not active. I attended protests at Lehman and at Central Park in New York City. On Monday, May 4th, 1970, students during a peaceful protest. faced Ohio National Guardsmen in gas masks on Kent State University's Commons. The National Guard opened fire on the unarmed college students killing four and injuring nine others. This confrontation, referred to as the Kent State Massacre, was a defining moment for a nation sharply divided over the protracted war, in which more than 50,000 Americans died. It sparked strikes by millions of students across the U.S., temporarily closing some 900 colleges and universities. The events also played a pivotal role, historians argue, in turning public opinion against the conflicts in Southeast Asia. At Lehman College, demonstrations were tense but non-violent. Students boycotted classes and took over Shuster Hall (the Administration Building) and the Library, but no one was hurt. Students eventually vacated the buildings when President Lief obtained a court order. The computer center remained intact.

2

As I mentioned earlier, the computer center's computing hardware consisted of an IBM 407 and an IBM 1130. So, the computer center's file systems were completely dependent upon card files. The IBM 407 had no storage capability and the IBM 1130 had three disk drives with a capacity to store 3 million bytes of data. There were no tape drives. Part of the disk storage, almost 500,000 bytes had to be reserved for the operating system and utility programs. An IBM (or Hollerith card) held 80 characters of data organized as columns and rows. Each column could hold one character. The simplest student record needed minimally several hundred characters including basic demographic, financial, admissions, and semester course data. The computer center didn't even try to create a full student information system because of the limitations in storage capacity. Just to maintain student records for a single semester involved multiple drawers of cards organized according to the three major schools of the college – the day session undergraduate program, the evening school of general studies, and graduate studies. To keep the cards for the three schools always separated, a color stripe on the top of each card (purple for day session, green for general studies and blue for graduate studies) was used as a code. To update any of the data on these cards required the data entry staff to keypunch a card and replace same in the appropriate card drawer. Producing a report required that a program be developed for the IBM 1130 (or the IBM 407) to read the cards and print the information. If the report had to be in a particular order (i.e., alphabetically by student name, numerically by student ID/social security number, or alphabetically by major) the cards would be sorted manually to specification on a card sorter. To manage and organize these cards took up much of my daily routine. However, I decided to hone my computer programming skills as well so that I might make greater use of the IBM 1130.

The IBM 1130, like all IBM equipment came with a full complement of user manuals. Typically, they were one-half inch thick, black and white, without covers. They were written in the most technical language possible and were geared for the individual who already knew what to do. Fortunately, I was able to locate a book written by Robert K. Loudon entitled, *Programming the IBM 1130 and 1800*. It was a godsend and was written in a clear simple style. The IBM 1130 machine was explained as well as the essentials of Fortran and assembler language programming. Given my limited training, Louden filled in many of the gaps I had. And so, I taught myself to be an IBM 1130 programmer.

As an aside, our other piece of computing hardware, the IBM 407 accounting machine taught me important principles of computer programming, especially for data processing applications. The plug-board control panel (approximately 24 inches by 30 inches) was a grid of holes into which a mass of wires and prongs could be attached. The grid of holes represented individual storage locations on cards and the printer controller. Just looking at it was a most intimidating experience, and only Bob Attianese and I were willing to program it. I had gained some experience for setting up the plug-boards with unit record equipment such as the sorter, collator, and interpreter. These machines had small plug boards about twelve inches high and six inches across. They all worked on the same principle of processing the characters of data on card columns. It was the classic systems concept of input, process, and output. The IBM 407 had one input device (card reader), one small processor or central processing unit (CPU) and one output device (printer). I never forgot this concept. When I look at any digital device, I still think immediately of input, process, and output. Later on in my career I would work with computer systems that had hundreds of input, process and output devices.

The Fortran programming language was based on algebra notation characterized by variable names and equal signs. All data were represented as variables that could be input, calculated and outputted. For example, here is a simple program that calculates the area and perimeter of a rectangle where the width and length are entered on a card and the answer is printed on a printer.

```
10 COMMENT PROGRAM CALCULATES THE AREA AND PERIME-
TER OF A RECTANGLE
20 INTEGER: LENGTH,WIDTH,AREA,PERI
30 PRINT*,"ENTER THE VALUE OF LENGTH & WIDTH"
40 PRINT*,"USE COMMA OR BLANK SPACE TO SEPARATE VALUE"
50 READ*,LENGTH,WIDTH
60 AREA=LENGTH*WIDTH;
70 PERI=2*(LENGTH+WIDTH);
80 PRINT*,"AREA IS=",AREA, "PERIMETER IS=",PERI
90 END PROGRAM AREA_PERIMETER
```

An important feature of Fortran was modular programming or the ability to develop a program in modules and gracefully share modules across other programs. Fortran accomplished this with its "subroutine" feature, in which small parts of programs could be used over and over again and shared. For instance, if you needed to calculate a student's grade point average in many different programs, you didn't have to reprogram the code in each application. All you had to do was develop the code once, save it as a subroutine, and call upon it in any other programs that needed it. Fortran also had its drawbacks. In the earliest versions of Fortran, a variable name couldn't be longer than eight characters. In the example above, the variable "PERI" is an abbreviation of the value for the perimeter. While the programmer could include comment instructions explaining the full names of all the variables used, it would have been helpful if actual names of the variables could be used where they were executed in a program. Later versions of Fortran eliminated this limitation. Perhaps the greatest drawback of Fortran was that its "Read" and "Print" or "Write" instructions executed very slowly so reading 12,000 cards (number of students enrolled at Lehman College in 1970) could take many hours. We were able to get around this problem by using assembler language programming writing subroutines that could be used by the Fortran programs. Assembler code executes its instructions faster than any other programming language. The assembler subroutines we used reduced the time to read or write a deck of cards by tenfold. Later on, I wrote a Fortran subroutine that sped up significantly the time it took to search for an individual record on a file. Using binary search techniques (repeatedly dividing the file size by two), we were able to eliminate the need to sequentially search a file for an individual record.

Learning Fortran was an important experience for me. It was fortunate that I managed the operations in the computer center; that meant that I could use the IBM 1130 as much as I wanted. Computer programming is a skill and the more you do it, the better you become. I went through every chapter of the Loudon book and practiced every exercise. I became proficient enough that just about anybody who wanted to program the 1130 would ask me for advice and pointers. The faculty, including the one adjunct who taught the Fortran programming course, would seek me out for assistance. The students who were doing their homework assignments in the lab, would come to me daily with some "bug" in their programs that they couldn't figure out. I enjoyed working with them tremendously although I probably should have let them sweat it out a little more and figure out their own "bugs."

Bob Attianese left Lehman College in June of 1970, leaving myself and Anita Better as the only full-time employees in the center. By that time, we had ten part-time (mostly students) keypunch, unit record and computer operators, but I was the only programmer. I set about understanding all of the programs that Bob had written and if I didn't like them, I rewrote them. I also wrote a number of new programs that provided new reports for the college's administrative offices. Anita did a fabulous job with her staff and I never had to worry about the accuracy of the data cards coming through her data entry operation. With card-based files, this was crucial.

In October 1970, a new director was hired. Her name was Barbara Medina, a mathematician from New York University. It was clear from the beginning that she was going to direct the center and not do any programming or operations work. She was, however, able to convince the administration to hire three new full-time staff. They were Dan Rosich, Ben Rothman and Jeff LeGear. We set about to reprogram all of our operations in Fortran which essentially involved student and course recordkeeping applications. Ben, Jeff, and I added new admissions, bursar, and advisement applications to our operations, all of which were still card-based systems while Dan worked on making the IBM 1130 systems software more efficient. It was also at that time that admissions, graduate registrar, and the SEEK administrative offices were moved to Shuster Hall, the main administrative building at the college, and we were given their office space. For the first time in my career, I had my own office, even though it was in a Quonset hut.

3

The next major issue facing the computer center, as well as the college in general, was preparing for the increase in enrollment expected for fall 1971. The projection was that the college would enroll 1,300 new students, bringing the total to more than 13,000 students. We had requested and received funding for two additional disk drives, two tape drives and an additional 32,000 bytes of memory. Although the disk drives and tape drives provided more storage capability, these were basically system band aids and we still had to do much of the data processing with card files. At this time, given the extra disk capacity, we were able to purchase a "Sort" program that moved many of the sorting operations to the IBM 1130.

It was in spring 1971 that I met the CUNY Dean for Computing Technology, Robin Spock. He was visiting Barbara Medina and she introduced us. During our conversation, we learned that we both would be attending the Annual Association of Computing Machinery (ACM) Conference in Atlantic City in April. We decided to drive down and we spent a couple of days together. He was very knowledgeable and had a lot of experience working with computer technology. He was an engineer and previously had taught at Staten Island Community College (SICC) where he became the director of the computer center. I was amazed when he told me that he had developed a student transcript system that had complete data for every student who had ever attended SICC. H also told me that CUNY had just installed a RCA Spectre 7046 computer and was planning on supporting academic computing. Specifically, he explained that the Spectre ran a timeshare operating system (TSOS) that could support student programming across the university via dial-up and dedicated data communications facilities. Furthermore, the Spectre came with Fortran and BASIC (Beginners All Purpose Symbolic Instruction Code) interpreters, not compilers. He explained that programmers using interpreters entered their code line by line using as terminal device. Unlike a compiler which compiles and checks the completed program for errors, an interpreter checks a program as each line is written. If an error is made, the programmer is alerted immediately. It was his opinion that this would be a much more effective way for students to learn programming. I went to visit Robin at the CUNY Central Office and he and his assistant Renee Halperin gave me a demonstration. I was very impressed to say the least. Robin thought that he would start providing access to the broader CUNY community in fall 1971 or spring 1972 at the latest. He was looking for one or two colleges to use as test sites. I told him I would be happy to push for Lehman College when he was ready.

Robin never had the chance to test the Spectre system at any of the colleges. In September 1971, RCA announced that it was going out of the computer business entirely and that it would be selling the division to Sperry Univac. Shortly afterward, Robin left his position as the CUNY Dean of Computing Technology. For a while, however, CUNY was thinking of giving the Spectre to one of the colleges, and I told Barbara Medina we should try to get it and replace the IBM 1130. For about six months, the CUNY Central Office entertained our idea and allowed me to work with Renee Halperin on a one-day a week basis to become more familiar with the software. Unfortunately, in early spring 1972, CUNY decided that the Spectre would stay at the Central Office and I stopped my work with Renee. Regardless, it was a great learning experience, and as far as I was concerned, the TSOS was ahead of the pack when it came to academic software.

In 1971, Robert Kibbee was appointed Chancellor of CUNY. He had extensive administrative experience working in public university systems. It was also said that he was very much a data-driven decision maker and wasn't at all pleased with the data processing operations at the university. As a result, one of Kibbee's earliest administrative initiatives was the review of technological support for the entire university. Prior to his arrival, CUNY colleges were on their own in providing technology services to faculty and students. Some of the larger colleges had invested in mainframe computers to support administrative as well as academic computing, while others did very little. In part, CUNY's technology problems were related to a poorly-administered computer procurement process that had been established for all New York City agencies. A single individual in the Mayor's Office of Budget had to approve all computer acquisitions throughout the City (King, 2014, p. 2.15). The approval of any major piece of equipment would minimally take months if not years. In addition, all equipment had to be purchased, the Mayor's Office of the Budget didn't support leases or even lease purchases.

Overall, the situation was described as "desperate" to Ken King, who was recruited by Kibbee to rethink and re-imagine technology services at the university (King, 2014, p. 2). One aspect of the situation at CUNY was indeed desperate was the central administration's inability to collect reliable data from the colleges. Basic information on students, faculty, even finances was lacking. CUNY relied on the colleges to submit paper reports each semester containing critical information such as the number of students registered. While college administrators dutifully filled out forms, there was no audit or verification capability for the accuracy of these submissions. Critical student records were maintained locally with varying degrees of support from a college's computer center. Student tuition payments were generally check or cash transactions with little accountability. At best, colleges used basic retail cash registers to collect tuition with modest recording of individual student transactions. In the early 1970s some colleges didn't even have cash registers and simply collected money in strong boxes.

When Kibbee hired King in 1972 as the Dean of University Comput-ing with a charge to build an entirely new technology infrastructure for CUNY, he assured King of complete support in that "the City had substan-tially increased the University's budget because of open admissions." (King, 2014, p. 2.15) As a result, King was able to build a state-of-the-art comput-ing facility in rented space on 11th Avenue and 57th Street. IBM twin 370-168 computers were purchased for the new central facility. The emphasis of the new facility was on networking capability so that colleges and the university's offices could more gracefully communicate with one another via electronic file transfer and email, major advancements in the pre-Internet days of the 1970s. During this period, the colleges were supported financially and technologically as well in building and expanding their local computing facilities to connect to the central facility. CUNY became a national leader in network technology. During King's tenure and for years that followed under the direction of Ira Fuchs, the central computer center was a resource available to administrators, faculty and students. However, the responsibility for developing applications such as student record keeping or personnel database systems was left to other CUNY administrative offices or to those at the colleges. On the other hand, academic computing both for research and instruction received a significant boost from the new central computer facility. At Lehman, we started using the IBM 1130 as a remote job entry station to the CUNY central computer facility to run student programs. In the summer of 1972, we purchased a Data General Remote Job Entry Station that consisted of a card reader, a printer, and a data communications controller. We located it in the student keypunch laboratory where students could submit programs on their own and run them as much as they wanted using this dedicated piece of equipment.

References

King, K. (2014). *The early years of academic computing: A memoir by Ken King*. Ithaca, NY: The Internet-First University Press.

4

With Robert Kibbee as the CUNY chancellor, Ken King as the Dean of University Computing, and surging student enrollment driven by the 1969 Open Admissions policy, budgets for the colleges and funding for education technology were at an all-time high. In the five-year period between 1970 and 1975, student enrollment in CUNY increased 35 percent or 65,000 students, going from 185,000 to 250,000 (headcount). College computer centers were asked to put together three-year plans to upgrade their operations. Barbara Medina developed an extensive plan that would triple staffing and included the installation of a new, larger computer system. To everyone's amazement, much of the plan was approved. In addition, a new, although temporary, building would be constructed just to house computer operations. By the end of 1972 and into early 1973, the center was on a hiring spree that included four new programmers, three operations people, clerical staff, and two keypunch operators. Among the new staff were Bruce Kerievsky, Ro Clarke, Jerry Cohen, Lenny Richardson, Sylvia Chiu, Richard Stern, Juliette Viera, and Joe Kij. All of these individuals added significantly to the computer center's operation. On the equipment side, rather than purchasing new equipment for all of the colleges, CUNY would be reallocating hardware systems from other colleges, and so, Lehman College was to receive Brooklyn College's IBM 360-40. This made economic sense, because with over 30,000 students (headcount), Brooklyn had emerged as the largest enrolled college in CUNY and needed something larger. Also, since all equipment had been purchased outright per City policy, CUNY owned the equipment and couldn't easily resell it or trade it in.

The IBM 360-40 was a mid-range model in IBM's highly successful 360 series. The machine we were receiving from Brooklyn had 256,000 bytes of internal memory, a card reader/punch, two printers, four tape drives, and most important, six IBM 2314 disk drives, each capable of storing 30 million bytes of data. The added disk capacity put our operations into the mainstream. The 360 Disk Operating System (DOS) was very reliable, stable, and easy to learn. All programs and data swapped in and out of the systems' central processing unit from disk storage. The most important software feature for our administrative data processing work was that it had a COBOL (Common Business Oriented Language) compiler which had become the standard programming language for administrative and commercial applications. All of the programmers were more than happy to convert to COBOL from Fortran. It was an easy conversion although I must say I felt a certain nostalgia for Fortran. Among its many features, COBOL used English language commands rather than the mathematical equation style of Fortran. Also, its variable names could be up to thirty-two characters which made understanding COBOL programming code somewhat easier. However, all experienced programmers will tell you that it isn't the syntax of a program that is most important, but the algorithms developed to control the logic flow. That's where the creative aspect of programming manifests itself.

As fall 1973 approached, the staff got ready to move into its new building. We spent early August organizing and packaging equipment and card files for the move. The IBM 360-40 arrived in the middle of August just as our new building was being completed. The move to the new machine was graceful and without problems.

That August 1973, I also got a call from Dan Rosich who had worked with us for a year but left to join the faculty at Borough of Manhattan Community College (BMCC) in its data processing program. He needed an adjunct instructor to teach a basic introduction to technology course that met for six hours (two hours lecture, four hours lab work) on Tuesday and Thursday evenings and paid $4,800. I thought his offer over and decided to do it. BMCC had a good lab setup for students that included an IBM 360-30, twenty keypunch machines, and a Data General Remote Job Entry (RJE) Station exactly like the one we had at Lehman College. The IBM 360-30 was used to teach computer operations while the RJE Station was tied to the CUNY

Central Computer facility and used for students to run their own programs. I enjoyed the teaching and found the students incredible. They were working full-time jobs during the day and on weekends as seamstresses, busboys, dishwashers, and messengers in and around Manhattan. Some were parents and asked if they could bring their children to class. They inspired me and I tried hard to help them learn as much as they could so that if they finished the program they might have better jobs and better lives.

5

My undergraduate degree was in political science with a minor in history and a second minor in secondary education. Since 1971, I had enrolled in graduate courses at several of the CUNY colleges to fill some of my evening time. Computer science at City College, political science at Hunter College, and social studies at Lehman College. The computer science courses at City College were all mathematics and had little relationship to anything I was doing. I enjoyed the courses at Hunter and Lehman and managed to accumulate enough credits by June 1972 for a master's degree. For fall 1972, I decided to enroll in another master's degree program, this one at Bernard Baruch College in public administration. Two colleagues of mine at Lehman, John Antonaccio and Miriam Ramos, were enrolling in the same program. John was the assistant business manager and Miriam was the executive assistant to the dean for adult and continuing studies. The three of us were all thinking that a degree in public administration would help our careers. At Baruch, one of the faculty, Fred Lane, became a mentor for me and guided me well through some of my future choices. We have remained friends for five decades. The program at Baruch was very flexible and I took courses in higher education administration, operations research, and systems analysis. It turned out to be a very valuable degree as it gave me a good sense of administration in general as well as honing my analytical skills. I completed the program in 1975 with a master's in public administration (MPA).

During my first year at Baruch, important things were going on in the country as well. In November 1972, George McGovern, the Democratic presidential nominee lost to Richard Nixon. McGovern ran as a "peace" candidate but failed to generate large-scale support for his views. He promoted a campaign message of "coming together" and I attended one of his events at a standing-room only rally held at Madison Square Garden. In the election, he only carried the state of Massachusetts and the District of Columbia. On

January 23, 1973, the United States and North Vietnam signed the Paris Peace Accords ending any further direct United States military involvement in Vietnam.

On January 22, 1973, the U.S. Supreme Court issued a 7–2 decision in favor of "Jane Roe" (Norma McCorvey) that held that women in the United States have a fundamental right to choose whether or not to have abortions without excessive government restriction and struck down Texas's abortion ban as unconstitutional. This landmark decision that protected a pregnant woman's liberty to choose to have an abortion, prompted an ongoing national debate in the United States about whether and to what extent abortion should be legal, who should decide the legality of abortion, and what the role of religious and moral views in the political sphere should be. *Roe v. Wade* reshaped American politics, dividing much of the United States into abortion rights and anti-abortion groups, and activating major movements on both sides.

Meanwhile back at Lehman, it was in 1973 that I learned the Statistical Package for the Social Science (SPSS), one of the most useful tools ever developed for the social sciences and for the teaching of research methods. My interest in it at the time, had little to do with research and everything to do with reporting student data to the CUNY Central Office. For years, CUNY colleges were required to complete paper documents referred to as Form A (undergraduate students) and Form B (graduate students) every semester. They began as seven- and five-page documents respectively, providing summary information on students. These documents not only could be used for institutional research but were also the basis for the following year's college budgets. They were expected to be accurate although there was no real way of checking this. By 1973, Form A had ballooned to 35 pages and the reporting was getting more complicated. Student characteristics (gender, age, ethnicity, years in program, major, etc.) were reported in two- and three-dimensional tables. Every semester I found myself rewriting the program to generate this report. I dreaded getting the memo each August with specifications/rules for reporting these data. I had first been introduced to SPSS in spring 1972 while taking a course in political science at Hunter College. My professor, Ken Sherrill, required a statistical analysis project using a national database of voting behavior. He taught us the basics of SPSS in order to complete the assignment. Later in spring 1973, I was taking a course in research methods at Baruch College when the instructor, James Guyot, also introduced SPSS, and I made the connection between it and the Form A and Form B reports.

The project to build SPSS was started at Stanford University in the 1960s by three graduate students, Norman Nie, Dale Bent, and C. Hadlai Hull. Although the initial work on SPSS was done at Stanford University, in 1969, Nie joined the University of Chicago's National Opinion Research Center. The University of Chicago recognized SPSS as an important intellectual property and encouraged Nie's continuing development of the software system. Nie was successful in recruiting Hull to join him at the University of Chicago by encouraging him to take a position as the head of the University's Computation Center. Bent, a Canadian, decided not to join Nie and Hull in Chicago, and returned to Canada where he had an academic appointment at the University of Alberta. (About SPSS, Inc., 2009)

The speed with which SPSS caught on was nothing short of amazing. Prior to its advent, social science researchers doing data analysis were typically using manual equipment and calculators. Frequently, these researchers relied on other experts who knew the specifics of statistical procedures and had great dexterity in using manual equipment, since it was one thing to add a sum of numbers on a calculator, and it was quite another to do an analysis of variance. Nie and Hull decided to give the software away for the cost of making a duplicate of the program which initially consisted of a tray of punched cards. However, Nie, Bent, and Hull came to realize that SPSS users would need instructions or a manual to use the software properly. The original version of the SPSS manual, published in 1970, has been described as one of "sociology's most influential books," allowing ordinary researchers to do their own statistical analysis (Wellman, 1998). The manual became a best seller as tens of thousands of social scientists took charge of their own research destinies, learning the basics as well as the nuances of data analysis. SPSS provided the classic environment for learning by doing. The software, with the aid of the manual, was very user friendly and a conscientious student learned the statistical procedures as well as the SPSS coding to conduct the analysis.

It is difficult to assess SPSS's impact on the entire field of data analysis, but in less than a decade it became the mainstay of faculty teaching introduction to statistics in all of the disciplines. Furthermore, it allowed for collecting larger sample sizes because the drudgery of running statistical routines disappeared once the data were converted into electronic form. It was SPSS that changed the way statistical research was conducted. Students and researchers could now collect sample sizes numbering in the thousands. Government agencies could collect sample sizes in the hundreds of thousands and make the data available in SPSS format free to researchers and set the standard for a number of other statistical packages such as SAS and Stata. Agencies such as NASA, the Census Bureau, as well as corporate America became regular users of the software. Versions of SPSS would also be made available for a number of computer hardware platforms (IBM, Univac, and Control Data Corporation). A whole new style of research evolved based on collecting large quantities of data without necessarily having specific hypotheses or research questions and later searching the data for relationships and patterns. This approach has evolved into the present era of "big data".

I was determined to learn all I could about SPSS and its basic statistical routines. Form A and Form B were crosstabulations or contingency tables that easily fit SPSS output formats. My plan, back in1973, was to no longer write source programs to produce Form A and Form B, but instead to develop a student data file with all of the pertinent variables or data elements and run SPSS routines which would save hours and hours of programming effort. I taught one of the associate registrars how to read the SPSS output and she was ecstatic at learning this new tool. For the rest of my career, I continued to use

SPSS. Wherever I went and whatever I did, it became a basic tool for me as an administrator, instructor or researcher. After leaving Lehman, I delivered several papers in the later 1970s, on the use of SPSS for management data reporting at information technology and college administration conferences.

In 1975, Nie and Hull incorporated SPSS into a company and began to sell SPSS commercially. To its credit, SPSS, Inc. always provided student versions at substantial discounts. In 2003, SPSS, Inc. also developed predictive analytics products that were especially popular for marketing applications. In 2009, SPSS, Inc. was acquired for $1.2 billion by IBM which continues to market it under the SPSS brand.

References

About SPSS, Inc. (2009). Corporate history. Retrieved from: http://www.spss.com.hk/corpinfo/history.htm Accessed: April 8, 2020.

Wellman, B. (1998). Doing it ourselves: The SPSS manual as sociology's most influential recent book". In D. Clawson (Ed.), Required reading: Sociology's most influential books (pp. 71–78). Amherst: University of Massachusetts Press.

6

I n fall of 1973, the conversion of our Fortran programs to COBOL proceeded briskly. The programmers developed enough confidence to consider redesigning and redeveloping our student and course systems without worrying about the limitations of the IBM 1130. At this time, a new registrar, George Haag, was appointed who took a keen interest in our operation and had fresh ideas on how we could move forward. In the past, the needs of the administrative users were discussed as needed generally one-on-one at small meetings. At this time, I was taking a course in systems analysis with Dr. Arthur Levine at Baruch. Dr. Levine was a gifted professor who brought his previous experience working at NASA to enliven our classes. In one of the sessions, he espoused the need for team approaches in the design of new systems. This resonated with me. I discussed it with George and we organized a small users' group of representatives from four major administrative offices. I chaired the meetings and kept minutes. We decided to meet every two weeks to discuss all types of issues regarding the nature of the file systems, the relationship between one file and another, and the coding schemes that would be used. We discussed how to integrate the information systems with the manual office operations, something we had never done before. As our discussions proceeded, it was determined that the new system wouldn't just be for the registrar's office but for the entire college.

I began contacting colleagues at other colleges and sent out a survey to about 100 computer center directors inquiring about the extent of their student and course record information systems. Their replies were varied but they gave me and the users' group some ideas to ponder. One of the survey respondents suggested I look at materials developed by the National Center for Higher Education Management Systems (NCHEMS) that was part of the Western Interstate Commission for Higher Education (WICHE). I sent away for several of their documents including their recommendations for designing a complete college information system that would include student, course, personnel, finance, and facilities components. The material emphasized the elimination of data redundancy and the importance of standardization of data element names and coding schemes across all the information system files. It also introduced to me the need for documentation in the form of a data element dictionary for each file that would serve as a blueprint for the data organization and coding schemes used. I incorporated this concept in all of my file designs at Lehman and at other colleges in the years to come. All of this is quite common and well understood today, but back in the early 1970s this wasn't the case.

The users' group was charged with designing the student and course information systems and to proceed with the other three components at a later date. Within four months, a basic plan was developing that all the users could sign off on. The membership of the users' group also increased so that ten administrative offices at the college were represented. In late spring, the programming staff started to develop the COBOL programs and algorithms for creating, updating, and reporting on the student and course information systems (see Figure 6.1).

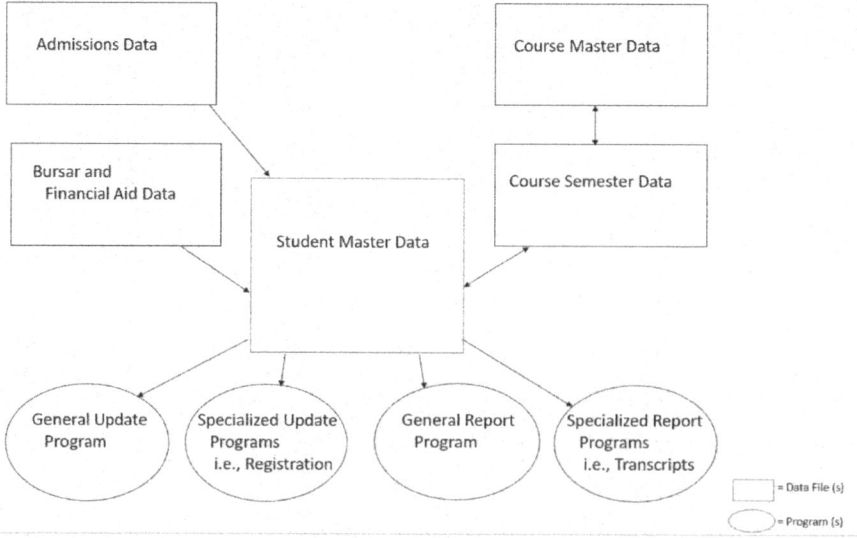

Figure 6.1 – Student and Course Information Systems

The course information system would have two files, one the course master file which would contain all of the information about any course that the college approved to be offered; the other, the course semester file which would contain all the information on each section of the courses offered in any given semester. The two files were completely integrated to eliminate any duplication of information. Each course had a key code that could be referred to by either file. As an example, the title and prerequisites for a course were only recorded on the course master file. However, these data could be accessed as needed by the course semester file without duplicating the information on both files.

The student information system was more complicated mainly because of its size. The decision was made to have one student master file containing all the information – admissions, registrar, bursar, advisement, etc. This file would be variable length which would allow semester data such as courses enrolled to be added as needed without taking up extensive amounts of disk space. The idea of creating a complete student transcript was put on hold until a plan could be developed to collect and gather historical data. At the time these data were recorded only on paper. In addition to programs that would support student registration and standard reports such as class rosters and grade reports, two general purpose programs were written. First, there was a program that could update any data element on the student master file by simply entering the student social security number (ID number), the data element code, and the necessary update data on a one-page form. The second was a general-purpose report program that could list up to ten student data elements and provide counts and sums if needed. Again, a single form was developed that required the user to enter the needed data elements and any conditional information such as specific gender or major. One person in the registrar's office coordinated all requests and reviewed forms for accuracy and completeness. These forms were delivered on a daily basis to the center's data entry staff and given priority for keypunching and running the reports.

Another important decision we made was to collect each semester's registration data from students using mark sense (fill in the bubble) technology. The IBM 360-40 was a good machine for doing batch operations but not particularly robust enough to manage a fully online registration system. I always felt that we had to settle for the mark-sense approach; it was by no means the most graceful or most efficient. Regardless, by fall 1974, the new student and course information systems were launched. The programming staff did an excellent job of developing the applications software for these systems, but it was the users especially the registrar's staff, who devoted hours of work collecting, recoding, and entering data onto the new files. In December 1974, I delivered my first paper at a professional conference entitled *A Committee Approach to the Design of a Student Information System.* It was well received.

7

I n 1974, one of the most significant events in American history was playing out in Washington, D.C.. President Nixon was the subject of inquiries and hearings as a result of Republican Party operatives breaking into the Democratic Party Headquarters in the Watergate Complex and stealing files. After two years of investigations, it was obvious that Nixon would be impeached. On August 9, 1974, Nixon resigned the presidency in disgrace and Gerald Ford assumed his position.

During the summer of 1974, administrative changes were going on Lehman College. Wilbur Edel, the Dean of Administration retired and was replaced by Jack Weiner, the Assistant Dean and former Business Manager. The administrative dynamic changed, and I sensed a different atmosphere within the college. Edel had been the dean since the college was founded in 1968 and commanded a lot of loyalty and support among the administrative staff. At a small farewell reception, he came up to me to ask how I was doing. While I had attended a lot of meetings where he presided, I had never spoken to him one-on-one. He thanked me for the work I had done in the computer center and asked what my future plans were. I told him about the MPA program at Baruch, my teaching at BMCC, and that I would like to pursue a college career. He told me that if I wanted to build a career, someone my age shouldn't think about staying at one college but should experience a number of institutions. Take advantage of all of the colleges here in New York City that employ thousands of administrators and faculty, he said. I never forgot his words.

Shortly after Dean Edel retired, Barbara Medina said she would be leaving Lehman also to take a position as director of computer services at Kutztown State College in Pennsylvania. In late 1974 and early 1975, a search was conducted for a replacement. I must say that I was a bit interested in the director's position but so were Bruce Kerievsky and Jerry Cohen, both of whom had many years more experience than I did. In any event, it was made clear to all three of us that Dean Weiner was interested in bringing in someone from the outside. Susan Kliavkoff, who was director of computing at Fordham University and a colleague of George Haag, was appointed to the position at Lehman. She was a nice enough individual and had a lot of experience.

Soon thereafter, John Antonaccio, my colleague in the business office and fellow student at Baruch, resigned his position to become the business manager at Medgar Evers College (MEC) in Brooklyn. We continued to see each other in classes and would go out for a drink every once in a while. He was quite happy with his new position. At one point, he asked if I might be interested in making a move to MEC. He said that the president was looking for a new director to develop their computer services. I decided to speak to Ira Fuchs and Joe Giannotti on Ken King's staff to see what they thought was going on at Medgar Evers in terms of computer services. It was their sense that very little had been established although the college had purchased a new Digital Equipment Corporations (DEC) PDP 11/45 minicomputer. I thought it over and in February 1975 decided to meet with the Dean of Administration, Don Watkins, at MEC. I was impressed with him. He was a former dean at Brooklyn College and moved to MEC because he wanted to work with the Central Brooklyn black community. Don was white and he gave me a friendly lesson on what it would be like to be white and work in a college where 95 percent of the student population was black and the faculty and staff were predominantly black as well. He also had me meet with Jim Grant, the Associate Dean of Administration, who was black, and to whom I would be reporting. Based on our conversation, I thought Jim was a class individual with whom I wouldn't mind working. Two weeks later I returned for a more formal interview and met with several of the administrators at MEC including the President, Richard Trent. Everyone with whom I met was black.

I learned that the DEC PDP 11/45 minicomputer had been sitting in storage. MEC had already hired and dismissed two directors and had yet to install the new equipment. Part of the problem was that the college didn't have a space for the machine that, among other things, needed a temperature-controlled environment. Don Watkins had assured me that the space problem was being solved and a substantial area in the basement of their main building was being renovated and near completion. The main building was the former Brooklyn Prep High School, a Catholic boy's school, acquired by CUNY in 1972. That explained all the stained-glass windows in the building that could be seen as you walked through the halls. There was little computer support for the college operations with the exception of some programs that were run on the CUNY central computer facility.

I decided to accept the position and negotiated a good salary along with lots of flexibility in terms of any decision making regarding the use of technology for administrative, research, and instructional activity.

At Lehman College, I told the programmers of my decision. It wasn't easy either for them or for me. We had learned a lot together and were proud of the work we had done at the college. The new student and course information systems that we had developed would continue to serve the college for twenty-five years until they were replaced by a CUNY central database system in 1999. Of the programmers, I would surely miss Lenny Richardson who started working with me as a student aide and developed into a first-rate programmer. He and I had designed and coded several of the critical programs for the new student and course information systems. We also played tennis together on Lehman College's red clay courts. He and I never played a game, set, or match. We just played each point. It was a great way to learn the game. Sadly, within two years, just about the entire programming staff with the exception of Joe Kij would leave for positions elsewhere. I then told the other staff about my leaving and all wished me luck. I knew that I would surely miss Anita Better with whom I had worked for five years. For a while we were the only two employees in the computer center and had been a part of its incredible growth and accomplishments. Once I told the staff, it was only a matter of hours before the rest of the college knew about my plans.

There were other people in the college who I would miss also. People in the business office who recommended my transfer to the computer center while I was still a student. The registrar's staff especially Charlie Schreiber who also started as a student aide, moved on the to be an assistant registrar, associate registrar and a couple of years after I left became the registrar. There were faculty and staff such as Bill Murdoch and Nat Kolodny with whom I played basketball on Friday nights in one of Lehman's gyms. That was a great way to end a week and blow off some energy.

The following morning, I got a call from Dean Weiner's assistant asking if I could come to his office and meet with the Dean. He asked me if what he had heard about my leaving was true. I told him that it was. He asked why I was leaving, and I said it was a good opportunity and a chance to advance my career. He then informed me that for someone in an administrative title to move from one CUNY college to another a request must be made by the receiving college to the home college. I didn't know that, and I told him that I would inform Don Watkins at MEC. A negotiation went on between the two deans and an agreement was made that I could leave, but it would have to be put on hold while the new director at Lehman, Susan Kliavkoff, became more familiar with our operations. This was expected to take about two months. As it turned out, Dean Weiner didn't agree to release me for almost seven long months.

PART II

Medgar Evers College
Brooklyn, New York
1975-1977

8

At the time of CUNY's establishment in 1961, the demography of New York City was changing. The manufacturing commercial sector was in decline resulting in significant loss of jobs. Urban renewal policies that demolished old ethnic neighborhoods resulted in large numbers of white residents leaving New York City for the suburbs. The "white flight" was substantial and saw middle-class and working-class families abandoning racially-mixed areas of the City that increasingly became home to poor minority communities. In response to these changes and pressure from community groups, the Board of Higher Education established several colleges to help provide stability and socio-economic stimulus to communities in the Bronx, Brooklyn and Queens that were experiencing demographic and physical upheaval and to provide opportunities for poorer populations that "traditionally had little access to higher education" (Roff, Cucchiara, & Dunlap, 2000, p.117). Medgar Evers College (MEC) was one of these institutions.

In the early 1960's, the community of Central Brooklyn recognized the need and desire for a local public college. Through community organizations including the Bedford-Stuyvesant Restoration Corporation, the Central Brooklyn Coordinating Council, and the NAACP, as well as through local elected officials, the residents of Central Brooklyn approached CUNY's Board of Higher Education with their request. Members of various community-based organizations constituted the Bedford-Stuyvesant Coalition on Educational Needs and Services which served as the primary vehicle for making the case to the Board of Higher Education. After many discussions, the Board of Higher Education, on November 17, 1967, "approved the sponsorship of Community College Number VII, with the intention to admit students in the fall of 1969" and on February 13, 1968, the Board of Higher Education announced that the college would be located in the Bedford-Stuyvesant/Crown Heights area of Brooklyn (Pollard, 2012, p. 21).

On January 27, 1969 the Board expanded the college's scope and approved the establishment of an experimental four-year college of professional studies offering both career and transfer associate degrees and the baccalaureate degree. On September 28, 1970, the Board approved the recommendation from the College's Community Council to name the college, Medgar Evers College, in honor of the martyred civil rights leader. During the 1970s, MEC operated in rented facilities on President Street, Carroll Street and Eastern Parkway in Central Brooklyn. In 1975, its enrollment was just over 3,000 students, the vast majority of whom were black. It had the largest percentage of students receiving Pell grants of any of the CUNY senior colleges.

By the time I arrived at MEC in November of 1975, Dean Watkins had kept his word and established an area for a computer facility in the basement of the Prep Building. I had made several visits to MEC prior to November and was kept abreast of the progress being made on the new space. I met with support staff from the Digital Equipment Corporation (DEC) who coordinated the equipment move once the basement area was completed. It was a generous space that easily housed the DEC PDP 11/45 and in addition, there was a reception area, a keypunch facility, and four offices. There was also an unfinished area that was to be used in the future for academic computing support should the college develop courses that needed access to technology. The college already was offering a two-year program in business administration that at some point would be expanded to offer introductory courses and/or programs in data processing and management information systems. The former director of the computer center was Nachman Bench, who was on the business faculty. He returned to teaching when I arrived and hoped to get technology-related courses off the ground in the program. The computer center staff included two COBOL programmers, two keypunch operators, a secretary and me. We also had four part-time student aides who did mostly keypunch work.

The PDP 11/45 was being used essentially as a remote job entry station to the CUNY Central Computer Center. It had two disk drives, two tape drives, a card reader and a high-speed printer. It had 256,000 bytes of semi-conductor memory. The system software was Resource Sharing Time Sharing (RSTS) which at the time only supported the Extended BASIC programming language. BASIC was fine for teaching computer programming because of its timeshare and interpreter characteristics but hadn't really been developed for doing administrative data processing applications. In many ways, it was similar to Fortran in its look and feel. The programming staff had written several COBOL programs to support the registrar's office that were card-based and were running on the CUNY Central Computer Center. An integrated student information system hadn't been developed. All of the college's administrative systems were essentially manual systems in need of technology support.

At the time of my arrival at MEC, New York City was experiencing a dire fiscal crisis and was literally running out of money. City and state political leaders had appealed to the federal government for assistance. One month earlier in October 1975, President Gerald Ford denied these requests, prompting the *New York Daily News* to run the infamous "Ford to City: Drop Dead" headline. Ford added that he would assist the City in declaring bankruptcy and criticized the City's uncontrolled and unwise spending policies including its tuition-free City University system.

References

Pollard, M.L. (2012). *Medgar Evers College institutional strategic plan: 2012 -2017*. Retrieved from: http://www.mec.cuny.edu/AboutMEC/pdf/MEC_Strategic_Plan_ISPC_Final_Draft_Post_Rev_9-14.aspx Accessed: June 17, 2020.

Roff, S.S., Cucchiara, A.M., & Dunlop, B.J. (2000). *From the Free Academy to CUNY*: New York: Fordham University Press.

9

My first major activity at MEC was to develop a plan for supporting administrative operations at the college. In conversation with the Deans and several department heads and with the approval of Don Watkins and Jim Grant, it was decided that we would first concentrate on supporting student applications in the registrar's office which at the time was a manual operation. Course registration was problematic, and the office hadn't been able to generate an official student transcript. The hope was to provide some support for the Spring 1976 semester, just a few short months away.

In my discussions with the two programmers, Joan Johnston and Ashok Idani, we concluded that if we were to do anything quickly, it would have to be done in COBOL and run on the CUNY Central Computer Center. Neither Joan, Ashok nor I had written any substantial programs in BASIC. It wasn't just a question of learning the language, we knew that BASIC wasn't designed for and never intended to do administrative file processing. We began to design a new system using COBOL.

To get started, I showed them the basic elements of the Lehman College student and course information systems. We believed that with some modifications that we could use them at MEC. So rather than writing programs from scratch, we converted the Lehman systems for MEC. The registrar was happy to get any kind of support she could from our center and left it to us to develop the system. With student registration starting in January 1976, we didn't have the time to convert both systems completely, but we did convert those programs that were most crucial to support student registration. As much as possible, we used existing MEC data coding schemes but also modified and enhanced them when necessary. In addition to programming, we also had to do a quick redesign of the paper forms that would be used by the registrar's office as well as the keypunch staff to get the student and course data into the systems. Once miraculously through registration, we used the rest of the Spring 1976 semester to convert programs as needed to support a host of student applications. We essentially were one week ahead of the registrar in developing the necessary programs. There were a couple of small glitches particularly with the data coding schemes but we all survived. By the end of the semester, the Lehman information systems were fully converted and operational at MEC. Ashok also made some rather nice enhancements to several of the converted modules, especially the main update and general report writing programs.

Ashok and I spent a good deal of the semester learning the PDP 11/45. While it had several fine features, we believed we should keep the administrative applications running on the CUNY Central Computer. The CUNY Central Computer Center also provided a very graceful text editor called WYLBUR. In addition to its text editor capability, WYLBUR provided access to word processing, remote job submission and retrieval, and an e-mail program that were easy to use and very reliable. We used it to develop our COBOL programs, for communications within our own center, and for submitting production jobs using the PDP 11/45 as a remote job entry station. Joan became very adept at using it to schedule our operations activities.

We used the new MEC student and course information systems to produce all of our reports including the Form A and Form B. By now, the two reports were about fifty pages long. Actually, we didn't have to do the Form B because graduate programs weren't offered at MEC. Alice Ryan, the Director for Management Reporting, coordinated Form A for the college and in the past, it was a manual operation that took about one month to complete. MEC was invariably late in submitting it to the CUNY Central Office. I described to Alice what I did at Lehman with SPSS and we took the same approach for MEC. I wrote the program to isolate the key data elements needed to do the Form A reporting and then ran the relevant SPSS programs to generate the data for Form A. At the same time, Alice learned SPSS and WYLBUR pretty much on her own and was able to complete the report with minimal assistance from me once I generated the file with the relevant data. MEC submitted the Form A on time, a first for the college.

10

While we were enjoying a good beginning in the MEC computer center in the spring of 1976, the same wasn't true for CUNY and for the City of New York, While CUNY was busy trying to accommodate tens of thousands of new students, its major funder, the City of New York was facing serious financial challenges. A deepening countrywide recession, an oil embargo, inflation, and an unemployment rate of 12 percent in New York had caused the bond market to grow skittish and made investors wary of buying New York City bonds. Mayor John Lindsay also came under increasing scrutiny for "gimmicks" he was using to balance the budget including "juggling books to shift state aid from one year to another, using fictitious surpluses, 'deferring' required payments, arbitrarily raising revenue estimates, borrowing against questionable receipts…borrowing just to pay back earlier borrowings." (McFadden, 2001) New York City's debt had grown during his tenure from $2.5 billion to $9 billion.

A year earlier in spring 1975, its pool of lenders was disappearing, and New York City reached the point where no one would buy its bonds. As a result, the City was unable to pay its bills, a default on outstanding debt was likely, and the specter of bankruptcy was very real. New York Governor Hugh Carey provided emergency funds to see the City through its crisis, but this only delayed the problem and didn't solve it. In fall 1975, Carey and Mayor Abraham Beame approached the federal government for assistance. As mentioned earlier, their appeal elicited a rebuke from President Gerald Ford, who cited CUNY's free tuition policy as an example of the City living beyond its means. He vowed to veto any bailout for New York. Governor Carey began working with New York State legislators and major figures from the banking and financial industry to find a solution. They proposed the establishment of the Municipal Assistance Corporation for the City of New York (MAC) endowed with the authority to borrow billions of dollars backed by State revenue and to exercise specific policing powers over City fiscal practices. In effect, MAC would become the fiscal oversight corporation for the City of New York. Carey's proposal was approved by both bodies of the State Legislature and became law on June 10, 1975. However, in fall 1975 and spring 1976, CUNY as well as MEC were already operating on an austerity budget. CUNY had held out hope for bailouts from the State of New York and the federal government but by January 1976, it was clear that the City and CUNY were in dire fiscal straits.

In February 1976, Chancellor Kibbee proposed a restructuring of the University which would have resulted in the closing, merger, or the conversion in status of five colleges. His proposal specifically called for closing Richmond College, John Jay College, and Hostos Community College, and changing the status of Medgar Evers College and York College from senior to community colleges. The Board of Higher Education deferred acting on this proposal. The colleges identified for closure or merger mounted an effective political action campaign with pressure to preserve their existence. Coordinated marches from the colleges culminated in massive rallies at City Hall. At MEC, a large contingent of faculty, students and staff including all of us in the computer center marched down Eastern Boulevard to Flatbush Avenue to the Brooklyn Bridge and to City Hall. Student activists throughout the University mounted strikes and sit-ins at almost all of the colleges to support sufficient funding for CUNY, to avoid college closings, and to demand increased funding from the State. The students at Hostos Community College, Medgar Evers College and York College were particularly adamant in their activism and desire to preserve their institutions.

In April 1976, the Board of Higher Education approved a modified version of the Kibbee Plan that included a merger of Hostos with Bronx Community College, consolidation of Richmond College and Staten Island Community College into the College of Staten Island, and the reduction of Medgar Evers College to a community college. John Jay College and York College would remain as senior colleges. Between April and June 1976, the New York State Legislature whose approval was required to make any permanent changes to CUNY's structure, governance, or financial model worked to find a compromise that would stabilize the crisis. Irwin Landes, the chair of the NYS Assembly's higher education committee became a major player in putting together a package or omnibus bill that would resolve a number of CUNY issues including the restructuring of colleges. In order to get support from the NYS Assembly and Senate a number of compromises were required. The NYS Legislature's Black and Puerto Rican Caucus made it clear that it would only support the Landes Bill if Medgar Evers College and Hostos Community College remained in existence. The Landes Bill passed on June 9, 1976 and included language that preserved the status of Medgar Evers College and Hostos Community College (History of Hostos Community College, 2016).

In May 1976, CUNY was about to run out of funds and negotiated an agreement with all parties involved including the MAC Board, the Professional Staff Congress and other unions, to defer two-weeks of employee pay. CUNY shut down the last two weeks of June 1976 and all employees were furloughed (Glazer, 1981, p. 564). J.S. Glazer's Dissertation (1981) *A case study of the decision in 1976 to initiate tuition for matriculated undergraduate students of the City University of New York* can be read for an in-depth study of CUNY and New York City's fiscal crisis. Furthermore, on May 24, 1976, the CUNY Board of Higher Education adopted *Guidelines and Procedures for Retrenchment* and also directed CUNY to implement cost-saving arrangements for consolidation of various noninstructional resources. The Guidelines ordered the president of each CUNY branch to "determine after consultation with appropriate faculty and student representatives what programs or activities are to be cut back or terminated;" required that the retrenchment plans "set forth the reasons why reduction or termination of academic or non-academic service is required with respect to each department or function;" and commanded that the "reasons must be related to financial needs and be directed at the needs of the college and department or function."

In June 1976, I was told by Dean Jim Grant that I had to develop a retrenchment plan for the computer center staff. Every existing full- and part-time position had to be justified and there had to be at least a twenty percent savings. I spoke to every staff member individually to discuss the situation. It was horrific. In the end every part-time employee and one full-time keypunch operator were retrenched. Every one of these individuals were black and single mothers. The elation that we had experienced earlier in the year was wiped out within six months. But the newly functioning computer center and the student system lived on. Throughout MEC and CUNY, the effects of retrenchment shattered morale among faculty, administrators, and students for several years to come.

References

Glazer, J.S. (1981). *A case study of the decision in 1976 to initiate tuition for matriculated undergraduate students of the City University of New York*. Dissertation completed at New York University.

History of Hostos Community College. (2011) Website of Hostos Community College. Retrieved from: http://www.hostos.cuny.edu/About-Hostos/The-History-of-Hostos Accessed: August 10, 2020.

McFadden, R.D. (February 11, 2001). Abraham Beame Is dead at 94; Mayor during 70's fiscal crisis. *New York Times*. Retrieved from: http://www.nytimes.com/2001/02/11/nyregion/abraham-beame-is-dead-at-94-mayor-during-70-s-fiscal-crisis.html?pagewanted=all Accessed: August 8, 2020.

11

Every dark cloud has a small silver lining. In May 1976, I was elected to the Pocantico Hills School District Board of Education where I was a resident. I would remain on this board until 1985 when I resigned after three terms. My time on the Board was interesting and stimulating. I got involved in a number of major issues related to education policy, special education, and education funding in Westchester County.

At MEC, despite the chaos of retrenchment, the Dean of Faculty Wendell Clement had put together a committee to apply for a United States Department of Education Title III Developing Institutions Grant, the purpose of which was to help struggling colleges to achieve self-sufficiency. At that point, MEC certainly qualified as "struggling." Dean Clement wanted to include a component that would address providing technological assistance to students who needed to enroll in remedial course work in reading, writing or mathematics. The vast majority of our students needed to take at least one remedial course and in many cases, two or more. I and one of the professors, Tobin Barrozo, were tasked with evaluating software that might be appropriate for establishing a computer-assisted-instruction (CAI) laboratory. I had read about CAI software but had never used it and had never seen such a lab since CAI was still in its beginning stages in the 1970s. Unlike present-day CAI that includes graphics and is media rich, the software in 1976 was essentially text-based. The technology wasn't readily available to develop quality digital media. The CAI software essentially guided students through lessons and tested them frequently to determine the level of mastery of the material. Once mastered, the CAI program directed the student to the next module. If not mastered, the program would identify the weakness(es) and provide the student with additional exercises on the same material. A good CAI program would also keep a file on how well a student was progressing which could be accessed and used by an instructor for follow-up.

Tobin and I evaluated two packages that we decided might be appropriate for our needs: PLATO (Programmed Logic for Automated Teaching Operations) and IBM's 1500 Instructional System using CAI software developed by the Computer Curriculum Corporation.

PLATO was developed by Donald L. Bitzer and his associates at the University of Illinois at Urbana-Champaign. It was a very impressive system, especially the plasma display monitor that was way ahead of its time. However, there were three important drawbacks. First, we would have to develop our own CAI software. We had neither the staff nor expertise to do this. Second, a PLATO workstation was expensive as much as $13,000. per unit with all the bells and whistles. Third, to use PLATO one had to time-share into Bitzer's Computer-Based Education Research Laboratory (CERL) and incur additional costs based on usage.

The IBM 1500 Instructional System ran on a computer very similar to the IBM 1130 computer I worked with at Lehman College. I was naturally drawn to the possibility of the IBM 1500 because of my experience with the hardware and software.. However, the IBM 1500 also proved to be expensive. We would have to buy the IBM 1500 system with each workstation costing as much as $10,000. apiece. We were hoping to establish a CAI laboratory with twenty stations. The Computer Curriculum Corporation (CCC) founded by Pat Suppes and Richard Atkinson, who worked at the Institute for Mathematical Studies in the Social Sciences at Stanford University, had developed a suite of CAI packages designed mainly for mathematics, reading and language arts instruction for a secondary education curriculum. Since the remedial courses at MEC were teaching high school level work, these packages would work for us. Suppes and Atkinson attracted a good deal of funding support from IBM, the National Science Foundation, the Carnegie Foundation, and the U.S. Office of Education. It was through their connection with IBM that they made their CAI software available for the IBM 1500. Tobin and I were even more interested in the IBM 1500 system because of the CCC software.

In July 1976, we received word that our Title III grant would be funded. The Title III award was for $100,000. (approximately $500,000. in 2020 dollars adjusting for inflation) in the first year for the CAI laboratory, and we could apply for additional funds in the following years. We knew that it was imperative that we establish the laboratory before the next cycle of the grant. By this time, we were most impressed with the CCC software, but the big problem was the hardware platform to deliver it. The IBM 1500 was expensive and beyond the grant's budget. In discussions with CCC, we shared our problem and its representatives indicated that they were just finishing negotiations with several minicomputer manufacturers to provide hardware platforms for its software. We thought we might be able to use the DEC PDP 11/45 but unfortunately, DEC wasn't one of the manufacturers. We finally concluded that the most cost-effective approach would be to get a new machine dedicated to running the CCC software. The CCC representatives recommended that we purchase a Cincinnati Milacron CIP/2200 for $30,000. with a configuration that would meet our needs for at least five years. The real savings was that we could use "dumb" terminals instead of the more expensive workstations. We purchased 21 Hazeltine terminals for $785. each. We used the rest of the funds to pay for the CCC CAI software, furniture, manuals, supplies and training. Lastly, we purchased 21 inexpensive toggle switches that allowed each terminal to access either the CIP/2200 or the MEC computer center's data communications controller that would also give students access to the CUNY Central Computer Center. My hope for the latter was that faculty would start using this facility for other academic applications. This data communications setup for the lab was the first coaxial cable network that was installed at the college (see Figure 11.1). MEC managed to provide college funds for a full-time coordinator for the lab and a part-time assistant. The part-time assistant was one of the staff retrenched in the summer. Tobin would work with the faculty to integrate the CCC material with the curricula of the college's remedial courses. One critical decision that had to be made was whether the CCC software replaced seat time in a remedial course or was used as a supplement.

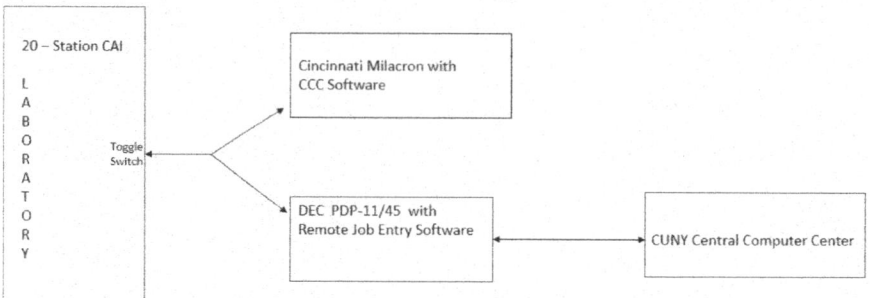

Figure 11.1 Twenty-Station CAI Laboratory

My staff and I were responsible for overseeing the installation and keeping the hardware and software running smoothly. The CAI laboratory was up and running by December 1976, with plans to have six sections of remedial classes test it for spring 1977. Tobin and I would do a basic implementation evaluation of the CCC software based on the student use of the software. As far as I knew, we were the only college in CUNY that had a dedicated CAI lab for students with remedial needs.

12

My work at MEC provided me many administrative, technological, and human relations experiences. The fiscal crisis had challenged all of us regardless of our positions, but I found the need to protect my staff from retrenchment a trying learning experience. I felt for the staff and the discussions that I had with mothers about possibly losing their jobs stayed with me my entire life.

Another important aspect of my growth at this time was my ongoing adjunct teaching at BMCC. Dan Rosich was still the deputy chairperson in the data processing program and called me regularly to teach a class in the evening. As I indicated earlier, the students in this program were wonderful and I tried my best to give them valuable experiences in my courses. During one of my classes in spring 1975, and before moving to MEC, I was observed by Marvin Kushner, who was the chairperson of the program. The personnel procedures at CUNY required that each adjunct faculty member be observed at least once during the semester. The observation was followed by a written report and a meeting with the observer. At the meeting, Professor Kushner said that he was pleased with my lesson and that his report would be very complimentary. He also asked what I was doing during the day, and I told him of my work at that time at Lehman College. In fall of 1975, Professor Kushner observed me again and during our follow-up meeting, asked if I was interested in teaching full-time. The offer was intriguing, but I told him I wasn't ready to move into full-time teaching.

In January 1976, I got a call from the Mt. Sinai School of Medicine asking if I might be interested in teaching a six-week evening course on computer technology in their hospital administration certificate program. I thought that I might be able to do it, but I asked how the caller got my name. He said that Professor Kushner from BMCC had recommended me. Over the course of the next year or so, I received a half a dozen calls from various colleges and organizations in New York asking if I might be available to teach a course or seminar. In every instance, Professor Kushner had recommended me.

My work at Mt. Sinai opened up another venue of teaching possibilities geared mostly to short-term (three-day to five-day) professional development seminars. My students at Mt. Sinai were a very mature group of individuals who had mid-level positions in hospitals across New York City. Most wanted to advance their careers similar to my goal in enrolling in the MPA program at Baruch. For my first course at Mt. Sinai, I did some research and integrated a number of examples and cases related to hospital administration. Actually, the data processing concepts for developing computer applications at a hospital weren't radically different from a college. As my students at Mt. Sinai went back to their hospitals, they recommended me for professional development activities in their own hospitals. I did four of these seminars over the next several months. I found it interesting work and enjoyed the experience.

Back at MEC, the fiscal crisis put a damper on all of our work. For 1975-76, the budget for all of CUNY was reduced from $539 million to $470 million. For MEC, the budget was reduced from $7.7 million to $6.2 million. However, as part of a new funding formula that would shift much of CUNY's budget to the State of New York, MEC was reduced to community college status for funding purposes. In addition, tuition was imposed for the first time in CUNY's history in fall 1976 and this created a need for new bursar and financial aid applications for which, fortunately, the CUNY Central Office assumed responsibility. In previous years, financial aid processing was a modest operation since with no tuition, there wasn't much need for financial aid information systems. With the imposition of tuition, enrollment plummeted twenty percent at CUNY and went from 250,784 to 200,737 students (headcount) in one year. MEC saw a very modest enrollment decrease from 3,090 to 2,945 students (headcount). In addition to budget cuts implemented at the start of the 1976-77 fiscal year, the drop in student enrollment exacerbated a bad situation for the entire university since the anticipated tuition revenue wouldn't be forthcoming. Tuition accounted for approximately one-third of the CUNY budget.

The vast majority of adjunct faculty at CUNY weren't reappointed for the Fall 1976 semester. At BMCC, I was told that the entire adjunct faculty had been let go. But in August 1976, just before classes were to start, I received a call from Professor Kushner asking if I was available to teach a course in the evening at BMCC. I was grateful for the offer and I said I would be happy to teach in his program, but that I thought that all of the adjuncts at BMCC weren't being reappointed. He said that was the case but that he had some limited research funds outside of the regular college budget from which he could pay me. For the Fall 1976 and Spring 1977 semesters I continued to teach at BMCC on research funds. I never forgot Professor Kushner's gesture and kindness towards me.

13

On January 20th, 1977, the Democratic Party candidate, Jimmy Carter was sworn in as the 39th President of the United States after defeating Gerald Ford, whose term was marred by the aftermath of the Nixon impeachment, resignation and pardon. On January 21st, Carter pardoned all Vietnam War draft evaders.

The Spring 1977 semester moved along fairly well. Although the budget situation dominated much of our discussions and planning, we were able to continue to develop and enhance the student and course information systems we implemented in the Spring 1976 semester. Ashok and Joan had really taken to the systems and kept them running smoothly. Using the CUNY Central Computer Center turned out to be a good decision; it was stable and reliable. Ashok and I continued to explore possibilities for the DEC PDP 11/45 but our conclusion was that at some point it would be used to support academic computing especially since the CAI Lab had access to it. However, with the budget situation being what it was, all academic programs were concerned with keeping what they had and weren't thinking about expansion.

In fall 1976 and into spring 1977, I became a member of a team of faculty and staff that participated in an IBM Business Alliance Program that sought to provide economic assistance to poorer neighborhoods in New York City. MEC's part in this program was to encourage students in the local Central Brooklyn high schools to graduate and to think about going to college. I participated in several of the activities including going to local high schools with other MEC faculty and administrators. I never had to say anything and usually one of the faculty would give a "pep" talk about the virtues of a good education. At the end of a talk, I would sit at a table with a colleague and answer student questions one-on-one about education and going on to college. Invariably the question of cost always came up and fortunately,

New York State had a good financial aid program that covered tuition. There were also the SEEK and College Discovery Programs (for community college students) that covered tuition plus stipends. I was a cheerleader for CUNY in general, since among its colleges just about every academic and career program of study on the undergraduate level was available. I learned a lot at these sessions and further came to understand the difficulties of the urban poor.

John Antonaccio, the Business Manager at MEC, and I had also become very good colleagues. We went to Baruch College together for our MPA degrees. John had recruited me to MEC. We carpooled to MEC together and lunched regularly. We played basketball on Friday nights. Professor Ronnie Bobb, chairperson of the Physical Education Department, organized Friday night basketball games for faculty and staff. John and I were regulars along with Dennis Johnson, the Dean of Students, Teddy Lachman and others. Ronnie also organized several faculty versus student varsity games which were quite intense and rigorous. After basketball, we would go to Dennis' office and send out for pizza or sandwiches and beer. Interestingly, I never had to provide much in the way of computer services to John or the Business Office because just as I got to MEC, CUNY decided to develop and implement a new university-wide financial accounting system that would run on the CUNY Central Computer Center. John asked me to attend meetings with his staff in case there were questions about the technical aspects of the new accounting system but neither I nor my staff would have any responsibility for it. It was during a ride home from MEC one night in May 1977 that John told me that he might be leaving the College. He was entertaining an offer from Publicker Industries, a large corporation in the distilling business, to be its chief financial officer. He said the financial compensation package would triple his salary. Naturally I congratulated him, but I was concerned about his leaving MEC. Not only had we been colleagues for over six years, I would be losing my closest friend at MEC. He said that he hadn't mentioned this to anyone else and to keep it quiet until he had. In July 1977, it was formally announced that John would be leaving MEC and that Teddy Lachman, his assistant would be the new business manager. Over the next year or so, I would hear about colleagues all over CUNY who had decided to leave for positions elsewhere. Given the New York City fiscal crisis and the financial situation at CUNY, it was to be expected. CUNY wasn't hiring; promotions were at a standstill and it was getting incredibly difficult to maintain basic administrative services. At the computer center, we were fortunate that we hadn't lost any more staff after the previous year's retrenchment, and in fact because of the Title III grant and the CAI lab, we were able to use research funds to keep our operations at a decent level.

14

The Fall 1977 semester was again budgetarily problematic all across CUNY. The effects of the retrenchment in 1976 were being felt. In CUNY, almost 6,000 full-time positions had been eliminated, most of these were the result of the hiring freeze that had been in effect for more than a year. Student enrollment across the university continued to drop from 200,737 in fall 1976 to 189,765 students (headcount) in fall 1977. At MEC for the same period, the student enrollment dropped from 2,945 to 2,774 students (headcount). The decrease in enrollment would also have a serious effect on budgets since once again expected tuition revenue wouldn't be forthcoming. Most of the administrative operations were just trying to keep their heads above water. As a side note, following the imposition of tuition in 1976, enrollment across the university would decrease from 250,784 to 172,229 students (headcount) over the next five years (1975 to 1980.) CUNY''s enrollment wouldn't reach its 1975 level again until 2010.

During this gloomy period, one bright spot was our CAI Laboratory. We were able to test and integrate the software with six courses in spring 1977. The CAI software was used as supplementary work in existing courses. The reading and arithmetic modules appeared to help students in the piloted courses. This wasn't true for the writing module. In fact, the writing module was deemed problematic by the instructors. Tobin would continue to work with the faculty teaching remedial courses and the plan was for six more classes to be added for fall 1977.

In the middle of September 1977, Ned Conway, a Dean from SUNY New Paltz, appeared at my office. He couldn't have come there by accident since our center was hidden in the basement. He introduced himself and came right to the point: he was the chair of a search committee for a new director of his college's computer services. This came completely out of the blue as

I hadn't indicated to anyone in anyplace that I was looking to leave MEC. I asked him how he got my name and said a colleague of his at the CUNY Central Office mentioned me to him. He didn't say who this colleague was. I told him I knew nothing about SUNY New Paltz. He gave me a candid rundown especially of the computer center operation which he thought was ready to implode. I gave him a tour of our facility and he was amazed with our operations and especially the CAI Laboratory. He asked me to think about making a visit to his college and that he would be in touch. I did indeed think about it and when contacted by the New Paltz president, Stan Coffman, I decided to make the visit in early October. I had breakfast with President Coffman who was very personable and forthcoming. He indicated that the previous director of the New Paltz computer center had resigned and gone to SUNY Albany. He had also taken with him his associate director, the operations manager and his senior programmer. I met with the search committee and the vice presidents including Bill Dempsey who was the VP for Administration and to whom I would be reporting. Bill had spent most of his career at SUNY Plattsburgh in administration. He too was honest and indicated that he thought the computer operation was a mess. I was given a tour of the campus that was very impressive. It had over two hundred acres with a combination of old and new buildings. The computer center was spacious and housed in the basement of the Haggerty Administration Building. For some unexplained reason there was a raised floor throughout the center even in the offices. When I made the tour, several of the offices were empty, indicative of the staff that had gone to SUNY Albany. I went into the computer room that housed a Burroughs 5700 computer. I had never worked on a Burroughs machine and knew very little about it. The long and short of it was that as attractive as the campus and computer center facilities were, I didn't think I wanted to come here.

When I returned to MEC, I decided to have a talk with my immediate supervisor, Jim Grant. He and I had a good relationship and I thought that I should share what was going on with New Paltz. I also didn't want someone from New Paltz possibly contacting someone at CUNY about me and getting word back to Jim. Jim let me know that the financial situation at MEC and CUNY wasn't positive and that it might not be until the 1980s that things might return to normal. He also suggested that I have a conversation with Don Watkins. When I spoke with Dean Watkins, he said he would be sorry to see me go but that I had to do what was best for me. His comments reminded me of my conversation with Dean Wilbur Edel at Lehman College. He also said that I was young, and I should gain experience at a number of different institutions if I wanted to make a career in higher education. This resonated with me and started me thinking about possibly making the move to New Paltz. The following week I received a call from Bill Dempsey who indicated that he was prepared to make an offer for me to come to New Paltz. It was a good conversation. We talked about salary and that the offer would be generous. I also suggested to him that I didn't want to make a strictly lateral move from one college to another. I asked if it would be possible to consider an assistant vice president position rather than the computer center director position. I had reviewed the administrative structure at New Paltz, and I knew the other two vice presidents had assistants, but Dempsey did not. He said he would have a talk with President Coffman about it. I said fine and to let me know when he was ready with the offer. Bill called the next day and said that President Coffman would consider giving me an assistant vice president title, but that it might it take six months to a year. I was disappointed about this, but I believed President Coffman was honest and wouldn't try to deceive me. I asked to have it all put in writing. I received a letter three days which spelled out everything that Bill and I discussed. I decided to accept the offer.

I let Jim Grant and Don Watkins know immediately of my decision. Then I shared the news with my staff. It was a sad day all around. I was to begin at New Paltz on November 14th, 1977.

PART III

State University of New York New Paltz
New Paltz, New York
1977-1979

15

The State University of New York (SUNY) New Paltz is located in Ulster County in the Hudson Valley of New York. It traces its history to 1828, when the New Paltz Classical School that offered Greek, Latin, reading, writing, and arithmetic began. In 1833, it was reorganized into an academy. One hundred years later, in 1932, the Classical School became a Normal School and then a four-year college in 1938 when it was renamed the State Teachers College of New Paltz. In 1947, graduate teacher education programs were added, and in 1961, the name was officially changed to the State University of New York College of Liberal Arts and Sciences at New Paltz. New Paltz was one of the fourteen four-year liberal arts colleges in SUNY which also included four university centers, ag/tech and community colleges, and other specialized schools. The enrollment at New Paltz when I arrived in fall 1977 was 7,543 students (headcount). There had been steady enrollment decreases since 1975 when the enrollment was 8,892 (headcount). Because a portion of the budgets of all the SUNY colleges were enrollment-driven, the SUNY Central Office had been requesting budget reductions at New Paltz for the past two years.

On November 15th, I had lunch with President Stan Coffman at his home overlooking the New Paltz Valley with the Shawangunk Mountains (part of the Catskill Mountain range) in the background. He impressed me as a seasoned, albeit low-keyed administrator. He made me aware early on that the SUNY Central Office was overly intrusive in the college's affairs. Every significant expense whether for personnel, equipment, contracts, or facilities had to be approved by the Central Office. All computer-related expenditures would have to be approved by the Assistant Vice Chancellor for Computer Services Harold Wakefield. He suggested I pay a visit to him as soon as possible. The following day I had lunch with Vice President Bill Dempsey and we hit it off very well. Most of his experience was at SUNY Plattsburgh where he had been the assistant vice president for administration. He knew the SUNY Central Staff well including Harold Wakefield and expanded on Coffman's view that they were very bureaucratic and functioned too much as "gate-keepers." They had a formula for every administrative office that determined the number of personnel and the limits on other-than-personnel service (OTPS) expenditures. He indicated it was difficult to get them to veer away from their formulae.

As I mentioned in the previous chapter, the computer center was located in the basement of the Haggerty Administration Building and was quite spacious. My office was 400 square feet with bookcases and a large wooden desk which I learned had been in the President's Office until about ten years ago. I also had a separate, adjoining conference room of 300 square feet. The programmers had their own offices although by the time I had arrived all of them were vacant. The data entry staff was intact, and the three keypunch operators were conscientious workers. Barry Stickel was the daytime computer operator who I would eventually promote to the operations manager position, also vacant when I arrived. He was knowledgeable about the equipment and had worked briefly for the Burroughs Corporation, a big boost that allowed us to keep the center running fairly well. He let me know that he wasn't happy with the previous computer center director who had hired away so many staff members. As a result, the programming staff consisted of two part-time students who were majoring in computer science at the college. Both were talented but lacked experience and were hoping to get a job at IBM when they graduated in the coming June. IBM was the major employer in the area with large facilities in Kingston, Poughkeepsie and Fishkill, all within fifteen-minute drives from the college. I had an administrative assistant, Kathy Johnson, who was excellent in keeping the office and all communications operating smoothly.

The Burroughs 5700 was part of the B5000 series of computers introduced in 1961. It had an MCP (Master Control Program) operating system that supported two compilers: COBOL and extended ALGOL (Algorithmic Language). All the programs being used in the center were written in COBOL. The MCP also supported a proprietary Data-Communications Processor (DCP) software that allowed for the control of terminals through a COBOL program. The Burroughs hardware was stable and Barry was able to keep it going, but if a part was ever needed, it could take days for it to arrive. I was disappointed to learn that preventive maintenance was unheard of at Burroughs, so we never had any forewarning that a part was wearing out.

New Paltz had a modest student information system that was quite old, and everyone recognized that it needed to be replaced. There had been a new student information system in the design phase but not implemented. There was a brand-new student admissions module which was good and worked well. In addition, there were several other small file processing applications for other administrative offices (bursar, financial aid, continuing education.) The college also had a small computer science program with modest facilities. There was a keypunch area in the computer science department and several slow-speed terminals connected to the SUNY Albany computer center. Our responsibility was to run student programs submitted on card decks through the Burroughs computer or remote job entry to the SUNY Albany computer. My priorities for the first several months were to develop a programming staff and begin assessing the college's computer needs.

16

Even though the college was under fiscal constraints, I was given approval to fill three staff vacancies. The nature of the positions was left to me. I decided to use all of them to hire programmers. I had to receive permission from Assistant Vice Chancellor Harold Wakefield, and I decided to use this as a reason to meet with him. It was a cordial meeting. Assistant Vice Chancellor Wakefield had a lot of experience in private industry and at SUNY. I filled him in on my background and he seemed impressed with the combination of administrative and academic computer experiences I had. He indicated that most of the SUNY colleges were doing okay on the administrative side of computing; but with the exception of the four university centers and a several other schools, weren't doing enough to develop the academic side. He also told me that Burroughs equipment was standard at all of the fourteen four-year liberal arts colleges in SUNY and would have to be replaced soon. But most importantly, he said he would approve my request for three new programmers.

I immediately advertised for the programmer positions and was able to hire three talented and very different individuals. Nick Galemo was a recent graduate of SUNY Plattsburgh in computer science. He was a talented programmer and knew the Burroughs software, especially the DCP, very well. He was a pure programmer who didn't want to spend much time talking with users. He preferred to be told what to do; he would do it on time; and it would be fully debugged. Phyllis Sturm had experience as a programmer, but her real strength was in understanding the needs of users. She had a good eye and instinct for applications and developed a rapport with other administrative offices in the college. Maura Kristofik was a recent graduate from Marist College in computer science and could code well. She had little experience but learned quickly. We also had two student programmers who were already working in the computer center when I arrived. As we entered the new year (1978), the computer center was staffed, and we could now develop applications for the college. Our first priority would be student and course information systems. Aren't they always?

The assistant vice president for student affairs and registrar, Jon Fackler, was completely devoted to the system designed by my predecessor and his staff. Nick, Phyllis and I reviewed the design and came to the conclusion that the student information component was workable but that the course component was weak. In consultation with Jon, we agreed that we would have the first phases of new systems completed by April. For the course system, we used the design that I had at Lehman College four years earlier, based on a course master file and a course semester file. For the student information system, we decided to combine the best elements of the student information system designed by my predecessor with the one from Lehman College. We saved a lot of time by using all of the coding schemes from the previous design since they were familiar to the registrar and other users. As we did at Medgar Evers College, we put a major effort into developing a comprehensive general update and a general report program. It took Nick, with help from me, about six weeks to build the general update program. Phyllis and Maura worked on the course information system, while two students maintained the existing programs that were in operation at the computer center. Barry was particularly helpful in determining any modifications that were needed for the existing programs. By the end of April as promised, we were ready to convert the old student and course files to the new student information and course system. We used the summer session to test the student registration and other transaction processing applications. Everything worked fairly well except that Nick believed he could do a better job with the online DCP portion of the general update program and rewrote large portions of it in July and August. The computer center would be ready to go into the Fall 1978 semester with the new systems and felt confident that they would be much better than what was previously designed. Jon Fackler and his staff were happy.

In late spring, Assistant Vice Chancellor Wakefield announced that SUNY would be issuing a request for proposal (RFP) to replace the Burroughs computers at all of the fourteen four-year liberal arts colleges including New Paltz. This created a bit of dilemma because there was no guarantee that Burroughs would get the contract. If another vendor got the contract, any applications developed on the Burroughs machine would have to go through a conversion or be rewritten. In the 1970s, the idea of standard software didn't exist, particularly if proprietary software such as DCP was used. Assistant Vice Chancellor Wakefield had indicated that he hoped a process for evaluating the RFP would begin in fall 1978 and a decision would be made by May 1979. He asked me and several other computer center directors to be members of the committee to develop the requirements for the RFP as well as evaluating vendor proposals.

17

I n June 1978, two major developments which evolved in California would have impact across the country. On June 6th, California voters approved a referendum (Proposition 13) that slashed property taxes by 60 percent. This was a signal to government leaders that the United States was moving towards a period of fiscal conservatism. On June 28th, the US Supreme Court issued its Regents of the University of California v. Bakke Decision which declared affirmative action in college admissions valid but invalidated the use of racial quotas. In this highly disputed ruling (six separate opinions were issued), the Court agreed that the University's use of strict racial quotas was unconstitutional and ordered that the California medical school admit Bakke, but it also contended that race could be used as one criterion in the admissions decisions of institutions of higher education. In sum, the decision barred quota systems in college admissions but affirmed the constitutionality of programs that gave advantages to minorities.

During that summer of 1978, a large space right next to the computer center that had been used as a storage area for the campus facilities department became available. I had been thinking about developing a space for students in the computer science program, so I spoke with Bill Dempsey and he thought the idea of an academic computer area was a good one. He checked with the campus facilities people and they had no plans for using the space. I then spoke with Richard Soghoian, the assistant vice president for academic affairs and Ned Conway, the dean of humanities, who both thought it a great idea. I then spoke with the computer science faculty especially Paul Zuckerman, who also was most supportive. I asked Paul what he would envision for the facility. Following these conversations, I wrote a small proposal requesting funds to convert the space into a student computer laboratory. Funds would be needed for renovating the space and purchasing equipment. The proposal included the renovation of the physical space, six computer terminals and a remote job entry station to connect to SUNY Albany's computer. We received funding for half of the proposal with a good chance that the rest would come in the next fiscal year. We were very efficient in using the funds for the renovation and relied as much as possible on in-house staff to do the work. The finished area wasn't a "showcase" computer laboratory, but it would do the job. We purchased six terminals, a small printer, furniture, and a dedicated data communication controller to connect to SUNY Albany. These would allow the students to work gracefully with several programming languages including BASIC and Fortran. We also moved two keypunch machines into the laboratory. The remote job entry station would have to wait until the next year. One of the computer science faculty also had an idea to set aside some of the area for students to build small personal computers using kits. At the time, personal computers manufactured by Apple, Commodore and Radio Shack were just coming on the market. However, "build your own computer" kits had been available for several years and cost just a few hundred dollars each. The faculty in computer science thought it would be a great experience for their students and put up the funding for the kits through their own department funds. We didn't have any funds for staffing but were able to get student aides from computer science to supervise the area. The computer laboratory opened in January 1979. It was a welcome addition to the computer science program, and we were delighted to have it as a next-door neighbor.

In August of 1978, around the same time we were developing the lab for the computer science program, Bill Dempsey told me that Hal Wakefield had contacted him about New Paltz being a test site for a new computerized financial aid system. He indicated that the system would be purchased by the Central Office and implemented by the vendor and that we would work with the financial aid office to integrate it into its operations. We wouldn't be responsible for programming but simply operating the system. I told him that we could consider this, but I questioned the timing since Wakefield had recently announced that SUNY would be issuing an RFP for new computer equipment at the four-year colleges next year. It seemed to me that we would implement the system and then possibly have to convert it within a year to run on new computer equipment. Bill indicated that it was Wakefield's decision and it would be beneficial for us to take him up on the offer. I said if that is what he wanted; it was okay with me. I asked our programmer Phyllis to be the point person on this. Privately, I wondered whether Wakefield had already assumed that Burroughs would be awarded the RFP contract.

In September of 1978, I was approached by Gerald Benjamin, a professor of political science who asked me if I was familiar with SPSS. He and several of his colleagues wanted to start doing more quantitative analysis for their own research as well to integrate it into their research methods courses. I told him I was familiar with the package and had used it at Medgar Evers College and at Lehman College. He asked if we could acquire SPSS for New Paltz. I said I would look into it but that I was skeptical about SPSS running on a Burroughs computer. I contacted Norman Nie, one of the developers of SPSS, at the University of Chicago. He said that indeed there was a version of SPSS that would run on Burroughs equipment and that I could request a free copy for New Paltz. I was ecstatic. I knew that the original SPSS, developed with funding from the federal government was freely available to legitimate researchers; I wasn't aware at that time that Nie and his associates had converted it to run on just about every mainframe manufacturer's equipment. I requested a copy and installed it on the Burroughs 5700. It was slow, but it ran without any technical problems. I did several one-day workshops for Benjamin and his colleagues on the basics of SPSS, including some of the control instructions needed for running it on a Burroughs machine. I also told them that they should purchase the SPSS Manual that Nie and his associates had published. Not only was it a great introduction to SPSS but one of the best books I had ever read about doing statistical analysis.

By the end of my first year, I was confident that the computer center was making progress and establishing its credibility with the main administrative users, and a small cadre of faculty, mostly those in computer science and political science. Ned Conway, who had originally recruited me to come to

New Paltz, would become an important support figure in the administration for our work.

18

As happy as I was with the progress of the computer center, I was concerned about the administrative leaders above me. As I suspected, Stan Coffman was a good president. I never had any problem with him or his executive assistant Gail Gallerie, who functioned like a fourth vice president in the college. President Coffman, as I indicated earlier was low-keyed and spoke softly, and had the best interests of his four-year liberal arts college in mind. He also connected with some of us in the administration by inviting us to his home on Saturday afternoons to watch college football games. I don't know who was invited at other times, but Ned Conway and Richard Soghoian were there every time I was present. I never saw any of the vice presidents at these social gatherings. My major concern was about my boss, Bill Dempsey. Shortly after my arrival in November 1977, he shared concerns he had about where the college was heading. He indicated that the college had a major budget problem that nobody, other than he, was interested in resolving anytime soon. The vibes I picked up were that he would leave as soon as something more to his liking came up. When I took the position at New Paltz, I was living in Westchester County and had a 70-minute commute by car. During my first few months I seriously considered moving my family nearer to the college but decided to wait until spring when the housing market is more robust. By spring, however, I was concerned about Bill leaving and decided to hold off on a move.

I had few interactions with the vice president for academic affairs, Peter Vukasian, and instead worked extensively with his assistant, Richard Soghoian. Richard was a solid administrator and we hit it off wonderfully. We also played tennis on a regular basis during lunch hours after which we'd go for a quick beer. He shared a lot with me that gave me a better understanding of the upper administration. Besides my staff, I spent more time with Richard than anyone else at New Paltz.

Eileen Farley was the vice president for student affairs, but I dealt most of the time with Jon Fackler, the assistant vice president for student affairs who was also in charge of the registrar's office. Jon could be demanding and had an attitude. He was sure that the main purpose of the computer center was to support the student services offices. I saw student services, especially registration, admissions, and financial aid as critical, but I was also interested in serving other areas of the college including the need to integrate technology into the academic programs. I was fortunate that I had the support of the academic deans especially Ned Conway.

It was September 1978, Bill Dempsey called me to his office to discuss several minor issues and ended by asking me if I was familiar with National Center for Higher Education Management Systems (NCHEMS). I told him that I had used its materials to design student and course information systems at Lehman College. He said he had contacts at NCHEMS and had been asked whether he would do a paid consultation at Saint Francis College in Brooklyn to help develop planning models. He indicated that it sounded a bit too technical for him but he thought that I might be interested. I told him I would be happy to speak with them, so he forwarded my name and I was contacted. I had a good conversation with the NCHEMS staff, and they thought I could do a good job for them. They also said they would send me material including updated documents on college information system design and a planning module called the "Induced Course Load Matrix". The latter was an academic management software tool to identify the most productive academic programs beyond simple enrollments and number of majors. I did the consultation and it worked out well. I subsequently did consultations for NCHEMS at Mercy College and Westchester Community College. Just after the consultation at Westchester, I received a call from the head of their academic program in information technology asking if I might consider an adjunct instructor position to teach computer systems in the evening in the fall. I decided to accept this mainly because the salary was very attractive. I also missed teaching since coming to New Paltz and thought this would be a good way to keep my skills honed.

In fall 1978, I also made the acquaintance of Sister Mary Genevieve Love who was an administrator at Mt. St. Mary's College across the river in Newburgh, New York. She just showed up at my door one morning and asked if she could speak with me for a few minutes. Given my Catholic background I could never refuse a nun especially one who still wore parts of the Dominican Sisters habit. She was very direct and shared a good deal with me about her college and her reason for visiting me. Mt. St. Mary's was struggling financially, and enrollment had been declining precipitously. Mt. St. Mary's was a former women's college that had decided to admit men in the mid-1970s. When many of the men's colleges had opened their schools to women during the early years of the women's liberation movement, there were many female applicants willing to enroll. The same hadn't been true for the women's colleges when they opened their doors to men. A number of the former women's colleges, particularly those that were tuition-driven, saw enrollment declines that put them in serious financial jeopardy. Sister Mary Genevieve also felt that her college's academic program had to be modernized and one of the areas into which she was hoping to expand was some form of business computer science even though she didn't have any computer equipment at her college. She was planning on applying for a United States Department of Education Title III grant to purchase equipment and staff up an academic computer center. She asked if I was familiar with Title III and I told her of my work at Medgar Evers College. On the spot, she asked me if I would consider helping her to draft the grant proposal; she was willing to pay me as consultant. I told her I would help her, but I didn't want remuneration. The grant proposal was submitted focusing on building a computer center and developing an information technology academic program. The following April, I got a call from Sister Genevieve telling me that the proposal was approved with three years of funding. I congratulated her and she asked to take me out to lunch to thank me. I told her yes we could do lunch later in the summer. I continued to work with Sister Mary Genevieve until the mid-1980s when she left Mt. St. Mary's to work with the poor in the Mississippi Delta. By 1981 the enrollment at Mt. St. Mary stabilized and began to increase in 1982.

In November 1978, I had a visit from Ethem Kok, the director of the computer center at the College of Staten Island. Ethem and I had been colleagues together and this was strictly a social visit. We had lunch and Ethem brought me up to date on all that was happening back in CUNY. I asked about Ken King and he told me that Ken had become a special assistant to New York City Mayor Abraham Beame on loan from CUNY. He was a member of a team that was to help the City develop its administrative systems and processes. Ethem was concerned about how things were developing at CUNY. The budget had been transferred to the State of New York for the senior colleges and basically they were operating with little financial relief from the disastrous New York City fiscal crisis. Computer center staff members were leaving CUNY because they couldn't get promotions or raises, and it was almost impossible to recruit new hires. I asked him if he had met my replacement at Medgar Evers College. He said that MEC had problems recruiting a new director and that Ken recommended appointing one of his staff, Bob Terdiman, at least temporarily. Ethem also said that Terdiman at meetings of the CUNY computer center directors, praised the MEC student and course information systems Ashok, Joan, and I had developed. He asked me how I liked working at New Paltz and I reviewed my past year. He was most interested in my description of the Burroughs computer and the new academic computer facility we were developing. It was a good visit and said we would do it again.

19

The Fall 1978 semester started well as the new student and course information systems the programming staff developed ran without a hitch and the student registration went smoothly. In November, Harold Wakefield called the first meeting of the committee to develop and evaluate an RFP for the new computer systems for the fourteen liberal arts colleges. Wakefield's staff had drawn up a boiler plate RFP that conformed with SUNY policies and our work began. By January 1979, detailed hardware and software specifications were developed that all bids had to meet. The proposed computer systems had to be in existence and couldn't be in design stages or otherwise not available for immediate delivery upon award of a contract. A series of benchmarks for hardware and software performance were also developed including the all-important cost for purchase and maintenance contracts. Lastly, there were several difficult to assess criteria such as costs to convert existing systems to new hardware and software and vendor reputation for technical support. The conversion criterion gave Burroughs a decided edge. On the other hand, Burroughs would have trouble defending its reputation for technical support, especially hardware support. The RFP Committee was meeting at least once a month, and this would continue through the spring. Most of these meetings were held at the colleges and not at the SUNY Central Office. In several cases, I had to stay overnight because New Paltz was several hundred miles south of many of the SUNY campuses.

Just before the winter break, Bill Dempsey told me he was leaving for a vice president's position at Ryder College in New Jersey. It was a good move for him in that he had never been happy working at New Paltz. He would be starting on February 1st, 1979. In the middle of January 1979, President Coffman called me to his office to tell me that Dick Debus would be the acting vice president of administration to fill Bill's position. Dick had a long career at the SUNY Central Office and was recommended by one of the SUNY vice chancellors. He asked that I give Dick my cooperation. President Coffman also indicated that he would be promoting me to assistant vice president as promised on February 1st.

On January 1st, 1979, the United States and the People's Republic of China established full diplomatic relations. It was the culmination of seven years of diplomacy that started with President Richard Nixon's visit to China in 1972 and his meeting with Chairman Mao Zedong. It marked a new era of economic cooperation between the two countries. On March 26th, in a ceremony at the White House, President Anwar Sadat of Egypt and Prime Minister Menachem Begin of Israel signed the Egyptian–Israeli Peace Treaty ending the years of war. This treaty evolved from the Camp David Accords hosted by President Carter in 1978. Things were looking up in Washington, but not necessarily so in New Paltz.

When Dick Debus arrived, we had several meetings and lunches. His background was accounting and he worked most of his career at the SUNY Central Office. It was my sense that his main priority was to get the college's budget under control. It was becoming clear to many of us that the financial situation at the college was becoming dire and that the new fiscal year which would begin on April 1st would be very difficult. The major concern was that the fall 1978 enrollment decline to 6,747 (headcount), down 796 students from fall 1977, might have been the last straw as far as the Central Office was concerned. Debus said the computer center was safe but that other areas in the college might be asked to take substantial budget reductions.

On March 28th, 1979, President Coffman called a meeting of the vice presidents, assistant vice presidents and deans. He laid out a very serious financial picture for the coming year. All hiring would be frozen, and equipment and contractual budgets severely curtailed. The real budgetary "bomb" was that at the next day's meeting of the Academic Senate, he would be announcing the retrenchment of eighteen faculty members, several of whom were tenured. The decision regarding which faculty would be retrenched was based entirely on college need and not on seniority or tenure status which was the generally accepted fiscal exigency policy in academia. I had rarely ever attended an Academic Senate meeting, but I attended this one. The announcement of the retrenchment came as a terrible shock to the faculty. When the list of faculty positions in the academic departments was read out, there was anger particularly since it was obvious that seniority or tenure didn't matter. On Friday afternoon, March 30th, President Coffman again called the senior administrators to his office and announced that he was handing in his letter of resignation immediately to the SUNY Chancellor. He suggested that all of us go about our work as usual and that he and Vice President Vukasian would be meeting with various faculty groups and representatives over the coming weeks. There was dead silence in the room. I never saw anything like this before or after.

20

The following week I had lunch with Richard Soghoian. He knew the budget was bad but had only learned in late March how bad it would be. He indicated that the SUNY Central Office had demanded that a retrenchment take place. He thought that for the next year or two or at least until there was a new president, the situation would be dire. It sounded to me like he was going to start looking for another position.

In the meantime, I was busy working on the RFP process. The committee was meeting just about every week now. We received proposals from most of the major mainframe manufacturers as well as several minicomputer manufacturers such as Hewlitt-Packard and Digital Equipment Corporation. I was impressed with the minicomputer proposals. They included a lot of hardware at low cost. However, there was little business-type software available and the existing college applications would likely have to be rewritten. At these meetings, I developed good relationships with several of the other SUNY computer center directors including Jack Horan (Potsdam), Ray Chamberlain (Buffalo State) and Bob Kilcourse (Oneonta). The four of us always met up in the evenings for dinner or a drink at the hotel bar to discuss all kind of things but especially where we thought the RFP was going. They all thought it would be very difficult to move away from the Burroughs systems. I was hoping that IBM would get the bid. I had worked with its equipment in my previous positions and given New Paltz's location in the middle of several major IBM facilities, it was a natural fit. But there were two big issues. First, as reliable as its equipment was and its stellar record of maintenance and service, IBM was expensive compared to other manufacturers. In addition, most of my colleagues on the committee were very leery of converting all of their administrative systems from their Burroughs machines. One colleague, Norm Plyter, from SUNY Brockport, supported me and mentioned that we should take into consideration the industry position of the various manufacturers, especially the fact that IBM controlled about 80 percent of the mainframe market. At this time, there were rumors that companies such as Burroughs, Control Data Corporation, and NCR were financially struggling to stay in the computer business. I also related several times the story of Robin Spock to the group and how RCA went out of business shortly after selling CUNY a high-end Spectre 7046 computer on Robin's recommendation.

In April, President Coffman opened up the search for Bill Dempsey's replacement. There were several applicants but not a very large pool. I met with all of the candidates and I have to confess I wasn't impressed with any of them. At the end of May, President Coffman called me to his office to review the candidates with me. He had come down to two possibilities, Dick Debus, the interim vice president for administration, and Jon Fackler, the assistant vice president for student affairs. He asked my opinion and I had to say candidly that I didn't think either one of them was up to the job. Dick had a singular focus on finance and knew little about broad college administration (personnel, institutional research, facilities). I thought he would make a good business manager. Jon's entire experience was in student services, specifically the registrar's office. However, he had developed good relationships with a number of faculty who were lobbying for him to get the position. I thought he would be a disaster and I told the president so. President Coffman asked me if I knew anyone in CUNY who might be interested in the position. I told him I would make some calls.

I contacted several acquaintances at the CUNY Central Office, who suggested a couple of possibilities in the central administration. I thought about it, but concluded I wanted to work with someone who had college experience. I then contacted Don Watkins, the Dean of Administration at Medgar Evers College (MEC). He said that things were pretty bad fiscally at MEC and CUNY in general. I told him why I was calling, and he said that if he were younger he would consider applying. He then said that while he would hate to see him go, he thought that Jim Grant, my former supervisor and the Associate Dean of Administration, might be interested. I asked Don if he would be upset if I contacted Jim and he said not at all. I thanked him and telephoned Jim immediately. After catching up a bit, I told him of the vacancy at New Paltz. He said he had been looking for a new position and would love to come up to meet the president. I told him I would get back to him. The next day I spoke with President Coffman and told him everything I knew about Jim. Coffman asked me several questions including whether I would enjoy working with him. I told him absolutely.

President Coffman set up a day of interviews for Jim. He also told Jim his own situation and that he would be leaving on July 1st. Coffman also told him that the interim president would be Jerome Komisar, a vice chancellor at SUNY. Jim was offered the position and he accepted. He started as Vice President on June 15th.

21

While the college was still reeling from the retrenchment, its fiscal problems, and the impending departure of the president, I continued to work on the RFP committee whose work was drawing to a conclusion. The majority of the members of the committee agreed to recommend the Burroughs proposal. Assistant Vice Chancellor Wakefield announced the decision in June 1979 and set up an implementation plan. New Paltz would receive a new Burroughs machine in the latter half of 1980.

In July, I received a phone call from Ed Volpe, the President of the College of Staten Island (CSI), asking if I might meet with him to discuss a position as the director of computer services. He told me that Ken King had recommended me. I thanked him for considering me, but I told him I was an assistant vice president and wouldn't take any backward steps in my administrative career. He persisted but I told him no thank you. He called back a week later and said he was prepared to offer me a very attractive salary and responsibility for several administrative departments. He again asked if I would just come to meet with him. I agreed and met with him and the provost, Felix Cardegna. The discussion was pleasant, and the offer was quite attractive. In addition to a very substantial salary increase, I would be responsible for computer services, the registrar's office and the financial aid office. I asked him what my title would be, and he said that he not figured that out yet. He then asked me to meet with the search committee which I agreed to do but by this time, it was pro forma. I contacted several people in CUNY including Ethem Kok who had been the computer center director at CSI. Ethem, now the director of computer services at Borough of Manhattan Community College, was critical of his former immediate supervisor. Others weren't encouraging mainly because CSI had recently gone through a merger and a very difficult retrenchment of both faculty and administrators. I decided to give Ken King a call and to ask him what he thought of the position. He was brutally honest and said that the administrative side of the college was in trouble and he wasn't sure if he was doing me a favor by recommending me. But he also said that he would very much like to have me back at CUNY and that he was hoping to issue an RFP for common computer systems for all the colleges. He also indicated that if I took the position, I would have his full support. The last part of the conversation made me think more seriously about the position. Ken was now a senior CUNY administrator and because of his work in assisting New York City during it fiscal crisis carried a lot of influence in the university. I had one more meeting with Ed Volpe and he described further my responsibilities and title which would be manager of administrative operations, but he also told that he would try to change the title within a year or so. I heard this once before at New Paltz and it worked out. I decided to take the position.

The following week I told my staff and it was once again a sad occasion. Nick especially felt bad, but he would blossom into a top-notch programmer who would go on to have an incredibly successful career. My discussion with Jim Grant was by far the most difficult, since he had barely started at New Paltz, but he had already heard through the CUNY grapevine that I was being considered for the position at CSI. He made it easy for me. I met with Richard Soghoian who told me he was also leaving also to become provost at Manhattanville College. We wished each other luck and said we would keep in touch. The following week, Interim President Komisar sent a very gracious letter to the college community in which he thanked both Richard and me for our service to New Paltz. Interestingly, in fall of 1979, student enrollment increased at New Paltz for the first time in five years. Alice Chandler, who had been the provost at City College in CUNY, was selected as New Paltz's new president where she would remain for sixteen years until her retirement in 1996. One of her most successful initiatives was to develop a relationship with IBM and its corporate leaders in the Hudson Valley.

On October 17th, President Jimmy Carter signed legislation establishing the US Department of Education. I left New Paltz at the beginning of November. In September 1986, Burroughs Corporation merged with Sperry Corporation to form Unisys.

PART IV

The College of Staten Island
Staten Island, New York
1979-1985

22

The College of Staten Island (CSI) was formed in the heat of the New York City fiscal crisis in the late 1970s through the merger of Staten Island Community College (SICC) and Richmond College. These two institutions couldn't have been more different in their missions, cultures, and faculties. Staten Island was the oldest community college (1956) in New York City and had over twenty years established a well-respected academic program geared to career, professional, and technical areas as well as a traditional liberal arts transfer program. Richmond was a relatively new, upper division college created in 1968 that focused on the liberal arts and sciences. The merger of these two disparate institutions that began in 1976 was difficult. Mirella Affron (2017), a member of the Richmond College faculty at the time of the merger who later became provost of the merged CSI, observed that the College's SICC folks saw their Sunnyside Campus as their own, while the Richmond College faculty and staff saw the facilities in the St. George section of the Island as theirs. This psychological and physical separation made it difficult for the newly combined/consolidated institution to move forward with new initiatives and projects. Even under the best circumstances, a merger would test the ability of the most seasoned and experienced administrators; during a severe fiscal crisis, it was insufferable. Before coming to Richmond College in 1974, Edmund Volpe, who was chosen as the president of the new college, had been an elected chairperson of the English Department at City College (CUNY) and had never held broad administrative responsibilities.

The merger of Staten Island Community College and Richmond College was in fact the only major restructuring to occur at CUNY during the New York City fiscal crisis. While the budget reductions and retrenchments were painful at all of CUNY, they were particularly so at these two institutions. Not only were they required to accept their share of the reductions, but they were also forced to pare down all duplicative academic and administrative functions. On the administrative side, all offices were merged, and staffs reduced fifty percent. For example, if Richmond College's Registrar's Office had a staff of six professional people and Staten Island Community College's Registrar's Office had a professional staff of six people, the new College of Staten Island Registrar's Office would only have six people and the remainder were retrenched. On the academic side, duplicative academic departments were merged, but given its relative newness, many of the faculty at Richmond College didn't have tenure and that made many more of them eligible for retrenchment. In 1975, the student headcount enrollments at SICC and Richmond College were 11,633 and 3,558 respectively for a total of 15,191. By 1980, the enrollment at the merged CSI would be 10,608 students, a thirty percent decline. This was comparable to what happened to enrollments across most of the colleges in CUNY.

On November 4th, 1979, United States President Jimmy Carter faced the most difficult crisis during his term in office after the seizure of the American embassy in Tehran by Iranian students. In response to exiled Muhammad Reza Shah Pahlevi's admission to the United States in September 1979 for medical treatment, a crowd of about 500 took over the embassy. Of the approximately 90 people inside the embassy, 52 remained as hostages for over a year. Carter's failure to resolve the crisis remained in the news for the rest of his presidency and contributed to Ronald Reagan's winning the presidential election in November 1980.

On November 5th, 1979, I met with President Volpe on my first day at CSI. It was a good meeting and he made it clear that he really wanted me to make a major contribution to his administration. The senior administration consisted of the president, provost, dean of faculty, dean of students, vice president for administration, and dean of administration. I was to report officially to the vice president for administration; however, it quickly became obvious to me that the president and provost would be very much involved in influencing everything I did. President Volpe described that present reporting relationships among the vice president, the dean of administration, and me as overlapping, but noted he hoped to resolve this situation within a year. During the rest of the week, I met with the other senior administrators, and all of the department heads and their assistants who reported directly to me. I was in charge of the administrative computer center, the registrar's office, the financial aid office, a budget planning office, and a to-be-created office for institutional research. The only wrinkle during my first week was my proposed office arrangement. President Volpe wanted me to have an office in the administrative computer center. I told him that wouldn't work and that it would be especially unfair to the other department heads reporting to me to feel that they reported to the computer center director. He understood and quickly arranged for me to have two offices, one at the old SICC or Sunnyside Campus right next to the dean of faculty and one at the old Richmond College or St. George Campus across the hall from the president. The Sunnyside Campus was a small "green" campus in the middle of Staten Island with four three-story buildings and four temporary buildings. The St. George Campus, near various government buildings on Staten Island, overlooked New York Harbor and occupied three rented buildings. One of the most important priorities for CSI was to merge the two campuses into one location.

The administrative computer center was on the Sunnyside Campus. CSI had well-established academic technology programs that originated from both SICC and Richmond College. There were two academic computer laboratories, one for each campus, that supported the two-year and four-year technology programs. A director of academic computing supervised these two facilities and reported to the dean of faculty. While the technology-based academic departments at CSI had been merged, the academic programs themselves were still in various stages of merging. The administrative computer center housed an IBM 360-30 computer that ran the IBM 360 Disk Operating System (DOS). This was basically the same equipment and system software that I worked with at Lehman College. The major administrative applications supported student record keeping for the registrar's office and other student service operations. I was most impressed that the center had developed and maintained a full student transcript system that could generate a transcript for any student who ever attended CSI or its predecessor institutions. This was the only such application in all of CUNY. In fact, very few colleges or universities at this time anyplace had computerized student transcript systems. All of these applications were based on card entry and student files stored on magnetic disk or tape. The IBM 360-30 had limited data communications capability and the machine itself was too slow to support a robust online environment. I was happy with what I saw on the hardware and software end, especially since I knew that Ken King would soon be issuing an RFP for new computer systems for all of the CUNY colleges.

References

Affron, M. (2017). Statement made regarding the merger of Staten Island Community College and Richmond College (February 7th).

23

Most of the upper administration consisted of individuals who had been with one of the predecessor colleges before the merger. Felix Cardegna, the provost, Arthur Kaufman, the vice president for administration, and Grace Petrone, the dean of students, came from SICC. Barry Bressler, the dean of faculty, was from Richmond College. Arnie Riback, the dean of administration, was the exception and came from the CUNY Central Office. Officially, I reported to Arthur Kaufman, but as I mentioned earlier, there was a certain lack of clarity in the reporting structure. All concerned appeared to have the best interests of the college at heart, however, they, like everyone else at CSI, were quick to let you know whether they were from SICC or Richmond. At meetings, you could feel the underlying tension that existed between the two camps. At the time of the merger, administrative directors from Richmond College had been chosen to supervise each of the offices now under my direction. By the time I arrived, my staff consisted entirely of individuals who originally worked at SICC. Every one of them was competent and dedicated to the new merged CSI.

In the computer center, there was a crew of excellent programmers. Lou Addeo led this group. He was knowledgeable and well-liked by the other programmers. Bill Canary and Ron Marcinkiewitz likewise were talented programmers. All three of these individuals had spent their entire careers at SICC/CSI. The operations and data entry staffs likewise were life-long employees of the college who took pride in their work. I promoted Lou Addeo to director of the administrative computer center. Prior to my coming, Lou was the interim director of the administrative computer center and reported to Arnie Riback.

Elaine Bowden was the registrar. Her entire career was at SICC/CSI. She was knowledgeable, could articulate her office's needs to the computer center staff, and was well-liked by both the programming and operations staff. Two years earlier, she took a one-year sabbatical and spent it studying computer information systems courses at one of the New Jersey state colleges so that she would be more technologically knowledgeable. She also understood well all of the policies and systems that were important to her office. She was assisted by Fran Draeger and Frank Delly, both of whom had excellent skills for handling complex student registration and scheduling processes.

Sherman Whipkey, also from SICC, was the financial aid director. He knew the intricacies of federal and state policies thoroughly. He also had an excellent support staff working with him who provided courteous and thorough services to students applying for and receiving financial aid.

Mike Bloomberg had spent his entire career at SICC/CSI and had a wealth of knowledge about the institution. Prior to my arrival, he had worked under Arthur Kaufman and had the registrar and financial aid director reporting to him. He wore several hats, but he was most knowledgeable about the college budget although he never had direct responsibility for that function. Instead, he analyzed various budget issues facing the college and could articulate strategies for seeking additional funding.

Lorraine Priester was my assistant and was very efficient. She knew everybody at CSI and was excellent at facilitating my meeting with people beyond those reporting to me. Lorraine, however, had worked for ten years in the administrative computer center and wanted very much to return to be with her colleagues. She would be replaced the following year by Terri Penna, who was competent, efficient, and had incredibly well-developed people skills.

I couldn't have been more pleased with the individuals working directly with me. They were among the most competent with whom I would ever work.

In late November, I had lunch with Ken King and his executive assistant Marie Drobin. I wanted to thank him for recommending me for the CSI position. He chose a Japanese sushi restaurant, which at the time were few and far between even for cosmopolitan New York City. He brought me up to date on all the goings on in CUNY. The funding for the senior colleges was firmly established with the State of New York, however, there was no indication that the funding would ever be restored to pre-fiscal crisis levels. We spent a good deal of time discussing the RFP for common computing equipment that he hoped to issue within months. He asked that I be on the evaluation committee along with Marie, Ira Fuchs, and George Goulandris, formerly of Queensborough Community College and now working in the Central Office. He described the need behind the RFP, namely, that there was absolutely no uniformity of equipment at the colleges. As a result, it was impossible for college computer centers to share their software to any major degree. IBM machines were dominant, but there also existed Xerox, National Cash Register, Burroughs, Univac, and Digital Equipment Corporation computers at various colleges as well. He also told me that politically both outside and inside CUNY, this was going to be a difficult undertaking. In fact, the New York State Division of the Budget wasn't supporting a major expenditure for computer equipment at all seventeen CUNY colleges. At the same time, presidents and computer center directors were leery that some of their autonomy and independence from the CUNY Central Office would be compromised by having common computer systems. I spent a part of the two-hour lunch describing the RFP process at SUNY and told Ken that it had pretty much been pre-determined that Burroughs Corporation would get the bid. Ken said to me that while he was open-minded, he couldn't envision the CUNY RFP going to any company but IBM. We would meet on the RFP regularly for the next six months and made several trips to Albany to visit with staff from the New York State Division of the Budget who had to approve the entire process. Interestingly, I would get a telephone call every once in a while from John Riordan, who was one of the examiners in the New York State Division of the Budget, asking me how the process was evolving. I had encountered John on several occasions while on the SUNY RFP committee. Every time John called me, I would let Ken know.

So far, I was happy that I made the move to CSI.

24

My first major initiative was to determine the nature of the student computer systems that were operating at CSI. Elaine Bowden and Lou Addeo were happy with the student file systems that had been established. There were two main files: a student history or transcript file and a student semester or "960" file, named for the number of characters it stored, that maintained student data for each semester. At the end of the semester, the course information was transferred from the "960" file to the student transcript file. The major concern they had with these two files was that semester course information had to be collected each semester and there wasn't always consistency in course descriptions and other data. The student course information derived from one course file that was created from scratch each semester. In addition, with the merger of two colleges, there were duplicative academic programs and courses leading to confusion on the part of everyone including students. We discussed the possibility of creating a new course system with two files: a course master file and a course semester file. This was the same approach I had taken at my three previous colleges. Elaine and Lou were all for it but they felt that there had to be the involvement of a number of users to take a fresh look at course description consistency, data elements and coding schemes. The other major concern they had related to the fact that all of the student systems were entirely batch oriented and relied on a lot of paper collection and keypunching. They would prefer to move to an online system. President Volpe mentioned to me during my meetings with him that he would love to see an online registration system. I told Elaine and Lou that an online system would have to wait for new computer hardware. Lou and I agreed that the IBM 360-30 wasn't fast or sophisticated enough to support intensive online processing. I told them of the CUNY RFP that might resolve this issue within the next year or so.

We decided to put together a users' committee that included representatives from all of the appropriate administrative, academic and student services' offices. I chaired this committee and we met every two weeks to discuss needs and specifically a new course information system that would have two files. The immediate task of this committee was to develop file layouts, coding schemes, and the relationship of the two files to each other and to the student files. After three months, we had the file designs in place and were ready to start programming the course information system. Lou and Bill Canary were effective on this committee and provided many details of the existing course system that proved helpful as we moved forward. The programming staff completed the major course information system programs and were ready for a first test for the Summer 1980 Semester registration. Elaine spent a good deal of time and effort working with the academic departments to standardize the course information and create and maintain a data element dictionary, a concept entirely new to CSI. The system was fully operational for fall 1980; we had our first major successful system design and implementation.

While the course information system development was going on at CSI, I was also busy working with Ken King and the committee on the RFP for the common computer hardware systems. We were provided an RFP template by the CUNY vice chancellor for financial affairs and we discussed the requirements. Marie Drobin crafted all of the language for the RFP. We made several trips to Albany to meet with representatives of the New York Division of the Budget and Ken did most of the talking. He was politically astute, and it was best that he spoke for us. John Riordan was at these meetings and several times referred to the RFP that SUNY had developed last year with nods to me. If I was asked a direct question, I answered it. These meetings weren't without stress. It was obvious that the Division of the Budget wanted to slow down the entire process, if not scuttle it all together. Paul Vliet, who was the chief budget examiner, made it clear he didn't think that all of the CUNY colleges should be included in the RFP. Given the small size of several of the colleges, he thought it would be more cost effective to have them do their administrative work through the CUNY central computer center. He also made a strong pitch that CUNY should be developing centralized information systems that all of the colleges could use, precluding the need for expensive mainframe systems at the individual colleges. At one of these meetings, Ken directly asked me if SUNY had centralized systems. I said that with the exception of several financial applications, the colleges developed all their own information systems. King handled Vliet's comments well, but having worked at Medgar Evers College for two years, I understood what Vliet was implying. It would have been difficult for the small staff at Medgar Evers, and probably at a number of other colleges, to maintain a mainframe computer. Vliet surmised that this RFP was likely to be awarded to IBM which would have one of the more expensive proposals. A compromise was worked out after several weeks of negotiation that the RFP could go forward but that the Division of the Budget would have final say on which colleges would install new computer systems as a result of it. This Division of the Budget requirement likely meant that a number of colleges wouldn't get new computer systems. It is interesting to note that the Federal Government had filed an antitrust suit against IBM in 1975, and the trial was in the process of winding down at the time of our RFP. The suit alleged that IBM violated Section 2 of the Sherman Act by monopolizing or attempting to monopolize the general purpose electronic digital computer system market. After thousands of hours of testimony (over 950 witnesses, 87 in court, the remainder by deposition), and the submission of tens of thousands of exhibits, word was that the trial would end with a favorable verdict for IBM. Several years later on January 8, 1982, the anti-trust case against IBM was finally withdrawn on the grounds that the case was "without merit."

On the four-hour car ride back to New York City, we discussed the meeting and Ken didn't seem worried. We had several such trips to Albany and each car ride proved to be an education on what was going on at CUNY. Ken, Ira, and Marie shared a lot about the personalities and policy activities going on at the given moment, all of which I carefully filed away in my memory. The discussions on technology, especially on future directions, were illuminating. Ira was focused entirely on computer networking. In his view, we were heading to a connected environment that would be international in scope. He indicated that he was working on such a system with colleagues at Yale University. Ira's mantra with regard to technology was to always look to the future and that it would be here quicker than you could imagine.

The final RFP was developed by our committee, approved by CUNY and the Division of the Budget, and distributed for bids. Several colleges resented the entire concept, mainly because CUNY had never unilaterally acquired computer equipment on a scale like this before. Sy Fischtal, for example, had installed a XEROX Sigma computer system at Queens College and wanted to make his own decisions about what would be the best for his campus. At the time of the RFP, Xerox had already sold its computer business to Honeywell, and it wasn't clear what would easily replace the Sigma system. CUNY received bids from all of the major manufacturers and evaluating the proposals was yet another learning experience. The bid was awarded to IBM which had proposed the IBM 4331 (for smaller colleges) and the 4341 (for the larger colleges) computer configurations. These had several options regarding the central processing unit (CPU) capabilities related to speed and memory capacity and hence cost. Most of the CUNY colleges waited anxiously for word from Ken and Marie as to when they might be able to receive a new computer system. I was told by Ken that CSI would be the first college to receive an IBM 4341. It would be paid for entirely by his office and was scheduled for delivery in early fall 1980.

25

In fall 1980, Lou and the computer center staff led the conversion of the application programs to the new IBM 4341 computer. It went smoothly and the staff was ready to consider new applications, especially an online registration system. The programming staff was adept at developing batch processing applications but had never tried to develop an online registration system. The critical software acquisition was a data communications system program that would integrate well with high-level programming languages such as COBOL and PL/1.

IBM provided a product called Customer Information Control System (CICS) that was designed to support rapid, online transaction processing. This IBM proprietary software could be integrated with a variety of high-level programming languages and used CICS-supplied language extensions to interact with hardware resources such as disk files and terminals. The programming staff and I looked at the CICS code and we all had to admit that it wasn't a user-friendly software package. We were contemplating sending a couple of the programmers to IBM school to learn CICS when Lou commented that a former CSI student named Bob Schullich had done a lot of work with CICS in private industry and might be willing to share his expertise with us. Lou, Bill Canary and I met with Bob to discuss the online registration system we were planning. I could tell immediately that Bob was a highly gifted programmer. While I still considered sending the programmers to school, Bob seemed generally interested in working with us as a consultant to develop the online registration system. Bob loved the college and was quite reasonable in terms of remuneration. I arranged to pay him $10,000. to help us develop the system. This turned out to be one of the best consultant investments I ever made in my career. Bob not only helped us, but he took on all of the heavy CICS programming work. He saved us at least 12 to 18 months of development time. Elaine served as the main go-to person for developing the specifications for the online registration. The result was that the computer center was ready to do a test by summer 1981. Elaine oversaw the testing of the system which consisted of using online terminals with card backup in the large gym facility that was normally used for registration.. She was pleased with the result. We decided to test the system again for the fall 1981 registration using the same approach. The system worked well again in the fall and we were ready to implement it fully for spring 1982. Elaine also recommended that CSI move to an early registration system in the fall. This move would require a new office configuration and would make the entire process more personal for the students. Rather than going into a large gym-like space with dozens of tables on the perimeter, students would be scheduled several hundred a day at specific times and come to an office where clerical staff would help each student with his/her registration. This change required major negotiation on the academic side and some modest renovation of available office space which was done in time to have an early fall 1982 registration take place in March/April of 1982.

When I first arrived at CSI, Vice President Arthur Kaufman shared with me the self-study that the college had prepared in advance of a Middle States Association accreditation visit that would take place in spring 1980. Despite having worked at three colleges, I wasn't familiar with accreditation. I decided to do some research. I also called Don Watkins at Medgar Evers College who gave me a good summary of the process and in general what to expect. I read the CSI self-study in parts especially as related to the offices that reported to me. The registrar and financial aid offices received lots of compliments in the self-study. The administrative computer center was characterized as performing poorly. I met with Vice President Kaufman about this and indicated that my opinion of the staff was that it was a competent and dedicated group of individuals. Kaufman indicated that the self-study had been written over a two-year period and that the comments reflected on the previous administration. I made the point that the former director was gone and that I didn't think that the staff should have to suffer for the performance of the previous director. I also told him that I had no desire to discuss what went on regarding the previous director with the visiting Middle States team. He understood what I was saying and the self-study was amended. The computer center staff were most appreciative of my efforts in this respect. When the Middle States accreditation team visited in spring 1980, the areas reporting to me received a good review with no substantive recommendations for improvement. The chair of the team referred to our administrative area as a "well-oiled machine." The accreditation report did comment that CSI needed to begin a process of systematically collecting data about student outcomes and academic programs. I noted this and planned to start working as soon as possible on the institutional research aspect of my responsibilities.

In October 1980, Ken King announced that he was resigning from CUNY and had taken a position at Cornell University in Ithaca, New York. I was very sorry to see him leave. He was so helpful to me in many ways and I would miss him. I got a call from him about a week after he made his announcement and asked me if I wanted to come with him to Cornell. The offer was attractive given Cornell's reputation and status as an Ivy League institution. I thanked him but decided to pass. Ken stayed with Cornell until 1987 when he left to become president of Educom, a national organization of information technology professionals who worked in higher education.

On January 20th, 1981, Ronald Reagan was sworn in as the 40th President of the United States. Minutes later, Iran released the 52 Americans held for 444 days, thus ending the Iran hostage crisis.

In spring 1981, Ira Fuchs announced the launch of BITNET (Because Its Time Network), a pre-Internet international network. CUNY's partners were Yale University (Greydon Freeman) and IBM. The first BITNET link was between CUNY and Yale and eventually would have more than 3,000 nodes around the world, all at educational organizations. In Canada, it was known as NetNorth, in Europe (EARN), in Israel (ISRALEARN), in India (VIDYANET) and in the Persian Gulf states (GulfNet). Part of the South African inter-university academic network, initially known as UNINET, and later TENET (Tertiary Education Network) was implemented using BITNET protocols in the late 1980s. In the years that followed, CUNY would go on to become an international leader in network technology and received a number of awards as one of the most wired universities in the country. BITNET provided a number of facilities including email, LISTSERV, and file transfer protocol (ftp), all of which would become standard features of the Internet in the 1990s.

That same spring of 1981, Arnie Riback resigned as Dean of Administration, and Vice President Kaufman announced that he would be retiring within the year. During that summer, President Volpe discussed with me a new administrative structure that would have most of the offices that reported to Riback and Kaufman reporting to me. I met with all of the department heads who were to begin reporting to me and while several were quite competent, others were problematic. I would spend a good deal of time over the next year working on personnel issues in these new areas. My new title would be Dean of Administration effective in fall 1981.

26

There hadn't been any institutional planning at CSI when setting up its data communications facilities: Academic departments and administrative offices had addressed their own individual needs with terminals using a mix of coaxial cable, dedicated telephone lines, and dial-up modems. I wanted to wire uniformly the two campuses and connect them to the University Central Computer Center. I met with Zafar Ahmed, the director of academic computer services, who was of the same mind and had already started thinking about the offices and facilities to wire. Academic computing supported two major programs at CSI. One was a two-year computer technology program housed at the Sunnyside Campus. A large laboratory with a Data General remote job entry station and twenty-five terminals was the main teaching facility for this program. The St. George campus housed a laboratory with a PDP-11/45 minicomputer and twenty terminals that supported a four-year computer science program. We agreed that we would wire all administrative offices, academic departments and academic laboratories. Zafar did a space inventory with help from the Campus Planning Office that was now reporting to me. We developed a plan that listed approximately one hundred offices/laboratories that would eventually be wired; that would connect the two campuses; and that would connect all facilities to the University Computer Center (see Figure 26.1). To save money, I approached the electrician's staff to see if they had the resources to string coaxial cable throughout the campuses. They said they could but would prefer to work on weekends when they wouldn't disrupt people when they were working. This of course meant overtime, but it was far cheaper than contracting out for the wiring. Within two months, most of the offices and laboratories were wired and were able to connect to CSI's own IBM 4341 computer, to the PDP 11/45, to a remote job entry station, or to a high-speed communications controller over a common network. The final part of the project was to connect the two campuses with high-speed lines and then to the University Computer Center. The St. George Campus was to connect to the Sunnyside Campus which in turn would connect to the CUNY University Computer Center in Manhattan. For this part of the project, we had to rely on the New York Telephone Company because they had a monopoly on any communications wiring going across public thoroughfares. Staten Island was essentially a residential community with few commercial enterprises, and we were the first customer to ask for dedicated T1 (1.5 Megabits per second)) communications lines. It took months of negotiation to get the utility company to install the necessary equipment to provide the high-speed service because it hadn't installed the infrastructure for a T1 line on Staten Island. We were actually asking for two T1 lines – one to connect St. George and Sunnyside and one to connect Sunnyside to the University Computer Center. I had to prevail on Ira Fuchs and CUNY to intervene for the college. It took the better part of a year but eventually the T1 lines were installed. While we were waiting for the T-1 lines, the New York Telephone Company installed two 56 KBS Digital Data Signal (DDS Lines). CSI students, faculty and administrators now had available a host of high-speed digital services including BITNET that many institutions wouldn't have until the coming of the Internet in the 1990s. The new, streamlined data communications network was far more manageable and saved CSI money by eliminating all of the previous disjointed individual dedicated lines and modem connections. I presented and published a paper in 1983 at the Annual CUMREC Conference in Waco, Texas on this project that was well-received. See reference at the end of this chapter for full citation.

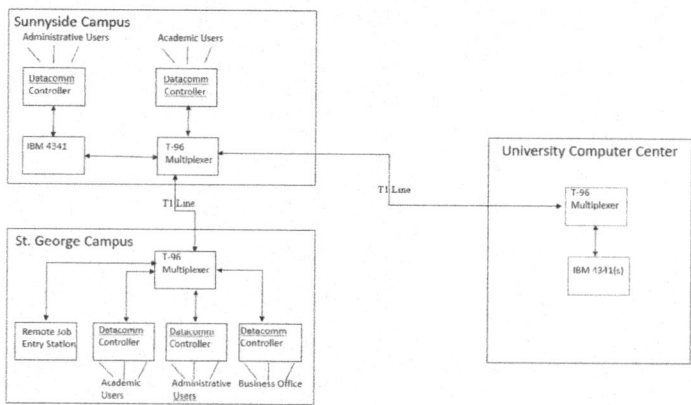

Figure 26.1 – CSI Data Communications Plan

In my new role as the dean of administration, I took an interest in the other areas of the college that had little to do with technology. The department heads and I met every Monday afternoon to discuss issues and to update me and each other on any concerns, activities, or events that were occurring. In summer 1982, I established a management by objectives (MBO) system wherein every department head established priorities and projects to be addressed for the coming year. As part of our weekly Monday afternoon meetings, the department heads reported regularly on their yearly objectives. After a while, I reorganized the meetings into separate groups: the technology and student oriented in one group, and the facilities in another.

In the first few months of my appointment as the dean of administration, I decided to make the facilities at CSI more attractive. The St. George buildings were long-term rental facilities that were fairly new and were maintained by an outside contractor. The Sunnyside Campus, on the other hand, had become an eyesore. CUNY's fiscal austerity of the late 1970s had taken its toll on maintenance of the physical spaces. I spent two days with Campus Planning and Campus Facilities staff walking the campus and all of the buildings. We came up with a list of about twenty projects that we would try to address. Ken Klintworth, George Tagovnik, Manny Esmilla, John DeCaro and John Whitman were helpful and supportive in developing our list and implementing the projects. Some of these were simple repairs; others would require substantial funding. Among the projects that we completed on the Sunnyside Campus were the following.

1. Fifty-five broken windows were replaced.
2. The lighting in the welcome sign at the entrance to the campus was repaired and the sign was used for the first time in years.
3. A good portion of the hallways on the main floor of the administration building was being used to store supplies on wooden pallets. These were all removed and placed in designated areas in the base-

ment. We also purchased a portable storage facility that was placed in a non-public part of the campus to alleviate the space crunch.

4. We replaced all of the dim incandescent lighting in the hallways of all of the buildings with fluorescent lights. In addition, all hallways were repainted a light tan color.

5. We purchased a large lawnmower for taking care of the grass areas on the campus and a regular mowing schedule was established. The testing of this new mower on the hilly terrain became the stuff of legend within the Campus Facilities department as one driver after another learned to trust the steering mechanisms that prevented it from tipping over.

6. We renovated several offices and facilities including the computer center.

7. With funding provided by the CUNY Central Office, we completely renovated the student dining room and the student club spaces.

8. A maintenance schedule was established for regularly mopping and waxing all floors in all buildings.

We did the small projects with CSI staff and modest assistance from outside contractors. The bigger projects such as the student dining room and club space, were funded through the CUNY Central Office. These required me to connect with a whole other cast of administrators at CUNY Central, especially those in facilities and capital projects. The CUNY Senior Vice Chancellor in charge of this area was Donal Farley, who had an incredible history with the university going back to the 1960s. I found him to be very helpful and a solid relationship developed between us.

During my first winter as the dean of administration, the staff had a very tough time getting the Sunnyside campus plowed during one of the heavier snowstorms since the one large truck that could be fitted with a plow was old and kept breaking down. At about the same time, the Security Director, Ed Paradise asked if I would consider purchasing a vehicle for him and his staff to drive between the two campuses. I hadn't considered this a priority and put it on hold until I decided to double-dip. Rather than buy a new truck, we decided to purchase two high-end SUVs that could be fitted with plows as needed. The SUVs were sky blue (the college's color) with silver "CSI Security" stenciled on the doors and came with a rack of flashing lights on top. Ed made sure the two SUVs were on full display with their lights ablaze at every night-time event at the campus. Everybody was happy with this arrangement.

I must admit I found these responsibilities rewarding. I will never forget when Dinitia Smith, the wife of one our faculty, David Nasaw, came up to me, having not been to the college in a year or so, to comment how attractive the campus had become. President Volpe also mentioned to me that he was getting compliments from the community people who lived in close proximity to the college.

The new departments that were reporting to me weren't without problems. There were three directors not performing as well as I or the college would have liked. Two of the directors held permanent positions comparable to tenure and were almost impossible to terminate. I worked with all three of them and was honest about their performance. One rededicated himself and turned his operation around. A second had serious personal issues that he couldn't overcome, so I decided to hire an assistant for him who would be the de facto director. The third, I gave a year to find a new position which he did, at a private college.

References

Picciano, A.G. (May 1983). Integration of data communications in a multi-campus environment.. *Proceedings of the 28th Annual College and University Machine Records Conference.* Waco, Texas.

27

I n 1981, the microcomputer revolution was in full swing. Mainframe manufacturers, including IBM were marketing PCs to compete with new companies like Apple, Commodore, and Tandy. The early years of microcomputers can only be characterized as unpredictable; companies came out every few months with new machines and new features. The earliest models were truly "personal" since individuals willing to learn a lot about technology could spend hours and hours developing simple programs. The software for most of the early microcomputers was lacking and it was difficult to integrate these machines into an administrative or academic operation. However, important breakthroughs occurred in the late 1970s with the introduction of word processing, electronic spreadsheets, and rudimentary database management software. We needed to consider this equipment at CSI.

In 1980, IBM had introduced the Displaywriter, a high-end microcomputer that was dedicated entirely to word processing applications. The software was stable, and it came with a high-quality printer, something that wasn't common on most of the other popular microcomputers of the day. Albeit a bit pricey, I decided to acquire one and have my assistant, Terri Penna, try it out. Within a week, she learned it, she loved it, and she would never go back to her IBM Selectric typewriter. I repeated this with two assistants in two other administrative offices and the results were the same. Within a year, about a dozen administrative offices had converted to Displaywriters.

In 1981, IBM introduced its PC microcomputer and the software for it blossomed as third-party vendors rushed to provide applications including word processing (Wordstar), spreadsheet (Visicalc), and simple file handling applications (dBase). Before long, many of the offices throughout the college were putting in purchase requests for this equipment. I recommended that all these requests pass through my office for approval. I wasn't interested in being a gatekeeper but I thought it would make sense to standardize this equipment so that we could more easily share applications, support services, and general knowledge. The president and the other senior administrators agreed, and I set the IBM PC as the standard in administrative offices. Under Lou Addeo, a new programmer was hired, who would specialize in assisting offices in developing simple applications, mostly file systems, on the PC.

It was at this time, I decided to put some effort into developing an institutional research operation at the college. Elaine Bowden responded to basic data requests, but I was more interested in conducting studies particularly on student performance. I contacted NCHEMS and was able to get survey materials that examined a variety of student outcomes. Using a combination of CSI's own data and surveys sent to samples of the student population, I undertook three studies, *Student Attrition/Retention, Recent Alumni,* and *Student Satisfaction.* I hired a part-time student assistant who did a lot of the data collection work including keying data from the surveys. About a year into these projects, I was able to hire a full-time director of institutional research, Ayshe Ergin, who was excellent at data analysis. These projects were completed over a span of about eighteen months. They were well-received by the college and by the CUNY Central Office. Two years later in 1983, when CSI had its three-year follow-up visit from the Middle States Association, Howard Simmons, its assistant director, mentioned the quality of the studies. In 1984, he invited me to be on a Middle States accreditation visit to Cheyney State College in Pennsylvania. It was an incredible experience and I met Jim Young, the chancellor of the University of Arkansas at Little Rock, who was co-chair of the team. He was the former president of SUNY Geneseo, and he shared a lot with me about the Middle States process. Later, he would come to New York City every once in a while and we would have lunch and catch up on what we were doing. Jim was a very informed individual and had worked in several different university systems. The discussions at these lunches were lessons for me on higher education administration and policy. My relationship with Middle States continued when Howard Simmons invited me to be on a team to evaluate three- or five-year reviews. This entailed two days in

Philadelphia where the team would evaluate a dozen or more college review reports. Reading details about how colleges were addressing issues and developing new plans was yet another incredible learning experience. During one of these visits, I had dinner with Howard and Bob Kirkwood, the Executive Director of the Middle States Association. Bob was a walking encyclopedia on the world of higher education.

In 1982, I was at a meeting of the CSI senior administrators, when President Volpe indicated that the college was thinking about applying for a United Stated Department of Education Title III grant. David Nasaw, a history professor, would coordinate this effort. I mentioned that I was familiar with Title III and had been funded at Medgar Evers College to establish a CAI lab. I also indicated that I worked as a consultant with Sister Mary Genevieve Love on a Title III project at Mt. St. Mary's College in Newburgh which was also funded. President Volpe asked if I would work with David. David did most of the writing and organized the grant tasks, for which I was most happy not to be doing. In speaking with my department directors in the student service areas, they indicated that there was a tremendous need to provide technology support for student advisement. CSI had an advisement office that did almost everything manually through dedicated help and faculty in the academic departments. Advisement systems that include graduation progress and ongoing degree audits aren't simple applications and are prone to a good deal of change as academic programs are modified. At CSI, academic advisement was especially complicated because of the merger when many of the academic programs developed at the two former institutions were integrated in a rather rushed manner. In addition, CSI offered a mix of associate and bachelor's degrees, some of which articulated well with one another and others that did not. We submitted the grant and received funding for the advisement project. Elaine Bowden worked with Fran Silvernail, the director of academic advisement to develop the specifications of the system. I spoke with Lou Addeo about programming support and he felt that the center was overloaded with requests from offices for data from the enhanced student and course information systems . He suggested that since

Bob Schullich had finished the online student registration system that he might be available to assist with an advisement system. Bob was contacted and he was happy to take on the project. The Title III money would pay for his services through 1984/85 and also provided funding for scanning equipment for student academic skills testing and intelligent terminals. Elaine, Fran, and Bob commenced immediately to start laying out the parameters of the project. Bob did an extensive review of the latest college catalog that contained all the various academic program requirements. He identified fifty-six questions and inconsistencies in the stated requirements that needed to be resolved, all of which involved numerous meetings for Elaine and Fran with academic administrators, department chairs, and program coordinators. These meetings went on for much of the academic year. Nothing will reveal the hidden flaws in an academic rule like attempting to encode it within a logical computerized system. Bob had only reviewed the current catalog but anyone who has ever done advisement or degree audits knows that students are automatically grandfathered into the academic program requirements at their time of admission. Previous college catalog reviews would therefore have to be conducted for at least the past five years. Regardless, the project had kicked off and was already serving CSI well by clarifying the academic program requirements.

At this juncture, our data communications and computer hardware were in place, and the agendas were set for the advisement and student information systems for the next several years.

28

During my last year at Medgar Evers College, back in 1977, I had started to think about doctoral programs in New York. I had two meetings with faculty at Columbia University Teachers College and was seriously considering enrolling there, but with my move to New Paltz, the traveling logistics would have made it impossible. In spring 1981, I started looking into the doctoral program again but found that the two professors with whom I wanted to work had both left Teachers College and were now working in the Texas University system. Just then, Fordham University opened a branch college on the Marymount College Campus in Westchester County about ten minutes from where I lived. The branch was to be dedicated to offering graduate professional degree programs. Fordham was offering its PhD program in education leadership at the Manhattan Lincoln Center Campus, however, some of the coursework as well as the summer residency could be completed at the Marymount Campus. I met with Tom Mulkeen, a faculty member in the PhD program in education leadership, and we hit it off immediately. He understood that I was interested in higher education and that I had a lot of administrative experience and technology in my background. He said he would be as flexible as possible with independent study and he would be happy to work with me. I enrolled in the program and Tom was as good as his word. He also took a genuine interest in me and my career and became yet another person in my life who would give me good professional advice. I finished the course work in three years and began my dissertation in 1983. I had spoken with Tom about topics and he thought that I should do something outside of CUNY. I told him of the relationship I had developed at Mount St. Mary's College in Newburgh and he thought there was the seed of a dissertation there. From 1983 to 1985, I visited and conducted five case studies of small colleges that were struggling financially and had introduced technology into their administrative decision making and planning. Entitled, *Computerized Support for Decision Making in Higher Education: Case Studies at Five Private Colleges,* my dissertation focused on the integration of data systems into planning and institutional development. My research was based in part on the work of Herbert Simon, Nobel laureate in economics (1978), who had developed a theory on the limits of rationality in decision processes also referred to as bounded rationality. In each of the five case studies, I examined and tried to determine how the "limits of rationality" in decision making were extended by data-informed processes. I would go on to complete my PhD from Fordham in 1985. I couldn't have asked for a better mentor than Tom Mulkeen. Sadly, he died one year later of a heart attack.

When I had returned to CUNY in 1979, I received a call from my old friend, Marvin Kushner asking if I wanted to teach as an adjunct at Borough Manhattan Community College. I thought about it but was too busy at CSI, and in any case, I needed the evenings to take coursework at Fordham. I enjoyed teaching and considered doing something at CSI but decided not to because of time conflicts. However, in 1981, Mike Petrides, the Associate Dean of Faculty and one of his program directors, Dorothy Brower, asked to meet with me about a new continuing education program they were planning entitled, *New Education Training for Work* (NetWORK). The focus of the program was to provide customized professional development for public agencies in New York City. In discussions with potential clients, they found there was a good deal of interest in technology and information systems. I told Mike and Dorothy of the work I had done at the Mt. Sinai School of Medicine in the 1970s and they thought that was exactly the kind of seminars they wanted to develop in NetWORK; short two to five-day intensive seminars that would have a workshop aspect to them wherein participants would develop or otherwise engage in activities in addition to the lectures. They asked if I would be available to develop and lead these seminars. I decided to discuss the time commitment for this with President Volpe and he was all in favor. Mike indicated that he was willing to pay me a special stipend from his own research funds to participate in this program. We had a deal and I developed a three-day, six-hour per day seminar for hospital administrators. This was an update of the work I had done at Mt. Sinai School of Medicine and involved a basic introduction to computer technology followed by group exercises in developing hospital-related information systems. Mike contracted with St. Vincent's Hospital on Staten Island for our first seminar. It turned out to be successful and Mike and Dorothy started contracting with hospitals all over Staten Island, Manhattan, and Brooklyn for similar seminars. By 1983, I was doing these seminars on a regular basis. Through my involvement with NetWORK, I conducted seminars with a number of public and private hospitals, the New York City Board of Education, CITICORP, New York City Community School Districts, the AFL-CIO, the New York City Department of Personnel, and the American Association of University Women. Mike and Dorothy did a great job with the NetWORK program and it was a success for CSI. I think the work I did was helpful in moving it forward. I also enjoyed teaching and learning about so many different organizations.

My seminars with NetWORK also opened up opportunities for consulting work. Most of these would be one- or two-day affairs followed by a written report. Over the next several years, I would consult with the New York City Department of Personnel, The New York City Board of Education, New York City Housing Authority, and the United States Coast Guard. The NYC Housing Authority became an on-going consultancy and we met every two weeks for almost two years. Joining me in this work was John Fuchs (Ira Fuchs' brother), who was a network communications specialist, and Jim Anastasio, who managed computer programming at Hunter College and was expert in database design.

In 1983, Ira Fuchs who was now a CUNY Vice Chancellor asked me to be on a committee to assist in the development of common university-wide administrative information systems. I told him I would be happy to lend my assistance but I didn't have the time to design new systems. He was fine with this since he planned to bring a third-party vendor to provide the basic information system which would be customized for CUNY. CUNY already had a financial accounting system that was installed in the late 1970s and that artic-ulated well with state and city funding agencies. There was little customiza-tion of the system and basically it did the job. Ira was hoping that something similar could be done for personnel and student information systems. Ira and other CUNY administrators decided to start with the personnel system and contracted with Deloitte Haskins & Sells, one of the major public account-ing firms in the country that was expanding into consulting and provid-ing information system software. Our committee met with representatives from Deloitte and our project commenced. As an aside, the project leader for Deloitte would be my predecessor in the SUNY New Paltz computer center who had resigned to take a position at SUNY Albany and had taken the senior staff with him. I still wonder what he was thinking the first time we met. The committee decided to meet every two weeks, which we did for several months. A number of issues occurred, the most serious being that CUNY Central Office staff as well as representatives from the colleges were requesting many modifications to the new City University Personnel System (CUPS). Every modification requested resulted in additional costs, some of which were quite substantial. After a year of modifications and cost over-runs, the CUPS project was suspended and replaced by several related simple file systems that generated CUNY Central Office reports. In no way was it complete or worth the cost and effort.

In May of 1983, after a small but potentially deadly fire on my property, I joined the volunteer fire company in my community and would serve as a fireman, first responder, officer, and a commissioner over the next thir-ty-three years.

29

I n spring 1985, several major events occurred in my professional life. First, in January, I received a phone call from someone representing New York Governor Mario Cuomo asking me if I was responsible for facilities and capital projects at CSI. I told him I was, and he went on to explain that there was a plan to close the Willowbrook State School for persons with emotional and intellectual disabilities, also known as the Staten Island Developmental Center. He also asked whether CSI was still considering consolidating its two campuses onto one site. I told him we were but that we didn't have the property or any funding. Since its merger, CSI had in fact pursued consolidating its two campuses without much success. He asked whether the college might consider the Willowbrook facility as a site and I told him I would consult with other administrators at CSI and CUNY. The Willowbrook facility sat on 375 acres in the middle of Staten Island. It opened in the 1940s primarily as an educational facility and at its peak housed more than 6,000 patients although it was built to house no more than 4,000. It was the subject of several scandals and Senator Robert Kennedy referred to it as a "snakepit". By the 1980s, New York State was in the process of closing all of its large-scale mental health institutions and Willowbrook's time had come. Governor Cuomo, however, wanted the closed facilities to be re-opened with a useful purpose. After receiving this call, I immediately contacted President Volpe and then Senior Vice Chancellor Don Farley. They were flabbergasted and knew nothing about the possibility of Willowbrook as a new campus. Farley contacted people in Albany to verify that the Governor was indeed interested in giving a substantial part of Willowbrook over to CUNY for CSI's campus. We paid several visits to Willowbrook which had been closed down and abandoned with the exception of its Institute for Basic Research for Developmental Disabilities. The interiors of the schools and the dormitories were unattractive and strewn with debris, fragments of toys, and broken furniture. During the decision-making process, I had the responsibility of escorting various CUNY and local officials on tours of the site and on one occasion I asked CUNY Chancellor Joe Murphy if he believed in "ghosts." He replied he did and "devils" also. The final approval of the property transfer would take a lot of negotiating, but by the end of 1985 we had an agreement of understanding that CSI would get 204 of the 330 acres as well as the buildings for its campus. It would take several more years before CSI developed the plans and received the New York State Dormitory Authority funding to build and retrofit the facility as a college campus.

The second major event was the announcement by Ira Fuchs that he was resigning as the Vice Chancellor for University Systems to become the Vice President for Computing and Information Technology at Princeton University. Ira was an important force for technology at CUNY and I had learned a lot from him. He had been a good colleague and I would miss him dearly. He would be replaced by Mike Ribaudo who would assume the title of CUNY Dean of Computer Information Systems and Chief Technology Officer.

The third major event in my professional life in 1985 was the successful defense of my dissertation in April and my graduation in May with a PhD in education leadership from Fordham University. It was a long five years, but well worth it.

Lastly, in August of 1985, I received a phone call from Ruth Weintraub who had been hired as a consultant to recruit a new vice president for administration at Hunter College. I knew the soon-to-be former vice president, John Tesoriero. In fact, he, along with three other vice presidents (Vince Tenaglia from the CUNY Graduate Center, Luther Johnson from New York City Technical College and Barney Levantino from York College) and I would have lunch regularly after CUNY's monthly meetings of chief administrative officers that were chaired by Egon Brenner, the Deputy Chancellor for CUNY. Brenner always introduced major new CUNY policies or procedures at these meetings. At our lunches, my colleagues and I would share what was going on in our respective colleges. I knew that John was retiring and planning to open a restaurant in Brooklyn, but I was also under the impression that his associate vice president, John Smith, would be taking his position. However, the president of Hunter College, Donna Shalala, wanted an open search. Dr. Weintraub, who had a long association with Hunter as a student, professor and dean before retiring, was hired to conduct the search. I told her that I wasn't looking to make a move and that I was embarking on a once in a career opportunity to participate in the design and building of a new college campus. She said she understood and our conversation ended there. About a week later, she called me again and asked if I would just come to Hunter to meet the president. Rather than be discourteous, I agreed. Donna Shalala, before becoming Hunter's president, was Undersecretary for Housing and Urban Development in President Jimmy Carter's administration. She also was the only woman on the Municipal Assistance Corporation (MAC) Board that was overseeing New York City's finances. MAC was created during the height of the fiscal crisis in the mid-1970s as the formal "watch dog" to make sure that the City lived within its financial means. President Shalala was persuasive and indicated that Hunter College needed a new set of eyes in the administration. After this meeting, I called John Tesoriero. He indicated that it was unlikely that John Smith would get the position and he would love it if someone he had confidence in became the vice president. He never said it, but I'm quite sure he recommended me to Ruth Weintraub. I never met with a search committee, but I had one more meeting with President Shalala and Ruth Weintraub. They offered me anything I wanted to come to Hunter. The long and short of it was that I would be a Deputy to the President along with the Provost Tilden LeMelle and would have all the administrative areas reporting to me. I decided to take the position.

Leaving CSI wasn't easy. I would miss working with the wonderful people who reported to me. My executive assistant Terri Penna; Elaine Bowden and the Registrar's staff; Lou Addeo and Bill Canary in the Computer Center; Sherman Whipkey in Financial Aid; Ayshe Ergin in Institutional Research; Ed Paradise, Ted Selby, and John Flaherty in Security; and Mike Metz in Reprographics. All were most competent and loyal for the six years I was at CSI.

PART V

Hunter College
New York, New York
1985-1989

30

Any discussion of public higher education in New York City during the 19th and early 20th centuries, pairs Hunter College with The City College of New York (CCNY) as the only two institutions offering citizens of modest means access to a college education. However, to assume that CCNY (founded 1847) and Hunter (founded 1870) were similar, would be a mistake. While both were public, free, and served large percentages of poorer students in New York City, they evolved in entirely different ways. CCNY from its beginning was meant to provide a broad liberal arts education along with practical programs of study in science and engineering to male students only. On the other hand, Hunter was originally established as a normal college where female students received certificates, not degrees, in their program of study and were licensed to teach in the public schools. The founding and early presidents of the institutions reflect their differences.

The first two presidents of CCNY, Horace Webster and Alexander Webb had military backgrounds. Webster, who served as president from 1847 to 1869, was a mathematics professor who graduated from and taught at West Point. Maintaining order and discipline were important to Webster (Roff, Cucchiara, & Dunlop, 2000, p. 8). Webb, who served from 1869 to 1902, was also a graduate of West Point and a recipient of the Congressional Medal of Honor for distinguished service during the Battle of Gettsyburg in the Civil War.

Thomas Hunter, the first president of the Female Normal College and High School, on the other hand, was a reformer of education who taught in and was a principal of a New York City high school. He was known for innovation and for impartiality with regard to race, religion, and ethnicity and maintained that the Normal College and School "must admit colored and white girls on equal terms" at a time when even New York's public schools were segregated (Williams, 2000, p. 7). He was passionate about the education of women, a position that dovetailed well with his advocacy for reforming teacher education. During this early period, cost wasn't the only matter that dissuaded immigrant families from sending young women into higher education. Cultural and social norms that originated in highly stratified European countries found their way into the neighborhoods of New York. Parents of young girls saw them as future wives and mothers and not as college graduates. Thomas Hunter became a spokesperson for the education of women both locally in New York and throughout the country. He held the post of president for thirty-seven years and left his mark on the institution, the name of which was changed in his honor in 1914. Hunter College remains the only senior college in the CUNY system to be named for an educator.

From its beginnings, expanding access to a higher education was a central focus of Hunter College. In 1910, it started offering courses at night and opened education centers in Brooklyn and Queens. In 1937, Hunter College in the Bronx was established on thirty acres of land next to the Jerome Park Reservoir in the North Bronx. The Bronx Campus served as a naval training ground for WAVES (Women Accepted for Voluntary Emergency Services) during World War II and the first meeting of the United Nations Security Council was held in its gymnasium in 1946. In 1951, after World War II, Hunter College began admitting men to the Bronx Campus in 1951 and became fully coeducational on both campuses in 1964. In its first fifty years, Hunter College distinguished itself in a number of ways. Its academic programs evolved to include the liberal arts and social work. The College, especially through its active alumnae association, became very much involved in community service and was active in the Settlement House Movement of the early 20th century (Greenblatt, 2012). Hunter College has had a number of distinguished graduates including two women Nobel Prize winners, Rosalyn Yallow (1977, Physiology/Medicine) and Gertrude Elion (1988, Physiology/Medicine).

When I arrived in November 1985, Hunter College was operating at four major locations, all of which were in Manhattan. As I mentioned in Chapter One, its Bronx Campus had been converted into Herbert Lehman College in 1968. The main campus was on 68th Street between Park and Lexington Avenues on some of the most valuable real estate in New York. The campus consisted of Thomas Hunter Hall; a Gothic structure built in the early 1900s, the North Building on Park Avenue built in the 1930s, and two new towers, the East and West Buildings connected by two distinctive sky bridges over Lexington Avenue that were opened in 1983. The Brookdale Campus occupied a square block on 25th Street and 1st Avenue and consisted of three buildings including dormitories. The property and the buildings had been donated to Hunter College and housed the nursing and health sciences programs. The nursing program had evolved in partnership with the Bellevue School of Nursing, the oldest such school in the country, dating back to 1873 that ceased its operation in 1969.

The Hunter College School of Social Work occupied a single building on 79th Street and Lexington Avenue. It was established in 1958 and was the oldest and largest public school of social work in New York. A driving force behind the School was Samuel "Bud" Silberman, a retired executive with the Consolidated Cigar Corporation, who donated the property and leased the building for $1 per year to Hunter College.

The Hunter College Campus Schools were located on 94th Street between Park and Madison Avenues, and included an elementary and secondary school. Originally, the Campus Schools were the laboratory schools of Hunter College's teacher education program and were among the premiere schools in the country dedicated to gifted and talented education.

In addition to the four major locations, the College also rented about 20,000 square feet of laboratory space at the Museum of Natural History where Psychology faculty conducted research.

When I arrived, Hunter was the largest college in CUNY with 18,600 students (headcount) and second in size to the University of Buffalo in all of New York State. Since opening its new towers, enrollment had been increasing approximately one thousand students per year. The Campus schools added another 1,600 students. The College comprised four schools – Arts and Sciences, Social Work, Nursing, and Health Sciences. Its extensive teacher education programs were housed in Arts and Sciences.

Compared to the previous colleges in which I worked, Hunter College had a more substantial administrative structure and staff. Hunter also was a main contributor to the CUNY Graduate Center's doctoral programs that operated on a consortial model with senior colleges contributing faculty and facilities. Hunter contributed much of the laboratory space for the doctoral programs in biology and chemistry.

References

Greenblatt, D. (2012). Unpublished paper: *The contributions of Normal College/Hunter College alumnae to the college and the community, 1872-1930.*

Roff, S.S., Cucchiara, A.M., & Dunlop, B.J. (2000). *From the Free Academy to CUNY*: New York: Fordham University Press.

Williams, J. (2000). Hunter College. Charleston, SC: Arcadia Publishing.

31

Donna Shalala was appointed Hunter College's president in 1980, after having served in President Jimmy Carter's administration as assistant secretary for housing and urban development. She also served on the New York City Municipal Assistance (MAC) Board that at the time had significant oversight over all New York financial operations. She had held faculty positions at Baruch College and Columbia University as well. The Hunter College presidency was her first administrative position in higher education. It became immediately apparent to me that she was a natural leader as well as a first-rate administrator. She was a presence at meetings, large or small, and knew how to delegate administrative responsibilities. She also instilled in all of her immediate staff a desire to work hard for the benefit of the college. Her primary directive to me was "to make the college look good" to the students, faculty and the outside world. During my interview, and given her high-level political background, I had asked her for how long she thought she would be staying at Hunter. She gave me a short smile and said, "Probably another three years."

In addition to myself, there were three other vice presidents. Tilden LeMelle was the provost and was responsible for the academic side of the college. Sylvia Fishman was the vice president for student affairs and had worked at the college for her entire career. Robin Elliot was the vice president for institutional advancement.

Reporting to me directly were my executive assistant Mary Ortiz, and one associate and two assistant vice presidents. Mary was the only other individual located in my office and was a calm, cordial and welcoming presence for anyone visiting or meeting with me. I was also fortunate to have three competent and effective associate/assistant vice presidents who handled the details within their respective areas. John Smith had finance, personnel, security, and facilities reporting to him. Ruth Weisgal supervised the registrar, admissions, office services and institutional research. Stan Sokol was responsible for information services. Each of the other campuses (Social Work, Brookdale, and the Campus Schools) were managed by deans and assistant deans but all non-academic matters relating to budget, personnel, security, facilities reported within my administrative structure.

The responsibilities of my new position were broad and deep, and to be honest during my time as Vice President at Hunter, I probably had the least interaction with educational technology of any other time in my career. Without a doubt, Stan had a powerhouse of talent working for him. Jim Anastasio was the manager of programming and was as knowledgeable as anyone could be about database management systems. Jim worked with me during my consultancy at the New York City Housing Authority and I knew his talents and abilities well. Working with him were first-rate programmers such as Gil Giannini, Stanley Lui, and Caryn Giananti. John McGloin was responsible for hardware systems and operations. He had decades of experience and technologically was very strong. And I couldn't have been happier than to have Anita Better, who worked with me for five years at Lehman College, responsible for user services and training. She had a top staff of technicians and trainers including Ralph Romanelli and Michael Nesbitt assisting her. Mark Watters who was responsible for telephone services, was well-versed in the movement of telephone systems to digital technology. With the exception for a major commitment of funds, these individuals carried out their responsibilities without me.

Hunter College was a much bigger operation than in my previous positions, so I'm going to indulge in extensive discussion of issues beyond technology. My day typically started at 8:00 am and I worked through 6:00 pm. President Shalala always encouraged the senior staff to participate in college evening events and I found myself attending a meeting, a dinner, or some other social activity several evenings a week. These could be with alumni, community groups, faculty and students as well as major political and social figures in New York City such as Mayor Ed Koch, Geraldine Ferrara, Bobby Wagner and Carol Bellamy. President Shalala would also ask me once in a while to represent her if she was unavailable or out of town. My favorite stand-in appearance was at a dinner party for about fifty people at the Bowery Savings Bank. The guest of honor was one of their spokespersons, the former Yankee great, Joe DiMaggio, who came to every table, spoke with us, and signed autographs, one of which was for a good friend of mine who was ill. President Shalala was also generous in having me participate in meetings with other CUNY presidents regardless of the venue – in her office, other colleges, or at the CUNY Central Office. In fact, I got to know several of the other presidents and assisted them with several projects at Borough of Manhattan Community College, York College and Hostos Community College.

32

For my first two months at Hunter, I planned to visit with as many individuals as I could, including the senior administrators, deans, department heads, staff, and representatives of faculty and student groups to determine which of their issues and needs that I could possibly address. These meetings included visits to all four campuses. Facilities and space issues rose to the top. While the administrators and faculty in the two new towers were essentially pleased with their new and expanded spaces, there were still some issues that they wanted the College to address. The students and faculty in the North Building and in Thomas Hunter Hall had enough space but much of it needed renovation, since the age of both buildings was beginning to show. All of the science programs were housed in the North Building and the faculty desperately wanted to upgrade their laboratory facilities. The School of Social Work had fine facilities but there was a deep desire on the part of the donor, Bud Silberman, to do a substantial expansion. The nursing and health sciences administrators and faculty had space at Brookdale but also wanted to do a renovation. The dormitory students had the typical requests for better dining facilities and more social spaces. The Campus Schools had a new building and didn't have any major demands. In meetings with my assistant vice presidents, facilities, personnel, and financial department heads, budget issues related to the new towers and the Brookdale Campus were high on their agenda. Construction delays and cost overruns for the new towers had caused the New York State Dormitory Authority, that issued the bonds and supervised the new construction, to use $13 million in the furniture and equipment budget for construction. We had come into possession of new facilities, but in many areas, the older equipment and furniture remained. There was also a "punch list" of small items that still needed to be addressed and required funding for repairs from the Dormitory Authority. Also, while we had the new towers, John Smith and Bob Salinardi, the

Budget Director, made the case that the College never received enough state funding for personnel to maintain the new buildings. They also mentioned that the Brookdale Campus was never funded properly for its maintenance, heating, and energy needs, an issue going back almost eight years. The New York State Division of the Budget had taken a position that income from the dormitories should pay for the latter budget items.

Besides facilities, several other issues arose as well. Eileen Webber, the Business Manager, raised a thorny issue about the state of our soft money gift accounts. She indicated that there were thousands of accounts, all of which were maintained in a manual system of paper files that needed a thorough review and audit. She had been in her position about a year and felt that no one at the College knew what was in those files and that we were vulnerable to some bad publicity should there ever be an audit by CUNY or another government agency. She wanted to undertake a three-year project to supervise the auditing of all these accounts and to set up a system whereby we could properly administer the funds, particularly those that were restricted gifts which had to be used per the donor's request. To assist with this, she preferred to hire an outside firm/consultant that specialized in doing this type of work. Stan Sokol and John McGloin indicated that the College could use a major upgrade to its computer facilities and that we were still using the original configuration that had been acquired via Ken King's RFP issued in 1980. Stan and Anita Better also indicated that there was a substantial need for an infusion of office automation throughout the College and its campuses. Ruth Weisgal asked for assistance with institutional research. She mentioned that while she was responsible for it, she had no staff and did the basic reports herself. Mark Watters wanted to convert the main telephone system to a new digital switching system.

Following these meetings, just before the New Year, I had a substantial discussion with President Shalala to present a list of possible projects we could tackle for the coming year. There would also be a budget request submitted in January for the coming fiscal year. She indicated that she had two "big ticket" priorities. One was to try and accommodate Bud Silberman and his desire to expand the School of Social Work. The other was to do renovations for the science programs. She indicated that she and the Dean of Sciences, Dick Mawe, were planning on submitting several major grants that would require expanding our laboratory facilities. She left it to me to prioritize the other issues.

The assistant vice presidents, the financial and facilities directors, and I came up with a list of six high-priority items:

1. Resolve the $13 million furniture and equipment shortfall with the Dormitory Authority;
2. Explore the possibility of funding an expansion of the School of Social Work;
3. Develop a plan to renovate laboratory spaces in the North Building;
4. Renegotiate the funding model for the Brookdale Campus;
5. Upgrade the College's computer facilities and develop a plan for office automation;
6. Audit the gift accounts.
7. Install a new telephone digital switching system.

I decided that if I could resolve the $13 million furniture and equipment issue, then I could use some of these funds for several of the other priorities especially Nos. 3 and 5. As 1986 began, I had these seven items written in large letters on a piece of yellow-ruled paper taped to the top of the left-hand drawer of my desk.

33

I n 1983, Hunter had begun moving into its two new seventeen story towers on the east and west sides of Lexington Avenue between 67th and 68th streets. These buildings, named appropriately if unimaginatively, the East and West Buildings, also extended four levels below ground and provided the College with a modern library, gymnasia, and much needed classroom and office space. The two sky bridges across Lexington Avenue also provided a distinctive view of the College from the north and south. Bridges connecting buildings in Manhattan are a rarity especially over a major avenue, and prior to their construction, people riding in cars, buses or taxicabs might have passed by Hunter without realizing that a college existed on 68th street. This was no longer the case.

Later in January 1986, I met with Don Farley, CUNY's Senior Vice Chancellor for Capital Projects and Facilities, to discuss approaching the Dormitory Authority to recoup the $13 million in furniture and equipment money. Don explained that when the New York City fiscal crisis occurred in 1975-76, all capital projects, including Hunter's two towers, were halted because the City had literally run out of money. These projects didn't commence again for several years and during that time, the cost of construction had increased considerably. Hunter's two towers had been the first of about six halted CUNY capital projects to commence again and he indicated that several colleges were facing a similar issue. Nevertheless, he was sympathetic and asked me to draft a statement of need and rationale for the $13 million request and we would meet again. He said to provide concrete examples of what funds would be used for responding to the "punch list" of repairs needed.

I drafted the statement, pleading a case, that it would be short-sighted on the part of the Dormitory Authority to have built these wonderful towers only to have them lacking in modern equipment and furniture. It was sad to enter these shiny new buildings and go into an office with a desk that was twenty years old. In addition, the academic programs and Library could use significant equipment upgrades for their activities. I also included a major request of $1 million dollars for desktop computers and office automation.

Don was on board with my rationale and said he would arrange a meeting with the Dormitory Authority to discuss the issue. We met in April in Don Farley's office. I didn't know any of the other people. Don made the case well and as I had learned when I was at meetings with Ken King and the New York State Budget officers, I didn't say anything unless asked a question. Don did all of the talking and the Dormitory Authority representatives did all of the questioning. I was specifically asked about the utility of the new towers and in every case I praised the design and construction. The Library, the gym facilities, the classroom and office space all worked well. I especially praised the extensive use of escalators in the towers as far more efficient than the elevators. They also asked how well we were maintaining the facilities and I invited them to come to Hunter and see for themselves how clean and attractive we were keeping the buildings. Before concluding, Don made the point that the same issue was occurring for all of the capital projects that were halted during the New York City fiscal crisis and that Hunter's request for $13 million was one of several that would need to be funded. The CUNY colleges, he said, were the victims of the New York City fiscal crisis and that the overruns were all due to inflation. When asked, Don indicated that the total additional cost for all of the halted CUNY projects would be about $50 million. The meeting had been cordial and ended after about ninety minutes. The Dormitory Authority representatives indicated that they would be back in touch with Don. Two months later, I received a phone call from Don indicating that the Dormitory Authority would fund our $13 million request and the funds would be available in the fall. I thanked him profusely.

I immediately let President Shalala know; she was most pleased. I told her that after we took care of the "punch list" repair items, we would have about $8 million for equipment and furniture. She asked if we could purchase laboratory equipment with these funds. I said technically, no, because the science labs were all in the North Building but that maybe we could get around it somehow. I then met with Stan Sokol and told him the news. His task was to develop a purchasing plan to upgrade or equip every office at the College with desktop computers and to connect them into a common network that would provide access to our own computer center or the CUNY central computer center. Next, I met with the provost, Tilden LeMelle, and told him of the Dormitory Authority funding and asked that he provide a list of his priorities. He asked about laboratory equipment and I told him the same thing I told President Shalala. However, I mentioned that the Library and the physical education facilities would be appropriate areas to fund.

By the end of the summer and after much discussion with other senior administrators, the deans, and my staff, a general plan for the purchase of equipment and furniture was developed. The list included a high-end electronic microscope, computer equipment, library equipment, a new digital telephone switch, and furniture such as modern carrels for the library. Judy Huertas, the executive assistant to the provost, suggested that it would be a nice touch to provide framed poster-size works of art for any offices that wanted them. This was added to the list and Judy coordinated the requests of which there were several hundred. She also negotiated a very good price for them since we were buying in bulk. The total price for the plan was $7 + million, leaving approximately $1 million.

34

Working with the Dormitory Authority was a new experience for me. It some ways it was a blessing and in other ways, "not so much." Purchasing equipment with Dormitory Authority funding bypassed the typical New York State and university procedures. Our purchase requisitions had only to be approved and processed through the Dormitory Authority. One real benefit of using Dormitory Authority funds was that we weren't required to expend the funds within a given fiscal year. The Dormitory Authority operated through long-term, multi-year funding of construction projects. Our equipment and furniture funds were considered to be an extension of the construction of the new towers. This proved helpful because it allowed us to take our time to make the best purchases possible. It also meant we could enter into longer-term purchase agreements that would allow us to acquire equipment over several years. On the other hand, the Dormitory Authority exercised its own discretion in approving our requisitions. This proved problematic in automating the offices and laboratories with new desk-top computers.

Almost $2 million of the Dormitory Authority funds would be spent on office automation. This included upgrades to our computer center, a digital telephone switch, wiring the campuses and hundreds of new desktop computers. There were no issues with the bigger items such as new disk equipment, more memory, and upgrades to the data-communications equipment, all of which would connect directly with the IBM 4341 mainframe which was housed in our own computer facility, However, when it came time to enter into a multi-year purchase for desktop computers, the Dormitory Authority became extensively involved. The mid-1980s saw a number of companies that manufactured IBM PC clones enter the market. These clone computers used the same DOS operating system and other software as an IBM PC but were somewhat cheaper than the IBM models. Depending upon the model, a clone could be purchased for several hundred dollars less. For purchasing 500-600 PCS, the savings could be a couple of hundred thousand dollars. Stan and his staff were of the mind that even though they were more expensive, we should stay with the IBM products. His main rationale was that IBM had good customer support and readily provided replacement parts if needed when making repairs or upgrades. I agreed and asked him to prepare a request for 600 IBM PCs plus peripherals to be acquired over 18-24 months. For logistical reasons, we couldn't acquire all these units at one time. The total cost estimate was approximately $900,000.

When the Dormitory Authority received our purchase requisition, their purchasing agents questioned why we weren't considering acquiring clones rather than IBM equipment. We explained the issue of maintenance and parts, but they weren't buying it. They suggested we get pricing from clone manufacturers and specifically from a company called Leading Edge. As technology professionals, neither Stan nor I had ever heard of Leading Edge but he contacted a sales representative and shared the purchase requisition for 600 units and assorted peripherals. The Leading Edge representative provided an unofficial quote for its Model D desktop computers that Stan estimated would be at least $200,000. less expensive than IBM. The Dormitory Authority representatives had an independent assessment of the savings and they were consistent. The Leading Edge Model D clone computer was also receiving accolades in the professional literature; *PC Magazine* declared it "a clear winner." The result was a two-month semi-dispute that included telephone calls, meetings, and correspondence. For a while I was leaning to the Leading Edge idea but Stan, Anita, and others were insisting on IBM. Finally, and I never understood why, the Dormitory Authority relented and approved the IBM acquisition. Soon, a good technology situation at Hunter became a better one as Stan and his staff made their services available online to the entire college community. Anita and her staff did an excellent job of scheduling delivery and installation of the IBM desk-top computers throughout the College. John McGloin and Mark Watters coordinated upgrades and installation of coaxial cable in the buildings where needed. Anita Better and her assistant Mike Nesbitt handled all the training needs of the faculty and staff.

The decision to go with IBM turned out to be the right-one. In 1989, Leading Edge filed for bankruptcy precipitating a number of lawsuits against the company from dealers who sold its products (Associated Press, February 14, 1989). Yet another acquisition disaster had been avoided during the course of my career.

References

Associated Press, (February 14, 1989). FBI To Investigate Leading Edge Finances.

Retrieved August 11, 2020 from: https://apnews. com/81a9378fe86e4af04a86937bdb51eed2

35

In early 1986, I started on developing a plan to expand the School of Social Work Building on 79th Street. President Shalala made clear that this was her high priority given that the Silberman Family was a major donor to the College. Bud, his wife Lois, and daughter Jane, all supported the School of Social Work going back to the 1960s when they initiated one of the first public-private partnerships to benefit the newly formed City University of New York. In 1964, the Silbermans had given Hunter:

- $4 million to develop a new building for the Hunter College School of Social Work (HCSSW);
- Development rights to a valuable family-owned site on East 79th Street, which the new building would occupy for an annual lease of $1.00;
- An endowment, the Samuel J. and Lois V. Silberman Fund, which would support HCSSW student scholarships in perpetuity.

These gifts plus several excellent administrative and faculty hires such as Hal Lewis, Rose Dobroff, Robert Salmon, and Florence Vigilante elevated HCSSW to one of the best in the country. The building that housed the HCSSW was seven stories high and rested on a parcel that was among the most valuable on New York's Upper Eastside. It seems that Bud had floated the idea of the expansion for at least two years but there had been no movement on it. The major sticking point being that Bud wasn't going to give up ownership of the building and lot and CUNY had no legal mechanism for doing a capital construction project on property that it did not own.

I met with Bud to get a better understanding of his proposal and expectations. I must say, I don't know that I had ever met a more generous, down-to earth individual. I learned that his family immigrated from Germany in the

1840s, settled in New York, and established a most successful business, the Consolidated Cigar Company, which at the time of our meeting was a subsidiary of Gulf & Western Industries. The family also invested in New York City real estate. He was now retired and was devoting his efforts to philanthropy with the HCSSW taking up much of his time, as well as the Silberman College of Business at Fairleigh Dickinson University. He had determined that the HCSSW building could be expanded three additional stories and widened a bit without seeking a variance from the zoning board of the City of New York. He didn't want to go for a variance and had little confidence in being able to get one given the location. He was sure that residents in the area would be totally against any expansion. He also was clear that he had no intention of giving up ownership of the property and that this was his way of making sure that the HCSSW would continue as a premiere institution. Given the politics of CUNY, New York City, and New York State, I didn't blame him for his caution. I think we both felt that the meeting was a successful start.

I met with Don Farley, who had been most helpful during the negotiations with the Dormitory Authority for the re-appropriation of the $13 million for equipment and furniture. Don wasn't sure a deal could be worked out. All capital projects at CUNY were funded through the Dormitory Authority which wouldn't issue construction bonds unless CUNY, New York City or New York State owned the property. Don did indicate that he had just started negotiations with New York State to do something similar at John Jay College, a CUNY four-year college that specialized in criminal justice and municipal service programs for police, fire, and corrections personnel. He suggested that I meet with Al Toscano, who handled all leases and rental agreements for CUNY. I met with Al. He was a well- informed and knowledgeable individual who knew funding, lease and rental property issues inside and out. He didn't have a solution, but he indicated that the John Jay College project might pave the way for the HCSSW. He asked me to provide as many of the details as possible.

I met again with Bud Silberman and he was delighted that there was some small hope for funding. He was also most understanding and indicated that he was willing to be as helpful as possible as long as he didn't have to give up ownership of the property. After my consultation with Bud, I submitted a tentative plan to Al Toscano essentially describing the HCSSW project as building an additional three stories of space that would house classrooms, a videoconferencing facility, and offices. He let me know that the John Jay College project was making progress and that Don Farley's plan was to add the HCSSW construction to the John Jay request, making it one CUNY-wide request. Al explained that the plan was to use a capital lease purchase approach called Certificates of Participation (COPs) that were tax-exempt bonds similar to municipal bonds. This approach had never been used before in New York State for capital projects and would need legislative approval. Al explained that the owner of the property would be responsible for design and construction and that CUNY would pay all costs in the form of rent over a twenty-five-year period with the property remaining in possession of the owner.

I discussed this with Bud Silberman and he seemed okay with it, although he would take on a lot more responsibility for the project. As a matter of fact, he liked the idea that he would be in charge of all design and construction rather than leaving it to a public agency. It took a bit longer to get the approval than anyone realized but before the end of the year, the required legislation was passed and approved by the Governor. John Jay College was able to elicit political support from several major public unions that represented police and fire-fighters. It was effective and the entire CUNY proposal had been approved by the Legislature. Bud and I started spending a good deal of time meeting architects and attorneys to draw up the design for the addition and to work out a contract. Bud was as good as his word and jumped into the design aspect of the project wholeheartedly. The legal aspect was another story. CUNY had no template for drawing up the contract since neither it nor the State of New York had ever processed a Certificate of Participation (COP) lease. There were resolutions for bonding, design plans needing approval, and of course the terms and conditions of payment. Everyone of these steps required approvals within CUNY and the State of New York. At one point, Bud confided to me that "this was the most incredible bureaucratic process I have ever seen." Fortunately, Al Toscano saw our work as a brand-new line of funding and operations for CUNY so he relished getting our plans and contracts approved as they worked their way through the various governing offices.

When we finally secured all approvals for a $6 million project, President Shalala and Bud sent out a joint notice about the project. While it was met with cheers within the College and CUNY, it was met with jeers within the immediate Upper Eastside community. We held several community meetings where the tone was very antagonistic to say the least. During one such meeting, Donna Shalala turned to me and whispered that she was ashamed of what she was hearing from the community. The residents who lived in close proximity didn't want their views of the city disturbed. There was nothing we could about that. There were also concerns whether the expansion would lead to a lot more students coming and going in the area. We assured the community that HCSSW was a graduate program and there were no plans for any major expansion. Regardless, a community group promised to file an injunction and even drafted the wording for it. One of our faculty who lived in the area was able to get a copy. The construction project started in March 1987 and there was a critical weekend in June when we needed to close 79th Street in order to bring in a crane to hoist material to the existing roof. It took two months to get this approval from the New York City Building Department. I was hoping that the injunction was not served before this crane did its job because if it had been, it would have taken at least five or six more months for the hearing before a judge. Fortunately, the community group never organized itself enough to file for the injunction and the project proceeded as planned. The new expanded HCSSW opened in 1988. I received a very touching thank you note from Bud and Lois Silberman indicating their appreciation for my efforts in seeing their dream for the building and the social work program come to pass.

36

On January 28, 1986, just as I began to move on the HCSSW project, I was just finishing a meeting with Stan Sokol and several people on his staff when Mary Ortiz interrupted me to say that President Shalala was on the phone. She had been away for several days and I had no idea what she wanted to talk to me about. When I got on the phone, she asked if I had seen what happened to the Space Shuttle Challenger. I said no and she told me that it had disintegrated and killed all on board. Among those killed was a high school teacher, Christa McAuliffe, who would have been the first teacher in space. She said that we needed to get a message out to the Hunter College Community immediately. She dictated a very heartfelt memo expressing the sorrow we all felt. In addition to the tragedy itself, I was struck by how emotional President Shalala had been. During the phone call and even after she returned to New York, I could tell that she felt terrible about the incident. Her empathy and sadness were so genuine and all of us who worked with her were affected for weeks afterwards.

Later in May 1986, the Dean of Sciences, Dick Mawe, announced that Hunter College would be receiving its first-ever National Institutes of Health (NIH) Research Centers in Minority Institutions (RCMI) grant. This grant would provide extensive funding over several years to encourage minority students to consider science research as a career. The grant proposal called for identifying talented minority students in the undergraduate program and shepherding them through graduate and doctoral studies, preparing them to become biologists or chemists. President Shalala, Provost LeMelle, Dean Mawe and the faculty in biology and chemistry were elated. There had been several earlier proposals but this was the first award of this type made to Hunter College. In previous years, the College had received several Minority Biomedical Research Support (MBRS) awards that were intended to encourage and increase participation of minority students in biomedical research at the undergraduate level. The program provided student salaries for part-time work as research assistants in experimental research projects sponsored by Hunter College faculty members. While we all recognized and celebrated this accomplishment, there were two issues that we needed to resolve. One was that the College was losing its only minority scientist, Professor Jim Wyche, who indicated he was leaving to take a visiting research professorship at Stanford University. Afterwards, he would be leaving to become an associate dean at Brown University. Not having a minority biologist or chemist would make it difficult to promote Hunter to funders as an institution supporting the development of minority scientists. The second and more complex issue was the fact that Hunter didn't have very good science research laboratories. All of the science labs and animal research facilities were in the older buildings namely, the North Building and Thomas Hunter Hall, and didn't meet safety standards. There would have to be a major investment in renovations of these facilities if the College didn't want to be cited for safety infractions.. In addition, the support of the latest science research required new equipment with environmental safeguards namely air-conditioning, ventilation, and emission controls. Tilden LeMelle and Dick Mawe were charged with recruiting a high-level minority science researcher and I was responsible for upgrading the facilities.

I had long discussions with John Smith and Ted Rieper who was in charge of capital improvements at Hunter. They expressed concerns about the cost and the difficulty of retrofitting or building the new science facilities in the older buildings, but they were willing to take on the task. In fact,, they had already started some work before my arrival at Hunter but the new RCMI grant meant this project would have to be expanded. It was at this time that John Smith told me that he would be leaving for a position as vice president for administration at John Jay College. I had known that it was only a matter of time before he would leave. I decided to hire a new assistant vice president whose sole responsibilities would be facilities, security and the management of the operations at the other three campuses. I would have the financial services report to me directly.

Tilden LeMelle and Dick Mawe had a difficult task in recruiting an experienced minority science researcher. There weren't that many willing to leave their A-list institutions to work at Hunter which didn't have the resources or recognition of a top research university, but they did have several leads. Robert Dottin was a research professor of biology at Johns Hopkins University and indicated that he would consider moving to New York given the right conditions. These included a new laboratory built to meet his research needs and a substantial compensation package. I indicated that we could probably divert approximately $500,000 in funds from capital projects already allocated to renovate other science facilities in the North Building for Dottin's needs. Tilden was willing to provide personnel support in the form of a laboratory technician as well as equipment and supplies from the RCMI grant. The major sticking point became Dottin's salary. CUNY had a collective bargaining contract that established salary schedules for all faculty positions and Dottin was already making above the maximum. President Shalala asked if there was some way we could get around this. I suggested we pay him additional (summer) salary as part of his RCMI grant work, but she and Tilden were hoping for more. Maybe rather than salary we could offer him a housing allowance similar to the CUNY presidents. I told them I wasn't sure that this had been done before for faculty, but the precedent was there for administrators. I called Vince Tenaglia, my counterpart at the CUNY Graduate Center, who told met that the Graduate Center sometimes made this type of arrangement, but that they paid the allowance through soft funds and not through the normal college operating budget. He said to make sure to let Joe Vivona, the CUNY Vice Chancellor for Budget, know what we were doing. President Shalala and Tilden liked the idea. The only questions left were how much to offer Dottin as a housing allowance, and who should do the final negotiation. I got the job. A lot of the preliminary negotiation had been done verbally and we needed to get all prior details down on paper. Once I received this, I contacted Dottin. We negotiated a "number", and he indicated that he thought we had a deal. I told him he would hear from either President Shalala or Tilden LeMelle. The deal was finalized the following week and we had an agreement. We would be hiring a first-rate minority scientist from Johns Hopkins University.

Building the new laboratory facilities went very differently. On the plus side, a comprehensive master plan had been developed at the College prior to my appointment. Following the move to the new East and West Buildings, the classroom, physical education, and other dedicated space used by the social sciences and other academic programs had been re-allocated to the sciences. So, the space was available and we wouldn't have to engage in a space negotiation among academic programs. However, as indicated earlier, the North Building and Thomas Hunter Hall were older buildings and not ideally suited for modern laboratories. There was no central air-conditioning just window units that dotted the exteriors. In addition, as I said earlier, the latest scientific equipment needed proper ventilation and emission controls, including careful planning and installation of hoods, ducts, and pollution control equipment. And any projects that involved breaking into or behind the walls might also require doing asbestos abatement. The result was that each laboratory renovation would be expensive and would be subject to a good deal of review by the New York City Building Department. Regardless, we were able to develop Dottin's new laboratory but at a cost much higher than we originally anticipated.

37

As the Vice President for Administration, I had continued to develop working relationships with CUNY Central staff and examiners at the New York State (NYS) Division of the Budget. This was especially important in seeking funding for the College's operating budget. I must say that two of the CUNY vice chancellors, Don Farley and Joe Vivona were very supportive and encouraging. I trusted them and would seek their advice on new funding requests. The NYS Division of the Budget was a different case although my experiences working with former Vice Chancellor Ken King helped me in negotiating with the budget examiners. There was a political side to these negotiations, some of which had nothing to do with Hunter, but was directed to the entire CUNY system. Although it wasn't explicitly stated, there was a limit each year for the entire University that pitted the colleges against each other. Each had to make the case that its college's needs were justified and more important than the other CUNY units. Sometimes we were successful and sometimes not.

Based on the difficulty I had encountered in obtaining funds to renovate our science labs, it was my sense that CUNY at the highest levels, didn't want Hunter to vie for major science grants, particularly RCMI-type funds. In fact, Chancellor Joseph Murphy assembled a taskforce, led by former Chancellor Al Bowker, to discuss whether Hunter should be making major moves into RCMI and other science grants directed at minority institutions. The task force report clearly stated that other units in CUNY and specifically City College would be more appropriate for this type of activity. While the University did not stop Hunter from applying for these grants, our requests for capital funding for laboratory renovations were slowed down and in some cases rejected by CUNY. This forced us to use other funds (i.e., gifts, research recovery funds, and continuing education surpluses) to fund our renovation projects. We became adept in assembling funding for renovations, tactics which appealed to some at the CUNY Central Office such as Don Farley but incurred the displeasure of the Chancellor and his immediate staff.

The two new towers were a boon to Hunter College. They were functional, attractive and most of the occupants were pleased with their new space. However, John Smith and Bob Salinardi kept harping on the fact that the College had never received any additional staff positions for maintaining these two new buildings. Requests had been made for new positions in previous years but were denied by the New York State Division of the Budget. I looked at the previous requests and I thought we could do a better job of stating our case and that we needed to meet with the NYS budget examiners to present our needs. We drafted a new request that essentially praised the new towers but contended that we were having difficulty keeping the facilities clean, secured, and well-maintained. In essence, we said that New York State, via the Dormitory Authority, had invested $100 million dollars in constructing the towers but wasn't willing to invest in maintaining them. I asked Don Farley to write a supporting letter for us. He did so, indicating that our request was important for the entire university. CUNY would be embarking on $1 billion of construction, and he wanted us to set the precedent for new maintenance funding. The budget examiners came to Hunter in January 1986 to meet with us. They toured the towers as well as the North Building and Thomas Hunter Hall. One of them commented that the buildings looked clean and in good shape. I said that we could do much better. I also mentioned issues with the heating/ventilation systems in the new towers that minimally needed fine-tuning and perhaps an upgrade. At the same time, as we were requesting new positions for the towers, Bob Salinardi drafted a request for an additional $750,000. to make up for a funding shortfall for energy needs at the Brookdale Center. The budget examiners had routinely rejected this request in the past on the grounds that the income from the dormitories should cover energy expenses. We redrafted the request and made the case that half of the usable space (one of three buildings) at Brookdale wasn't used for dormitories but for classroom and laboratory activities in our nursing and health sciences program.

In April 1986, when we received our budget for the new academic year (1986-87), we received funding for fifty-five new positions (lines) to maintain the new towers and $550,000. for energy costs at the Brookdale Campus. I congratulated Bob Salinardi for a job well-done and called Don Farley to thank him for his assistance with the new positions. I told President Shalala and Tilden LeMelle who immediately asked if we could use these positions for other than cleaning, security and maintenance. I told them we weren't supposed to but we would do what we could. In addition to new positions in plant maintenance, we funded new lines in other areas including institutional research, health and safety, and laboratory technicians. We snuck in a number of new faculty positions to support the RCMI and MBRS grants. All's fair in budgets and war!

38

At the end of 1986, CUNY embarked on a major initiative to develop centralized administrative computer systems for all the colleges. The Central Office had already developed a centralized financial accounting system that served the colleges well. There was also a modest centralized personnel system that provided very basic services. The major thrust of the new initiative would be a student information system. Stan Sokol and Jim Anastasio kept me up to date about this development. In fact, Jim was being recruited by CUNY to be a key player since they wanted his expertise in developing a new student system patterned after the one he had developed at Hunter College. Jim and I had a long relationship and he confessed that he was interested in working on the centralized system and wanted my opinion. I would never stand in the way of a colleague's career advancement but I questioned him about CUNY's expectations since it appeared to me that the organization for developing a centralized student system wasn't in place. While the Central Computer Center had done marvelous work in providing networking services to the university (i.e., BITNET), this wasn't the case when it came to student information systems. My advice to Jim was to get clarity as to exactly what his position would be in the central development before making a move.. The long and short of it was that indeed the organization for the development of a centralized student information was non-existent. Jim made himself available for committee work and consultation, but his primary responsibilities remained at Hunter.

In January 1987, Silvia Fine Kaye, the wife of the Hollywood actor, Danny Kaye, contacted President Shalala with the news that she might be willing to donate $1 million dollars for renovating the Hunter College Playhouse in exchange for renaming it the Kaye Playhouse. Mrs. Kaye was born and raised in Brooklyn and maintained a residence in Manhattan just a few blocks from Hunter College. Unbeknownst to us, she had attended many performances at the Playhouse. There was no doubt that the Playhouse could use a renovation but it wasn't clear at the time whether $1 million would be enough to do the job. While the Playhouse was a small intimate theater, the acoustics were not very good. It had a high circular ceiling that absorbed a lot of the sound coming from the stage and the audience in the back rows wasn't always able to hear the voices of actors and actresses. I contacted an engineering firm that specialized in theater renovations to provide estimates for improving the space. Their estimates starting at $1 million and went up to $5 million. Don Farley thought that we could get funding to match whatever Ms. Kaye would provide. President Shalala, Vice President for Development Robin Elliot, and I met several times with Ms. Kaye and we agreed that we would apply for the additional funding to match her gift. In the middle of these negotiations, on March 3, 1987, Danny Kaye died and shortly thereafter Sylvia Kaye became ill. The project was put on hold but we started making plans to apply for a $1 million match pending firm estimates and an agreement with Ms. Kaye for whatever the renovations would entail. When Ms. Kaye was well enough, we started discussions again about the gift and the renovation of the Playhouse. Our tentative plan was that, assuming we received funds in 1988-89, we could have the renovation completed in late 1990.

During my second summer at Hunter in 1987, President Shalala went on a two-month trek in the Himalayas and wouldn't be in contact with any of us in New York. Tilden was appointed the acting president and, for the most part, all went well except for a request from Chancellor Murphy to appoint a former president from one of the other CUNY colleges to a tenured full professorship in our School of Social Work. The appointments of former presidents to college positions weren't unusual and we had two previous CUNY presidents already on salary at Hunter. Usually, these appointments were for a specific period of time, perhaps five years. Tilden asked me what I thought about the Chancellor's request. I thought he could probably approve the appointment to a full professorship, but I wouldn't guarantee the tenure. I suggested that he hold out until President Shalala returned. For whatever reason, Tilden decided to make the appointment with tenure. When President Shalala returned, she was livid. I had never seen her so angry. She proceeded to undo the appointment citing that it didn't go through proper channels within the School of Social Work. Eventually she negotiated with the Chancellor an appointment for this president in the School of Health Sciences. My takeaway from this episode was that the relationship between President Shalala and Chancellor Murphy was deteriorating and had begun with the RCMI application and the Albert Bowker Committee recommendation.

Also, in the summer of 1987, I received a call from Don Farley asking whether I knew anything about New York City Technical College's (NYCTC) Voorhees Building on West 41st Street. I was aware of it but I had never been inside. He indicated that NYCTC had just opened a new campus in Downtown Brooklyn and would no longer need the Voorhees facility. CUNY didn't want to give up the property which would revert to the City of New York if it was not used for a higher education purpose, so he wanted in know whether Hunter College could use it. I told him that I would like to tour the facility and that as soon as President Shalala returned from her trek we could meet to discuss further the space. The Voorhees Building had been used for associate degree technology programs. It had a large multi-story open center space with offices and classrooms around the perimeter. It just so happened that Sandy Wurmfeld, the chair of Hunter's Art Department, was hoping to expand his relatively new M.F.A. program. I discussed the possibility of the space with him and he thought that the open center space would be ideal for large-scale student art studio projects, especially sculpture. When Donna returned, she was all for it assuming that we received full funding to support the building. Don Farley assured me that we would receive the funding we needed. I also mentioned to him that during my visit to Voorhees, I noticed that the heating system was ancient and might need replacement. He promised to absorb the cost of any repairs until a new system could be built. He also indicated that he would need some office space at the facility for CUNY Central employees and special programs. Don and I negotiated all of this on and off for about two months. We took control of the building in December

1987. Sandy Wurmfeld and the Art Department faculty were happy. President Shalala and Chancellor Murphy were pleased as well. Hunter had acquired its fifth site.

Around this time, Don Farley invited me to dinner with the Chancellor and several other CUNY administrators who had helped in securing a major bond issue for capital projects at a number of the campuses. The dinner was on Dillon Read and Company, a major banking company in New York, that had handled all of the investment negotiations. On several occasions, Don had asked to bring potential investors to see Hunter's new towers. I was happy to host them. If he would give me twenty-four hours-notice, I would make sure our buildings were sparkling inside and out. It was at this dinner that Don took me aside and asked if I might be interested in working with him at the CUNY Central Office. Henry Mortarotti, who was the Director of the Office of Facilities Planning, Construction & Management, had just resigned to take a position at Arizona State University. Henry directed the implementation part of Don Farley's operation. While it was an intriguing offer, I wasn't interested in leaving Hunter and saw my future working at a college where there were students and faculty.

In October 1987, Donna Shalala told Tilden LeMelle and me that she would be leaving to become the Chancellor of the University of Wisconsin at Madison. The announcement was made publicly a week later. While we were all happy for President Shalala, several of the senior administrators took it very hard. Within a couple of months Robin Elliot, the Vice President for Institutional Advancement, Jim Muyskens, the Associate Provost, Dick Mawe the Dean of Sciences, and Walter Weiss, the Dean of Social Sciences announced that they were retiring or otherwise leaving their positions. I was especially bothered that Dick Mawe was leaving. We had developed a good relationship during the RCMI projects and I thought he was much too young to retire. However, his avocation was to be an actor and he believed he had to make a clean break from Hunter in order to pursue his dream. Tilden and I both believed that our days would be numbered once a new president was hired. President Shalala continued on for several months. She cautioned me to be careful regardless of who the new president was and to do everything I could to keep what we had accomplished at Hunter going.

In December, President Shalala called me into her office for a quick chat. She told me that Donald Trump had just called her and asked if she would be interested in trading Hunter College's East and West Towers for a new campus with as much space as we wanted on the Westside of Manhattan. At first, I thought she was kidding me, but no, she was serious. In my opinion, Hunter College was part of the fabric of Manhattan's Upper Eastside and to move it to the Westside just didn't seem right, even though the idea of "all the space" we could want was attractive. I also mentioned that the decision wouldn't be ours. And having just gone through the takeover of the Voorhees Building, I reminded her that existing CUNY property no longer used for a public higher education purpose reverted back to the control of the City of New York. That pretty much ended the discussion. I thought she was going to tell me to call Donald Trump, but she called him herself.

Let me share a couple of other Donna stories before concluding this chapter. One afternoon as I came into the foyer where our elevators were located, Donna was waiting with a tall businesswoman. Immediately, Donna introduced me to Christie Hefner, Hugh Hefner's daughter. I made the connection and blurted out instantly: "Donna, don't tell me you are to be a *Playboy* centerfold?" The three of us had a good laugh. It seems that Ms. Hefner wanted to initiate a change to *Playboy* that would have it appeal to women and she was asking Donna's advice. Donna had the most interesting acquaintances.

On another unforgettable occasion, Joe Kiernan, the Director of Facilities at the Brookdale Campus, who was finishing up a renovation of a new student lounge on the top floor of one of the dormitory buildings, invited me to take a look at it. I asked Donna, Tilden and John Smith to come along. We drove down to 25th Street and Joe took us to the new lounge. We all thought it was quite well done., and before we left, Joe took us onto the outdoor patio area for a great view of the East River from thirteen stories above the street. When we went to return to the lounge, Joe's master key wouldn't work. The door had locked behind us and the construction company had put a temporary lock of their own on the door. There we were thirteen stories high in the age before cell phones, where no one would hear us if we yelled all day. The student lounge wasn't open yet, so no one would be coming by soon. With the entire senior administration of Hunter College stuck on the roof, Joe came up with the idea that if we could get to the door at the top of the elevator maintenance shaft, his master key would work. The only problem was that someone had to scale a twelve-foot wall to get to the elevator shaft. John suggested that we give someone a boost up the wall and Donna volunteered to be the one to do it, which made sense because she was by far the lightest person among us. On the other hand, she was wearing a skirt hemmed just above the knees and I couldn't figure how we could gracefully give her the boost we needed. Everyone but Donna thought this was a problem. Finally, we decided that Joe who was a good hundred pounds heavier than Donna would have to go up the wall. John Smith and I had the pleasure of giving Joe the boost while Donna cheered us on. He came back down a ladder inside the elevator shaft, opened the door to the patio, and let us back in. For months afterwards, we were retelling this story of our adventure up on the outdoor patio.

We had a grand farewell party for President Shalala and invited the entire college. We hired a band and I had the pleasure of dancing with her to Ritchie Valens hit song *Oh, Donna*. It went, "I had a girl, Donna was her name...." She surely was the most fun of any president I ever worked for.

Donna's position in Wisconsin began in January 1988. Tilden was named the interim president and a search for a new president began in the spring. Tilden would have loved to become the president but that wasn't in the cards.

39

In January 1988, I received a phone call from President Ed Volpe from the College of Staten Island (CSI). He and I had had several conversations over the past year regarding the building of a new campus for CSI at Willowbrook, and I assumed this call had something to do with this. After exchanging updates on colleagues of mine at CSI, he said the purpose of his call was to discuss the presidential vacancy at New York City Technical College. Ursula Schwerin had announced her retirement and a search was on for a replacement. Ed said he had spoken to several other presidents including Leonard Lief at Herbert Lehman College and Harold Proshansky at the Graduate Center and together they would be happy to nominate me for the position and support my candidacy. I had never dreamt about moving into a presidency and I didn't know what to say. He was very encouraging, but I told him I had to think about it and get back to him. This possibility forced me to think carefully about what I wanted to do for the rest of my career. I was forty years old and I believed I had a good twenty-five plus years of work left in me. Truth be told I was beginning to think about not spending them in administrative positions but in academic teaching positions. I had been teaching one or two courses a year in educational leadership at Hunter and I was enjoying it immensely. I thought I wouldn't mind doing this for a living. I was also greatly concerned with CUNY's tightening hold on the colleges. For most of my years of experience at CUNY colleges, the presidents and senior administrators had a lot of flexibility in setting goals and objectives as well as requesting funding to realize them. This had especially been true at a large college such as Hunter, but I detected a change at CUNY where more of the planning, decision making, and funding for the colleges was moving to the Central Office. I called President Volpe two days later and thanked him profusely for thinking about me but I told him I wasn't ready to move. He continued to try to persuade me to consider otherwise, but my mind was made up.

There were a number of excellent candidates to succeed Donna, and in the end, Paul LeClerc, the Provost at Bernard Baruch College and a close colleague of Chancellor Murphy, was hired as president. It was clear to Tilden and me that Hunter would come under the control of the Chancellor. The independence that President Shalala had fostered would be gone. She was fond of saying "let's not allow CUNY to stop us from doing what we want to do." This would no longer be the case. Paul LeClerc began his tenure as president on September 1, 1988. He asked to meet with me at 10:00 am and said he was meeting with Tilden at 9:00 am. President LeClerc came into my office on schedule and told me that he had just asked for Tilden's resignation. I assumed he would be asking for mine but that didn't happen. We had a good conversation. He hoped I would stay on. I thought I could work with him. We would see.

40

In December 1988, New York City would be hosting a visit by the Soviet Union's Premier Mikhail S. Gorbachev and his wife Raisa. Because of the United Nations, New York was adept at hosting the visits of foreign leaders. Gorbachev, however, was not just any other foreign leader; he was the United States' adversary in the Cold War. In addition, Gorbachev had been hinting he would like to see the relations between the two major powers improve and he appeared willing and able to institute major reforms in the Soviet Union that could lead to true détente and more peaceful involvement with the West.

Hunter College was involved in some of the discussions regarding the logistics of his visit because the Soviet embassy was just across 67th Street from Hunter East. Furthermore, Hunter East was the tallest building on the same block of mostly modest-sized apartment buildings and was a natural place for staging Gorbachev's security operation since he would be spending a good deal of time at the embassy. The Hunter Security staff and I met with New York City police as well as representatives from the U.S. Department of State. We were given a general briefing of Gorbachev's visit and events. We were asked if the police could take over the roof of Hunter East, a request I granted immediately. Every day of the visit, I would get a phone call or visit telling me which hours would be most important in terms of Gorbachev's comings or goings to and from the embassy. We cooperated in any way we could and also posted our own security guards in the stairwells and entrances to the Hunter East roof. Twice our guards stopped newspaper reporters who were looking to take photographs.

Gorbachev's visit came off without a hitch and we were proud of the small part we played during his stay. It should be mentioned that Gorbachev and his wife proved to be incredibly popular among New Yorkers. People lined the streets to see his 45-car motorcade day after day and warmly greeted them. Gorbachev and his wife, without regard for their own safety, would make impromptu stops on Broadway, at Bloomingdale's, on Times Square and the World Trade Center. In the years immediately following this visit, the United States and the Soviet Union enjoyed a period of cordial relationships culminating with the tearing down of the Berlin Wall in November 1989.

41

The next several months went by quickly but it was becoming more obvious to me that my time as the senior vice president at Hunter College would be coming to an end. Others around the university, including some from the CUNY Central Office inquired about my availability but I hadn't pursued any offers. I had two thoughts about my situation, First, it was clear that CUNY was embarking on a major initiative to gain greater control of the colleges. Yearly budget requests were now being approved by the Central Office and the budget hearings by individual colleges with the New York State Division of the Budget were eliminated. President LeClerc was fine with this but I was less than happy with this this type of bureaucratic environment. I had been doing college accreditation visits for the Middle States Association, at least two a year, and had become familiar with a number of public institutions in New Jersey and Maryland that might be attractive possibilities. I also thought about the non-public sector in and around New York but didn't have a lot of contacts at the private colleges and universities.

As I mentioned earlier, my second thought was whether I wanted to continue in an administrative career at all. President LeClerc and I were becoming increasingly unhappy with each other's styles. I had enjoyed teaching for the past eighteen years at several institutions and at several levels. I never tired of sharing what I knew with students whether they were undergraduates, graduates, public administrators, or businessmen. I also thought a lot about Dick Mawe's decision to leave the Dean of Sciences position to pursue his love of acting. I remember him saying that he had to make "a clean break." In May 1989, following several days of turmoil that left us at odds, President LeClerc and I had a discussion. I offered my resignation in return for a teaching position in Hunter College's education leadership program. After some negotiation, and with the full support of my family, I would begin my career as an associate professor teaching graduate courses in education leadership starting in fall 1989. It was one of the toughest and best decisions I ever made. And so, my administrative career came to an end!

PART VI

Hunter College
New York, New York
1989-1996

42

On Monday, August 28th, 1989, I began my career as a full-time faculty member in the Department of Curriculum & Teaching (C & T) in the Programs in Education in the School of Arts and Sciences at Hunter College. In addition to C & T, the Programs in Education housed programs in the Education Foundations and Special Education Departments.

My faculty colleagues in the department were most welcoming. Mae Gamble, the newly elected chairperson met with me in June to determine what my teaching schedule would be. I had known Mae when I was the Senior Vice President for Administration. She had asked for assistance the previous year in finding office space for the American Social History Project (ASHP) which had to move from its facilities at the CUNY Graduate Center. With help from Hunter's Department of Communications, we were able to real-locate two offices for the ASHP. She was most grateful, and it helped me as we met to lay out my new career. In discussing my teaching style with Mae, I indicated that I had done a lot of professional development in the 1970s and 1980s. I let her know that I rarely lectured for extensive parts of my lessons and instead incorporated problem-solving, case studies, data analysis, and collaborative group projects. Mae was most happy, maybe impressed, to hear how I described my teaching.

My teaching responsibilities for the coming academic year would be in the graduate program in education administration and supervision (ADSUP). It was a post-masters certificate program that upon graduation qualified the students to become school leaders such as principals, assistant principals and district-level administrators. It was a selective program admitting about 25 students per year. I was to teach a research methods course in the fall and an education policy course in the spring. I had already taught the research methods course in this program while in my administrative position. I was also asked if I could develop a new administrative technology and data-driven decision-making course. In addition to the ADSUP program, I would teach an instructional technology course in the graduate teacher education program. In reviewing the syllabi for these courses, I felt well-prepared to teach the courses in the ADSUP program, but I needed to bring my knowledge up to date a bit in the instructional technology course. A third of the course was a computer literacy component which I could easily make current using the material I had developed for professional development workshops in the NetWORK program at the College of Staten Island. For the rest of the course, I needed to become more familiar with the technology used in K-12 education. As a result, I developed a plan to become fully immersed in the K-12 technology world. I spent a number of days during the summer at the Marymount College Library near my home. The College had a good collection of journals on teacher education including technology. I needed to develop an inventory of software programs that were appropriate for K-12 students. In addition to commercial game simulation software like *The Oregon Trail* and *Where in the World is Carmen Sandiego*, I became fully acquainted with *Logo*, which was an immersive programming language developed by Seymour Papert at M.I.T. Written in LISP (LIST Processor), an early programming language used extensively in artificial intelligence, *Logo* brought a powerful learning experience to K-12 students who used a friendly turtle as its primary programming interface. It was a provocative and creative way for young students to learn how to program. Its major drawback was that the teacher had to become proficient in programming *Logo* and had to be willing to devote extensive amount of class time to allow students to learn it. I also became quite interested in interactive videodisc technology which allowed a degree of manipulation of images and full-motion video using random-access disc technology. Pioneer, Incorporated offered several excellent, affordable and easy to use videodisc players while companies such as Optical Data Corporation (ODC) provided education software. With its award-winning *Windows on Science* series, ODC offered entire courses for middle and secondary education using videodisc technology that were visually way ahead of their time.

While learning the various K-12 software, I contacted and developed a relationship with Professor John Niman who also taught instructional technology and who, with grant money and funding from the College, was overseeing the development of a new 20-station, IBM-PC instructional technology lab for the Department of Curriculum & Teaching. The lab also housed four Apple Macintosh computers. John had also been building a software library that I would need to teach the subject matter using a hands-on student approach. I spent a number of hours in this lab in August familiarizing myself with the software available, the teacher workstation and the large projection screen. I was able to get a copy of *Logo*, installed on my computer at home, and in a few days I was proficient enough to be able to teach it to my students. By the time the Fall 1989 semester started, I felt well-equipped to teach a course on instructional technology for K-12 teacher educators using a hands-on student approach based on regular computer activities.

The ADSUP research methods syllabus concentrated on research concepts and the evaluation of studies related to administrative issues. With the approval of the program coordinator, Hal Judenfriend, I decided to reduce the evaluation components and add a substantive hands-on experience using Excel and SPSS to analyze data. With John Niman's okay, I asked the College's technology support operation to load SPSS onto the IBM PCs in our computer lab. All of my courses for the fall would be taught in the new lab. Since John Niman taught all of his courses in the daytime and I would be teaching my courses in the evening, we never had a conflict over use of the lab.

In the Spring 1990 semester, I taught three courses, adding the ADSUP course on education policy to the same courses I taught in the fall. This was basically a discussion course wherein I covered a number of topics related to how education policy evolved in the country. I focused on major events such as the U.S. Supreme Court's Brown v. Board of Education Decision(1954), President Lyndon Johnson's War on Poverty/Great Society Programs and the Elementary and Secondary School Act of 1965, and President Ronald Reagan's *A Nation at Risk* Report (1983). I also included material on current New York State and New York City school policy related to community control of education, bilingual education and special education. For most of the students, despite having undergraduate and master's degrees in teacher education, policy was a new subject area. I used modest amounts of video to allow the students to hear and see events, as well as policy makers and others discussing education policy issues. Blackside's *Eyes on the Prize* series provided a plethora of well-done video material on education and civil rights issues. I again used the computer laboratory to teach all of my courses including the education policy course.

43

In June 1990, our Chair, Mae Gamble asked to meet with me about a new experimental, grant-funded undergraduate teacher education program called Quality Urban Education Student Teachers or QUEST. She was happy with all of the hands-on/workshop activities that I had integrated into my teaching and wanted me to bring some of that to the QUEST program. She told me that as much as possible the QUEST education courses would be taught in the field at cooperating local public schools. I knew right away that might be a problem depending upon whether the schools had appropriate computer facilities. She understood and asked to me review the three public schools (P.S. 171, P.S. 108, and the Schomburg School) in which we would be working in East Harlem to determine their suitability for teaching instructional technology. She also asked if, in addition to an instructional technology course, would I be willing to teach a social foundations course in the same program. I had never taught social foundations and I thought it was normally taught by faculty in the Education Foundations Department. She said it was, but she was having difficulty recruiting faculty to teach in QUEST from Education Foundations. She also thought that I could use some of the material that I had developed for the ADSUP education policy course. I visited all three schools and only the Schomburg School had a good functioning computer lab. Even then the time during the day necessary for me to use it would be a problem. I met with Mae again in late June and gave her my review of the computer lab situation in the three cooperating sites and we agreed that I could continue to use our own computer lab for as much of the teaching as I saw fit, but that we would also try to integrate some of it into one of the cooperating schools. As a result, I would teach instructional technology at P.S. 171 or Hunter College in the mornings and social foundations at P.S. 171 in the afternoon. My schedule for the Fall 1990 semester was now set and in addition to the two QUEST courses, I would teach the research methods course in ADSUP. QUEST was assigned two rooms at P.S. 171 for the entire day on Tuesdays and Thursdays for use as classrooms and for faculty-student meetings and consultations.

My experiences in teaching in QUEST were incredibly beneficial to my own development as a faculty member for several reasons. First, it allowed me to teach undergraduates and I came to understand the differences in their approach to their studies versus graduate students. The undergraduates needed much more guidance and advisement, since most of them had no experience teaching in public schools. And unlike my graduate students, all of whom were educators with years of teaching who had developed a repertoire of pedagogical skills, the undergraduates had never worked with public school students. Many of them lacked confidence and needed to be encouraged to follow their instincts and passions. Above all I stressed the importance of being well-organized and prepared for their lessons.

Second, there is no better way to understand an environment than to live in it for a while. I was spending one full day a week working in P.S. 171. I wasn't just teaching the undergraduates, but I was also seeing and working with the administrators, public school teachers, a plethora of K-5 students, parents, security guards, and other support staff. I was made aware of their successes and problems. For example, technology was at a minimum. There were no technicians at the school and the one teacher responsible for developing a technology program was trained and worked half of his time as an art teacher. Creating a stable technology teaching environment was difficult to say the least. I resorted to teaching about 50 percent of the technology course at Hunter.

Third, in addition to spending the day with our undergraduates at P.S. 171, I was also working closely with other Hunter colleagues to develop activities for our students beyond our college courses. They could student teach, tutor K-5 students, and assist public school teachers to develop special programs. We did all we could to develop a supportive community for the school. George Gonzalez was my Hunter College co-teacher at P.S. 171, and I couldn't have asked for a better partner. He was affable, supportive of our work and knew P.S. 171 well, having been a teacher there prior to joining the faculty at Hunter. Kimberly Kinsler also became a fine QUEST colleague and was generous in sharing with me her ideas for teaching the social foundations course. I would go on to co-author two brief articles with George and Kimberly on our experiences teaching in QUEST.

References

Picciano, A.G. and Kinsler, K. (1991). Hunter College's QUEST Program, computers and urban education," *Computers in the Schools, 6*(1-3), pp. 175-177.

Gonzalez, G. and Picciano, A.G. (1993). QUEST: Developing competence, commitment, and an understanding of a community in a fieldbased, urban teacher education program," *Equity and Choice, 9*(2), pp. 3843.

44

In October 1990, I had a visit from Steve Epstein who was a representative with IBM's Academic Information Systems group (ACIS). The role of ACIS was to develop hardware and software products for teaching and learning in higher education but not to sell them directly. That was left to IBM's regular sales force. Steve was referred to me by Mike Ribaudo, CUNY Dean of Computer Information Systems and Chief Technology Officer. Since assuming the position of University Dean in 1985, Mike and I had served on a number of committees together and we had a fine professional relationship.

Steve wanted to demonstrate a new hardware/software product that ACIS had developed and wasn't yet on the market. We set up a meeting at Mike Ribaudo's office at the CUNY University Computer Center where Steve demonstrated what he referred to as a multimedia PC. It was an IBM PS/2-70 (386 Processor) with a M-Motion Board that could be programmed and customized to control audio-video devices. It was connected to a Pioneer 8000 videodisc player. The application software was Asymetrix's Toolbook with Multimedia Extensions and Clipmaker. Toolbook was similar to Apple's HyperCard software with a book and page comparable to a stack and card. This version of Toolbook had multimedia extensions compatible with the IBM hardware. These extensions allowed the user to control the videodisc down to the individual frames. Furthermore, the IBM M-Motion Board could play the selected clip at 30 frames per second which was above the standard for high-quality analog video. In 1990, digital video was still developing and typically displayed at 10 frames per second with a postage-stamp size cell or image. The IBM M-Motion Board allowed for displaying video clips on the entire PS/2-70 computer screen with fully synchronized audio. I was quite impressed. Steve indicated that he would entertain a grant request for developing a multimedia instruction software application based on the IBM PS/2-70 with the M-Motion Board.

With some basic training on the software provided by ACIS, I was immediately able to visualize developing an instructional application. The only problem I had was access to quality video. A few months earlier, I had attended a presentation by the American Social History Project (ASHP) of a videotape-based history module entitled, *The Five Points*. The module focused in part on events depicted in Herbert Asbury's 1927 nonfiction book *The Gangs of New York* which would later be made into a movie with the same name in 2002 starring Daniel Day-Lewis and Leonardo DeCaprio. The videotape developed by ASHP had images and voice-over narrations of a riot that took place in the notorious Five Points section of New York in 1857. It was approximately thirty minutes long and was meant to be shown in its entirety with a discussion/question-and-answer period to follow. I thought it would make for an interesting interactive lesson if I could repurpose the videotape into short video clips that the viewer (student) could pick and choose from to view and question in any order. I approached Steve Brier, the Director of ASHP and shared my idea with him. He was interested and we had a follow-up meeting with his ASHP colleagues Josh Brown and Bret Eynon who were all for it. I drafted the grant proposal to develop *The Five Points: A Multimedia Program in Social History* and submitted it to IBM's Steve Epstein. It was approved quickly and soon the IBM PS/2-70 was delivered. Steve, Josh, Bret and I met regularly for several weeks. We decided to convert *The Five Points* videotape to videodisc and to develop a software simulation program in which a reporter in 1857 is writing a newspaper article about the causes of the riot in New York City. The clips, extracted from the original video, included eyewitness accounts, descriptions of the neighborhood, and background information on immigrants who lived in the Five Points and were the main participants in the riot. The student activity was to assume the role of the newspaper reporter and write an article based upon the information in the clips and other material that would be provided in the program.

To accomplish our objectives, the simulation was organized into five major sections (see Figure 44.1):

1. Introduction
2. Eyewitness accounts (see Figure 44.2)
3. Archive room
4. Draft(s) of a newspaper article
5. Relating the historical events to the present day.

Figure 44.1 Outline of the Five Points

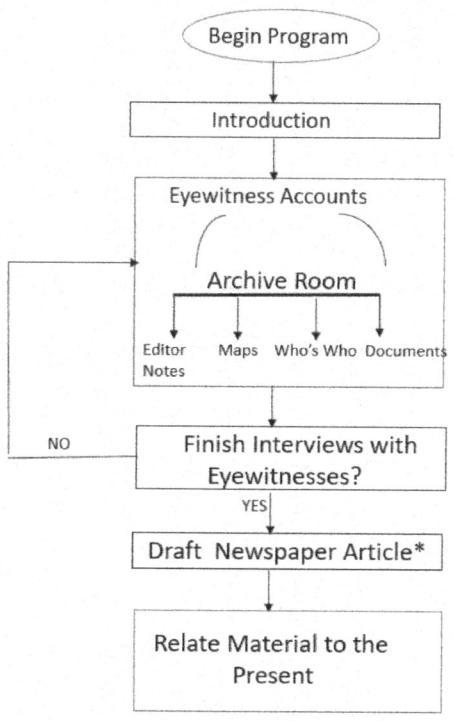

*NOTE: An electronic notebook is available for all modules to keep notes and to draft the article.

Figure 44.2 Five Points Eyewitness Accounts Section

Introduction

The multimedia program opens with a series of nine "tease" clips of approximately seven to ten seconds in length that serve to arouse curiosity about the "mayhem" that occurred in our "heaven-blessed" city on July 4, 1857. These clips serve the same function as the opening chapter of a mystery novel. Following these clips is an actual headline "Rioting and Bloodshed – Streets Barricaded" and an article that describes how twelve people were killed and hundreds injured when local Irish Catholics rioted against a new temperance law. The last part of the introduction assigns to the student the role of a reporter who has to write a feature article on the "real causes" of the riot.

Eyewitness Accounts

The Eyewitness Accounts section contained twenty video clips of six eyewitnesses to the riot: The Reverend Louis Pease, four members of the Mulvahill family, and Tom McGivigan, a volunteer fireman. Five clips are readily available to the student on the opening screen of the Eyewitness Accounts, but the other fifteen only become selectively available as the student contacts the "editor" of the newspaper who suggests further investigation. Rev. Pease relates the sad conditions of abandoned children, prostitutes, and too much liquor "coursing through the points." Mike Mulvahill, the father, tells of his difficulty in finding work. The mother, Mary, and her teenage daughter, Elizabeth, describe life from the women's perspective. The young son, Matty, boasts of his life on the street as a member of a gang. Tom recounts the importance of helping local ward bosses at election time. To keep notes, students were provided a basic word processing program integrated into the simulation.

The Archive Room

An important addition in the multimedia program that wasn't available in the original videotape was an archive room. This "room " was a Toolbook page depicting a reference room or office. Old-fashioned desks, a grandfather's clock and oil lamps reinforced the idea that the student was in the 1850s. The student could go to the archive room at any time and look up over one hundred documents, maps, charts, a who's who, and statistical data from the period. There is an actual memorandum from a police chief for example dated 1850, that comments on the rise of juvenile delinquency. There is a letter from a wife left behind in Ireland pleading for her husband to send for her. All of the material in the Archive Room comes from historically accurate sources from the period. As exciting as video and audio material are, the Archive Room provided alternative material that was meant to be read and analyzed.

Draft of an Article

Writing the article forces the student to become more fully involved in the multimedia program. Students, as they put their thoughts to "paper" organize and come to learn about their own attitudes. The word processing program used for keeping notes, as mentioned earlier, was also there for the students to draft their article.

Relating the Material to the Present

After completing and submitting an article, the student is brought back to the present and is asked to respond to questions regarding current events such as the Detroit riots of 1967 and the Los Angeles riots of 1992.

Once we had the beta version of the multimedia program completed, we had students in Hunter College's education foundations courses view and recommend changes. Bret Eynon arranged for a more formal evaluation of *The Five Points* in a field-test at LaGuardia Community College. We adjusted and fine-tuned the program accordingly. IBM was pleased with the outcome and arranged for us to give presentations to colleges and universities all over the country. It was at one of these presentations at Syracuse University that I met Karen Swan from SUNY Albany who was also developing multimedia using IBM's M-Motion Board software. Our discussion on instructional technology has evolved into a thirty-year collegial relationship that continues to this day. Perhaps the most interesting of my presentations was at Harvard University to a full house in the Kennedy School of Government's atrium. *The Five Points...* was also selected to be part of several national exhibits including "New Learning Technologies" held in San Diego, California in June 1992. I published an article providing a rich description of the development and evaluation of the program that appeared in the *Journal of Education Multimedia and Hypermedia.*

Steve, Josh, Bret and I received another grant to do a second multimedia program: *Heaven Will Protect the Working Girl.* Using *The Five Points..* as a model, this program allowed students to examine conditions in the sweatshops of Lower Manhattan where Jewish and Italian seamstresses worked in the early 1900s. I did one additional multimedia program, this time with the cooperation of Blackside Incorporated, using material from its award-winning documentary series, *Eyes on the Prize.* The subject of this program was the integration of Little Rock's Central High School in 1957. As a result of all of this multimedia development, I was approached by several companies if I might be interested in doing work for them. I passed on these offers.

IBM was in serious financial difficulty and unfortunately in 1993, began to lay-off hundreds of thousands of employees. The ACIS Group was pretty much eliminated and gone by 1995. Support for the PS/2-70 with the M-Motion Board ended. While I was fortunate to have learned a great deal about multimedia and simulation software development, neither the hardware nor the software platforms for *The Five Points..* has survived. Regardless, this was a tremendous learning experience that provided insights about using multimedia technology in teaching and learning.

In December 1990, I also embarked on a small research project relating to what I was observing in the New York City public schools, namely that access to technology was limited or non-existent. This was quite different from the schools in my home county of Westchester County where one district after another had started new technology initiatives. With the help of a couple of my graduate students, I conducted a study, the purpose of which was to provide a descriptive analysis of the use of computers for instruction in the public schools of a large, urban area, namely New York City, and to compare same with the public schools of a suburban area, namely Westchester County. I placed particular emphasis on the availability of hardware, the nature of the software used for instruction, and the perceived progress or problems encountered in integrating computers into the curriculum. A key finding was the disparity in the student per microcomputer ratio in the urban versus suburban areas. A table in the report clearly illustrated that while all schools had started acquiring equipment, and at a similar rate in many cases, the fact that the New York City schools had much larger enrollments reduced significantly the access urban students had to the technology. The student per microcomputer ratio between urban and suburban schools was more than double (22.57 to 10.90). Other issues related to software and support were also very evident. While a small study, it illustrated the "digital divide" that existed in public schools. I published an article based on this study in *The Urban Review* in 1991.

References

Picciano, A.G. (1991). Computers, city and suburb: A Study of New York City and Westchester County Public Schools," *The Urban Review, 23*(3), pp. 191-206.

Picciano, A.G. (1993). The Five Points: The design of a multimedia program on social history. *Journal of Educational Multimedia and Hypermedia, 2* (2), pp. 129147.

45

1991 would prove to be an incredibly newsworthy year. The Soviet Union dissolved. Nelson Mandela was freed after serving twenty-seven years in prison in South Africa. Saddam Hussein would direct the Iraqi Army to invade Kuwait thereby setting the stage for the Persian Gulf War. In October, Arkansas Governor Bill Clinton announced that he would be running for President of the United States. He would go on to defeat the incumbent, George H.W. Bush. Clinton's election ended twelve years of Republican control of the White House. He would go on to win re-election in 1996 and end his tenure embroiled in the Monika Lewinsky scandal, during which he was impeached.

With the development of *The Five Points...*, Mike Ribaudo and Colette Wagner, the Assistant Dean for Computer Information Systems at CUNY, approached me about sharing my work with other faculty in CUNY. I was amenable and as a result, Mike and Colette took on half of my Hunter College teaching load and named me a Faculty Fellow at the newly established CUNY Open Systems Laboratory. This Laboratory was charged with providing technology assistance to CUNY, public agencies and businesses in the greater New York City Metropolitan area. Starting in 1994 and for the next eight years, I developed and conducted a number of professional development workshops for the Laboratory on a range of topics related to technology including multimedia, presentation software, using the Statistical Package for the Social Sciences, the Internet, and online and blended learning. This arrangement was quite generous and allowed me a good deal of free time to tinker with newer technologies. I was given an office at the University Computer Center complete with just about any hardware and software I wanted. I also had complete access to the new Laboratory that housed fifteen microcomputer workstations, a presentation system, and an interactive video conferencing facility. Within a month, I developed and started giving presentations on a regular basis. Colette did an excellent job of promoting my work via newsletters and personal contacts so that I always had excellent attendances. I modified some of these workshops into 90-minute presentations that I gave at the colleges and in the field to government and corporate audiences. Colette estimated that in one year, attendance in the workshops and presentations approached approximately one thousand faculty and other professionals. Mike and Colette also expanded the Faculty Fellows program. I was joined by other CUNY faculty including Michael Fitzgerald from Medgar Evers College and Bruce Naples from Queensborough Community College, both of whom became good colleagues of mine. On a number of occasions, we did joint presentations for faculty and other professional organizations.

With half of my workload now devoted to working in the Open Systems Laboratory, I gave ap some of my teaching at Hunter. After discussions with Mae Gamble, it was decided that I would teach only in the ADSUP program, since the Programs in Education had recently hired several new faculty who could teach the courses (instructional technology, social foundations) that I had been teaching in QUEST. In addition, the nature of QUEST changed dramatically in 1994 when CUNY faced severe financial issues. Teaching in the field entitled each faculty member to one extra workload unit per course. As a cost savings, this extra unit was eliminated and most of the faculty were no longer willing to teach their courses in the field. Enrollment in the New York City public schools was increasing significantly and our partner public schools could no longer devote classroom space to QUEST. As a result, almost all of the teaching that had been done in the field was now returned to the College. I would always be appreciative of the teaching I did in QUEST. It gave me insight into the issues that existed and continue to exist in public schools in impoverished areas of New York.

In addition to my University work in technology, I also developed an interest in historical research at the Rockefeller Archive Center in Tarrytown, New York, not far from where I lived. A friend of mine, Erwin Levold, was the associate archivist at the Center and he mentioned that the Rockefeller family had recently released a trove of material on progressive education in the early 20th century specifically related to Abraham Flexner and The Lincoln School. I was aware of The Lincoln School, progressive education, and John Dewey but knew nothing about Flexner. I had never done any archival research and decided to give it a try. For about a year, I spent a few hours each week at the Center and came to appreciate the tedious work required in doing archival research. Pouring over documents, memoranda, and news articles, I tried to piece together a story line. Flexner without a doubt was a most interesting individual. He did major work in reforming education in this country especially medical education in the early part of the 20th century. He also founded the Institute for Advanced Study in Princeton, New Jersey, and was its first director in the early 1930s. During his tenure there, he succeeded in bringing to the United States a number of European scientists including Albert Einstein who would likely have suffered persecution by the Nazi regime in Germany. I was most interested, however, in Flexner's work with the Rockefeller General Education Board and the creation of The Lincoln School which opened in 1917 and continued until 1940. The Lincoln School, affiliated with Columbia Teachers College, had a progressive curriculum focusing on modern subject matter that was more practical than the classical high school curriculum of the period. Major figures in education such as Charles Eliot, Otis Caldwell and Harold Rugg contributed to the development of its program. I came to understand that archival research is a major time-drain and while incredibly interesting, particularly when you come across a significant document after days of searching, I wasn't sure that I was willing to devote the effort necessary to do this work well. I did manage to publish one short article on The Lincoln School based upon my work at the Archive Center and would always be grateful to Erwin for giving me the opportunity to experience this type of research.

In 1994, I had my first book published entitled, *Computers in the Schools: A Guide to Planning and Administration* (Macmillan/Merrill Publishing). According to my editor, Linda Sullivan, it was one of the best sellers on the topic of planning and administering technology in K-12 education. This book would go on to have four new editions. I also published an article entitled, *Technology and the evolving educational-industrial complex* (Picciano, 1994) that looked at the influence technology companies were having on education policy. At the time I was sure I was the first to acknowledge the "educational-industrial" relationship between "Big Tech" and education policy, although a few months after I published this piece, Albert Shanker, the President of the AFT, had a column basically making the same connection.

Since the 1980s, I had continued to do site visits for the Middle States Association of Colleges and Universities. I generally did one or two a year. In December 1994, and upon its 75th Anniversary, I was one of seventy-five individuals honored for our service to the Association. I would continue to do site visits well into the 2000s.

In 1995, I was asked to be one of the project coordinators at Hunter College for a grant entitled, *New York City Collaborative for Excellence in Teacher Preparation*, a $5 million NSF funded project designed to improve the teaching of science, mathematics, and technology. Five CUNY colleges and New York University participated in this Collaborative. I worked with a number of colleagues in science and mathematics to determine how we would better prepare K-12 teachers for what today we would refer to as STEM subjects. The six colleges developed a plan to identify specific courses and develop models for improving their teaching. At Hunter College, we identified several courses and I teamed with Rod Varley, a professor in Physics to reconceptualize the teaching of basic astronomy. We chose this course because in reviewing the transcripts of students who majored in education, Astronomy 100 was the course most frequently taken to meet the general science requirement. Rod and I reviewed the syllabus and I also attended a number of classes, all of which were delivered in large, lecture hall settings. There was a laboratory activity each week that focused on problem solving and mathematics. I thought the lectures were quite boring and used very little in the way of media or images to convey the subject matter. Rod and I agreed that we could improve significantly on the delivery of this course by integrating media that would illustrate the wonders of the universe. Rod shared the subject matter for each week's lesson and I developed a number of Astound (a precursor to PowerPoint) presentations and simulations that were rich in video and images to accompany the lectures. I learned a great deal about astronomy and enjoyed every minute of it. Rod and I developed a total of twelve new media-rich lessons. Rod also developed new exercises for the lab component of the course that included visits to the Hayden Planetarium across Central Park from Hunter College. About one year into the project, we demonstrated our new Astronomy 100 course and our colleagues in the Collaborative were quite impressed. NSF, around that time scheduled an external progress review of the Collaborative's work during which we demonstrated our projects to an evaluation team. The lead evaluator for our Astronomy 100 course was a physicist from California and, to say the least he wasn't impressed. He indicated that students should be doing more field work and going up on the roof of Hunter College and looking at the stars and planets. We explained that Hunter College didn't have a telescope or an observatory and even if it did, the ambient light and the cold winter nights in the middle of Manhattan would make star gazing very difficult. The evaluator didn't want to hear about these difficulties. Rod and I were dismayed. Rod, however, thought we had done incredible work and asked if I would be interested in conducting the lectures for the Astronomy 100 course. I declined not because I wasn't interested, but because I was becoming increasingly involved with one of the most significant technological developments of the 20th century – the Internet.

References

Picciano, A.G. (1994). The Lincoln School and the General Education Board, *Rockefeller Archive Center Newsletter*, Fall 1994, pp. 35.

Picciano, A.G. (1994). *Computers in the schools: A guide to planning and administration*. New York: Macmillan/Merrill Publishing.

Picciano, A.G. (1994). Technology and the evolving educational-industrial complex, *Computers in the Schools, 11*(2), pp. 85101.

PART VII

Hunter College
New York, New York
1997-2007

46

started experimenting with the Internet in the early 1990s, however, I continued to use BITNET for email and file-transfers. With the development of the World Wide Web by Tim Berners-Lee and its subsequent availability to the general public, all of us BITNET users started to migrate our activity to the Internet. The Corporation for Research and Educational Networking (the governing body of BITNET) formally ended support for the network in 1996, although some BITNET users were still accessing its facilities as late as 2007 when it ceased all operations. I started using the Internet essentially for email and file transfers, but I also learned Hypertext Markup Language (HTML) in order to develop simple webpages. There were several individuals at the CUNY Central Computer Center who had become proficient in programming in HTML and I could go to them for questions and help if needed. As I became more comfortable with HTML, I started putting course reference materials on the Web, but I was intrigued by the idea that I could actually teach part or all of a course on the Internet.

By early 1996, I was developing tutorial material for the ADSUP research methods course I was teaching. At first, the material I developed was text-based, but then I moved to including images and even dabbled with brief videos. The text and images loaded quickly enough but the video took forever on slow-speed and dial-up modems. In any case, everything I was doing was passive with little interaction other than inviting students to email me if they had questions. I was surprised by the number of students in these courses, almost all of whom were teachers in K-12 schools, who were connecting to the Internet. I embarked on an ambitious project to develop thirteen modules on descriptive statistics using text and images. In addition to making these available on the web, I also used them to teach concepts in my face-to-face classes. During this time, I was still trying to figure out the best way to actual teach on the web.

It seems that there were several of us at CUNY experimenting with online learning. Tom Suprenant was teaching library science at Queens College, Joe Rachlin in biology at Lehman College, and Mike Fitzgerald in philosophy at Medgar Evers College. Through discussions with colleagues, I did learn that software such as *FirstClass*, an early course management system was available, but it was quite expensive. I had started to use LISTSERV (a group email system) in my regular face-to-face classes to send out messages or provide handout attachments to my students. Most of them had access to an Internet connection either in their schools or on dial-up modems at home. In fall 1996, I asked a group of my ADSUP students if they wanted to participate in an experiment in which I would teach part of our course online using webpages and LISTSERV software. While skeptical, they agreed to try it. For two weeks in October, I conducted my ADSUP research methods course online using an asynchronous model that started on Sunday and continued through the week to Saturday. While the LISTSERV was a bit clunky, it worked, and we were able to interact with one another. At first, all of the interactions were between me and the students, but that was corrected by requiring students to respond to each other. When I later met face-to-face again with my students, we spent the better part of the class discussing this new way of teaching and learning. I was buoyed by their enthusiasm and interest in doing more.

It was at this time that I happened to bump into Mike Kress in the hallway at the University Computer Center. He was a colleague who was a faculty member in the Computer Science Department at the College of Staten Island. I hadn't seen him for several years and we shared what we were doing. I told him that I just started experimenting with teaching online using the web. I also mentioned that the students were finding the LISTSERV software a little difficult for keeping track of interactions. He thought that I might be able to get a beta version of LISTSERV that in addition to generating group emails, had an option to create a webpage with threaded messages so that students could respond on the list rather than via email. I thought this would work wonderfully and thanked him for the tip. I sought out Victor Viggiano, the

Director of the University Computer Center, and asked if he could have one of his staff install the beta LISTSERV version for me to use. Victor always responsive to any request I made and that afternoon he emailed me to tell me it would be installed the following week. I discussed what I was doing with Mike Ribaudo who also mentioned that if I wanted to continue teaching online, I might look into the Alfred P. Sloan Foundation's grant program for funding online learning projects in colleges and universities. I went to the Sloan Foundation website and sure enough, a grant program entitled, *Anytime, Anyplace Learning,* had been established. It included the email address of A. Frank Mayadas, who was the program officer for this grant.

47

I emailed Dr. Mayadas and he responded the same day that he would be happy to meet with me to discuss the possibility for an *Anytime, Anyplace Learning* grant. The Sloan Foundation's Office was located at Rockefeller Center on Fifth Avenue in Manhattan and it was easy for me to accommodate his schedule. Dr. Mayadas' webpage at the Sloan Foundation website indicated that he had spent his entire career at IBM, working with Ralph Gomory who was now the President of the Sloan Foundation. In 1992, it was Dr. Gomory's who initiated the *Learning Outside the Classroom Program*, later renamed the *Anytime, Anyplace Learning Program*. Dr. Mayadas and I met the first week of December 1996.

Dr. Mayadas asked me about CUNY and specifically whether it had established any distance learning programs. I told him that as far as I knew there were a couple of half-hearted attempts including Sunrise Semester, but that CUNY really had very little activity in this area. I described our programs in education at Hunter and gave him a long upbeat spiel about our history, reputation, and the diversity of its students and programs. He asked why Hunter would need to do online education. I told him quite frankly that we didn't need to do online education, but that I saw it as an interesting use of Internet technology that could provide convenient learning experiences for students. I told him that all of my students worked full-time in New York City K-12 schools, had families, and were trying to advance their careers through higher education. For them, the distance wasn't measured in miles, but in time. They led incredibly busy days coordinating family, travel, work and education. It was my sense that if we could reduce the need to travel to Hunter College, even one night a week, it would help them. Mayadas suggested that I write an exploratory grant proposal. I could ask for approximately $10,000. to convert an existing course to substantially online delivery; and up to $30,000. to convert a total of three courses. He also asked that

I get the proposal to him before December 31ˢᵗ. Before I left, he told me that his wife taught at the Hunter College Campus Schools, and that he had asked her to check my reputation for him in advance of our meeting. He also told me to call him Frank.

I emailed the grant application on Friday, December 27ᵗʰ, 1996. It asked for $30,000. to convert three courses in the ADSUP program to online delivery. In addition to the support of Dean Mike Ribaudo and Assistant Dean Colette Wagner, I also had the support of David Caputo, the President of Hunter College. My plan was to convert one course in each of the three coming semesters (Spring 1997, Fall 1997, and Spring 1998). My first attempt for spring 1997, would be a course for which I had already done some Website development. I received a positive reply on January 8ᵗʰ, 1997. The major focus of my grant application was to use asynchronous learning to meet the needs of busy urban professionals whose "distance" wasn't geography but time. Frank said that this was a new rationale that he hadn't seen previously in other grant applicants.

Eventually, the use of online learning to conquer time constraints would come to be well-accepted, but at the time it represented a new idea.

The first course I converted was *Administration and Supervision of the Public Schools - The Principalship*, a required course in the ADSUP Program. I used an asynchronous learning model based on the websites I had developed in HTML and LISTSERV software for student interaction. Another section of the same course was offered in traditional face-to-face mode. The seventeen enrollees in the online version of the course could be characterized as typical part-time students and full-time working professionals. First, all of them were adults who delicately balanced studies, careers, and families in their daily lives. In this respect, they represented an urban student population that would benefit from the convenience of asynchronous learning. Second, all of the students commuted to Hunter College and participated in the course via equipment located in their homes and offices. As a result, the model had to accept a wide variety of on-line services as the means of participation. Third, these students didn't possess extensive technical skills and could be classified as new to intermediate in terms of expertise. This required that the model employ simple software interfaces that would minimize student frustration due to technical difficulties. Lastly, all of these students already had earned master's degrees and were teachers in the New York City metropolitan area. They had a good command of reading and writing and as experienced teachers, they were attuned to pedagogy and could provide valuable insights into the instructional components of the model.

At the end of the course, I conducted an evaluation and wrote a paper based on the student perceptions of the quality of the online components of the course. With regard to participation and student satisfaction, quantitative and qualitative data were collected. A full description of the techniques used in this course as well as the results of the evaluation were published in an article in 1998 entitled, *Developing an Asynchronous Course Model at a Large, Urban University.* The entire article is available in Appendix A. This was the first of what would be my many publications on online learning. It would also serve as required reading for faculty professional seminars that I would be giving at the CUNY Open Systems Laboratory. Here is a sample of the student feedback regarding the convenience of taking an online course:

Convenience of Taking an Asynchronous Course

"As graduate students, most of us work. It is hard to travel from point A to point

B...Asynchronous classes are a solution to our high-paced, hectic lives."----Rick

"It is a more flexible form of class and allows one to participate around one's personal life."----Devorah

"The fact that I can log on at my convenience and as often as I want...I can work at my own pace."----Mirza

"[While] it reduces travel time, saves money, and people can work in the privacy of their homes, as a full-time working mother and student, it has been difficult to find the time every night to participate. In [a traditional] class, there are not disturbances from members of the family."---Teresa

(Picciano, 1998)

I was buoyed by the student responses to this course and I was convinced that online learning could be a major benefit for my students. I continued to refine the model for the next year as I converted two more courses.

In January 1997, I received an invitation from Skip Ward, the Director of the American Studies Center in Salzburg, Austria, to be a guest faculty member at a ten-day seminar entitled, *Distance Education: A Cutting-Edge Classroom Resource.* The seminar was attended by English as a Foreign Language (EFL) educators from countries in Europe, Asia and Africa. Two other faculty joined me, one from the United States and one from the United Kingdom. I was the "technology" expert while my two colleagues were specialists in the pedagogy of teaching English as a second language. The twenty-two seminar participants were selected by ministries of education in their respective countries. I found all of them incredibly eager to learn about instructional technology and especially online learning. This was a once in a lifetime experience as I shared meals, camaraderie, and knowledge with an international group of educators in the beautiful Schloss Leopoldskron overlooking lakes and the Alps. The Schloss had been commissioned by the Archbishop of Salzburg in 1746. The grounds in and around the Schloss had served as the backdrop for a number of scenes in Robert Wise's 1964 film, *The Sound of Music,* starring Julie Andrews. During the weekend included in our stay, we were treated to bus tours of the surrounding Alpine towns and villages, many of which still had snow on the hills and valleys.

At the end of each day's work, we would go to the Bierstube in the basement where there was an upright piano and a refrigerator that was well-stocked each day with Austrian beer. Hauk, an educator from Iceland, would play the piano to entertain us. He was joined by a colleague from Moldova who played guitar. The music ranged from the folk songs of the different countries to Broadway musicals, and soft rock. We sang and dance until midnight every evening. On the last night of our seminar, we sang John Lennon's *Imagine* four times before retiring at around 3:00 am.

48

Spring 1997 and fall 1998 were incredibly busy semesters. I was working on converting my courses to online learning as well as conducting presentations as a Faculty Fellow in the CUNY Open Systems Laboratory. At the time, faculty, instructional designers and administrators were eager to know more about online learning and I was averaging one presentation a week, all of which were well-attended. A major focus of these presentations was a running commentary of my experiences in teaching online. I also continued evaluating my online courses and was able to provide data on student outcomes and perceptions. All of this was going along well, when in June 1997, the Professional Staff Congress (CUNY faculty union) declared a moratorium on all "distance learning" activities at CUNY. What this came down to this was a moratorium on the work of three or four CUNY faculty, including me. I met with the PSC President Irwin Polishook and other officers in the union to discuss the issues. Polishook said that the PSC had declared the moratorium because there were no provisions in the collective bargaining agreement regarding distance learning. I sensed that he was flexible and didn't really have a problem with a small group of faculty continuing to experiment with online learning. Mike Ribaudo told me he had a discussion with the Acting Chancellor Christoph Kimmich who was also supportive of our work in online learning. As an aside, Chancellor Kimmich went out of his way to become familiar with everything we were doing with online learning and saw it as important for CUNY and its students. The upshot was that in fall 1997, a committee would be established to develop recommendations on how to proceed with distance learning. In the interim, a limited amount of experimental online learning could continue.

This online learning committee was comprised of five PSC representatives and five CUNY appointees. I was elected its chair. We met monthly from fall 1997 through spring 1999. In retrospect, the PSC was right in calling for this moratorium because CUNY had no policies of any type regarding distance learning. Issues about intellectual property, compensation, and workload were left to individual colleges to negotiate on ad hoc basis with the few faculty doing any type of online instruction. As part of my work on this Committee, I volunteered to meet with faculty and administrators throughout CUNY to discuss the issues that were emerging regarding online learning activities. Over the course of almost two years, the Committee collected data from the colleges regarding present and future plans for online learning. The Committee also reviewed my student evaluation data which now was in the form of the article mentioned in the previous chapter. In fall 1998, the Committee drafted a two-page memorandum (see below) of understanding that would serve as the guidelines for developing online learning in CUNY. This memorandum was adopted in March 1999 as official policy for two years and was later extended for one more year.

MEMORANDUM

March 22, 1999

TO: The Presidents of the Colleges
               The Dean of The CUNY Law School
               The Dean of The Sophie Davis School of
               Biomedical Education
FROM: Interim Chancellor Christoph M. Kimmich
SUBJECT: Distance Learning

On Thursday, 18 March 1999, the Delegate Assembly of the PSC voted to modify the union's moratorium on distance learning and to open a two-year window of experimentation under guidelines that address concerns expressed by members of the instructional staff. I commend the Delegate Assembly's action and applaud Dr. Polishook's leadership in this matter.

Modification of the union's moratorium on distance learning activities was one of the first recommendations that Dr. Polishook and I received from the Educational Technology Committee established under the 1996-2000 PSC/CUNY collective bargaining agreement. The members of the committee are: Dr. David

Arnow, Professor in the Department of Computer and Information Science at Brooklyn College, Dr. Jane Davenport, Assistant Professor in the Library Department at John Jay College, Mr. Peter Hoberman, PSC Vice President of Cross Campus Units, Dr. Russell Hotzler, University Dean for Academic Planning and Programs, Raymond F. O'Brien, Esq., Director of Instructional Staff Labor Relations, Dr. Anthony Picciano, Professor in the Department of Curriculum and Teaching at Hunter College, Dr. Michael Ribaudo, University Dean for Instructional Technology and Industry & Government Partnerships, Mr. Sam Santiago, PSC CLT Chapter Vice President, Mr. Ronald Spalter, Vice President and Dean for Administration and Planning at Borough of Manhattan Community College and Dr. Rosanne Wille, Provost at Lehman College. Dr. Picciano serves as Chair of the Committee.

During the two-year period of experimentation, the Committee will collect and analyze data from the colleges to inform the recommendations it will make to the Professional Staff Congress and the University in accordance with its mandate under the collective bargaining agreement. I ask that you give full cooperation to the Committee and respond to its data requests on your distance learning experiments. The experiments are to be conducted in accordance with guidelines the Committee recommended in two letters sent to Dr. Polishook and me; they are also reflected in the resolution adopted by the PSC's Delegate Assembly last week. Copies of the three documents are attached. If you have any questions, please call Mr. Raymond F. O'Brien in the Office of Faculty and Staff Relations at (212) 794-5386.

The PSC's decision to lift its moratorium on distance learning to permit a period of experimentation should eliminate any hesitation among members of the faculty wishing to participate in such activities. The University now has an opportunity to experiment with new distance learning modalities and to explore appropriate terms and conditions of employment that would apply to such modalities. I encourage you to seize the opportunity.

Resolution on Waiving PSC Moratorium on Distance Learning

Passed by the PSC Executive Council: February 4, 1999
Passed by the PSC Delegate Assembly: March 18, 1999

WHEREAS, the PSC Delegate Assembly on June 3, 1997, voted for a moratorium on distance learning projects at CUNY, and

WHEREAS, the PSC and CUNY established an Educational Technology labor-management committee in the new 1996-2000 collective bargaining agreement, and

WHEREAS, this committee comprised of an equal number of PSC members and CUNY managers, held its first meeting on December 4, 1998, and

WHEREAS, the chair of this joint labor-management Educational Technology Committee, Professor Anthony G. Picciano of Hunter College, has written to Chancellor Kimmich and President Polishook, indicating a consensus of the committee to gather data on distance learning at CUNY over a two-year period in order to develop future voting recommendations to the PSC and to CUNY, and

WHEREAS, in this letter the Chancellor is asked to encourage distance learning experiments, without constituting binding precedents for employment related policies, and

WHEREAS, this letter requests President Polishook to recommend a resolution to the Delegate Assembly to modify its moratorium on distance learning, therefore be it

RESOLVED, for a period of two years (January 1, 1999 through December 31, 2000) the Delegate Assembly waives its June 3, 1997 resolution on distance learning so that the joint PSC/CUNY labor-management committee can gather data for future policy recommendations to the PSC and to the University, and

BE IT FURTHER RESOLVED, that nothing in this process shall be construed as altering in any way existing campus-based policies on governance and curriculum or the PSC Collective Bargaining Agreement, and

BE IT FURTHER RESOLVED, that the following stipulations shall direct PSC policy during the two-year period in which the waiver of the Delegate Assembly moratorium is in place:

1. Faculty shall participate in distance learning projects only on a voluntary basis.

2. Reassigned time, compensation, enrollment limits, and workload issues, shall be determined at the local level, with the agreement of the Instructor, subject to the provisions and authority of the PSC/CUNY contract.

3. The copyright on materials generated by faculty shall remain with the faculty member(s) unless those materials are specifically contracted for at the inception of the project.

4. In implementing distance learning projects, the usual school-based policies on governance and curriculum will be followed.

5. The PSC encourages campus governance bodies to participate in assessing distance learning projects on their campuses.

6. The PSC urges faculty to ensure that their participation and decisions relating to the use of educational technology at CUNY be implemented in concert with academic departments and faculty governing bodies.

7. The PSC representatives to the joint labor-management committee on Educational Technology shall report to the PSC Delegate Assembly on the implementation of distance learning projects, no later than the December 1999 meeting of the Delegate Assembly.

8. The PSC shall inform college presidents and faculty governance leaders that the period ending December 31, 2000, is a time for experimental projects, data gathering, and assessment. The PSC shall state that colleges must recognize that experimental distance learning programs should not become permanent until the end of the experimental period and the joint committee has issued its final report and the PSC and University have agreed upon its guidelines.

By 2000, a new CUNY chancellor, Matt Goldstein, was appointed and a new president of the PSC, Barbara Bowen, was elected. The Memorandum of Agreement was allowed to lapse but online learning in CUNY had begun to take root. In the years following, there would be additional CUNY committees and other discussions about policies regarding online learning particularly involving intellectual property. The guidelines developed earlier, especially Item No. 3 on intellectual property and copyright continued to be referenced in many of these discussions. Eventually, CUNY and the PSC reached agreement on a number of distance learning issues and faculty were free to develop online courses with the approval of college presidents or their designees.

In 1999, with the encouragement of Frank Mayadas, CUNY applied for and started to receive major grants from the Sloan Foundation to grow its online learning efforts. Colette Wagner and George Otte were the principal PIs of these grants. I was involved in writing the grants and served as the go-between with the Foundation. Our colleagues at the SUNY Learning Network (SLN) especially Eric Fredericksen and Chris Haile, were incredibly generous with their assistance and advice. These grants totaled several million dollars over their lifetime and enabled CUNY to purchase a site license for Blackboard (Course Management System), establish CUNY Online (a major faculty professional development program), and sow the seeds for designing fully online programs at the CUNY School of Professional Studies.

49

I n 1998, Frank Mayadas invited me to attend a meeting of Sloan Foundation *Anytime, Anyplace Learning* grant recipients that was being held in Lower Manhattan. There were about ninety attendees. This meeting brought together a group of individuals, all of whom were "pioneers" in developing and supporting online learning activities including Gary Miller (Penn State World Campus), John Bourne (Vanderbilt University), and Burks Oakley (University of Illinois – Urban-Champaign). There were presentations and small group meetings that focused on traditional distance education programs that already existed in institutions such as the Penn State World Campus and University of Maryland – University College. Several of us who attended this meeting continued to communicate and contact each other to discuss a variety of issues related to online learning.

In March 1999, Frank contacted me and asked what I thought about having a small workshop of about thirty people in the summer to have everyone participate and share their online learning experiences. I thought this was a grand idea. Burks Oakley organized the event to be held in August in Urbana-Champaign. Each attendee had to deliver a paper or formally respond to someone else's paper. This was an incredible experience where in two and a half days participants learned what was going on around the country in online learning. It was at this workshop that I came to meet Chuck Dziuban, Joel Hartman and Steve Sorg from the University of Central Florida (UCF). In addition to using online learning to reach large commuter populations, UCF was embarking on significant online learning research. Chuck and I especially hit it off; and we would go on to co-author four books and give numerous presentations at professional conferences in the years to come. These summer workshops continued for several years and took place in Lake George, Boston, Victoria Island, and Baltimore. They were the thought incubators of the early years of online learning and were instrumental in knowledge-sharing and community building. The intimacy of these three-day workshops was incredibly beneficial to understanding and moving online learning activities forward. They were strikingly effective for sharing knowledge and experiences, for planning future directions, and for developing ideas for joint research projects. They also helped identify individuals with expertise who could assist other colleges and universities embarking on online learning programs.

At one of these summer meetings, Frank Mayadas, John Bourne, Burks Oakley, Gary Miller and I met and discussed the possibility of starting a consortium of colleges and universities dedicated to the practice and research of online learning. Frank was willing to have the Sloan Foundation fund it and John offered to be the lead administrator for the new organization. John was ideally suited for this. He had a small group of part-time people working with him on several Sloan Foundation projects including publishing the *Journal of Asynchronous Learning Networks* (JALN) which later would be renamed the *Online Learning Journal.* JALN was the first free refereed journal devoted entirely to online learning. It was at this meeting that the Alfred P. Sloan Consortium of Colleges and Universities was conceived. It continues today as the Online Learning Consortium or OLC.

The Sloan Consortium became the largest recipient of funding from the *Anytime, Anyplace Learning Program.* From the beginning, one major focus of the Consortium was to promote quality in the development and delivery of online learning, which in its early years was viewed skeptically by many segments of academia. As an example, the Consortium's *Five Pillars of Quality Online Learning* (see Appendix B) was the first framework for developing goals, objectives and metrics for evaluating online programs. This framework continues to be widely used and cited by a wide variety of practitioners and education policy makers.

In addition to issues of quality, the Consortium played a pivotal role in providing support for many of the activities related to community building.

The Sloan Consortium functioned well in this role because of the generous funding ($700,000 to $1 million per year) provided by the Foundation as well as the commitment of individuals who became national leaders in the field of ALN, many of whom have served on its Board of Directors.

At this same time, with funding from the Sloan Foundation, I published *Distance Learning: Making Connections Across Virtual Space and Time* (2001, Simon & Schuster/Prentice-Hall), one of the first books devoted entirely on online learning. In 2002, I published an article entitled, *Beyond student perceptions: Issues of interaction, presence, and performance in an online course* in the *Journal of Asynchronous Learning Networks (JALN)*, 6(1). It would go on to be the most read article ever published in JALN and has been cited in over 2,000 articles in peer-refereed professional journals. This article is available as a free download at: https://olj.onlinelearningconsortium.org/index. php/olj/article/view/1870/701

Several years later, in 2006, I published a well-received article entitled, *Blended learning: Implications for growth and access* in JALN, 10(3), which defined and predicted the importance of the blended learning model. I received inquiries and communications about this article from colleagues all over the globe. Chuck Dziuban and I in 2006 held meeting at an event sponsored by the Sloan Foundation and invited anyone in attendance interested in sharing research on blended learning to meet with us. About thirty individuals attended. It was a very informative and went on for almost three hours. Chuck and I decided to invite these individuals to share their work in a book on blended learning research. With Chuck and I as editors, the first edition of *Blended Learning: Research Perspectives* was published in 2007. Two more editions of this book would be published in the years to come. Charles Graham and Patsy Moskal joined us as editors of the subsequent editions.

50

I n November 2000, I received a call from Don Watkins, the former Dean of Administration at Medgar Evers College. We hadn't spoken with each other for several years and it was good to catch up. Don was involved with organizing an on-going Sino-American Conference and co-leading groups of educators from CUNY and other education institutions in New York to visit Shanxi Province in the People's Republic of China. He told me that the Conference meets for 2-3 weeks every other year going back and forth between New York and Shanxi. He was organizing the next meeting of the Conference to Shanxi in June 2001. His counterpart in Shanxi was interested in having discussions about education technology, so Don was reaching out to me to see if I would be interested in joining his group for an 18-day visit to Shanxi in June 2001. All expenses would be paid by CUNY. I thought it over for a couple of days, discussed it with my family, and let him know I would be happy to make the trip with him.

Between November 2000 and June 2001, the twenty-five members of the group met once a month to discuss the logistics, the overall schedule in Shanxi, and the topics for discussion. There were a number of my colleagues from around CUNY who would be joining this group including George Otte, Bret Eynon, Manfred Philipp, Mike Kress, Ron Spalter, and Y.C. Chen. George was originally from Baruch College and had succeeded Colette Wagner as the CUNY assistant dean for technology. Bret, with whom I worked on The *Five Points* multimedia project when he was with the American Social History Project, was a dean at LaGuardia Community College. Manfred was a chemist from Herbert Lehman College who was doing a lot of work integrating technology into teaching science. Mike was a computer scientist who I knew from my years at the College of Staten Island. Ron Spalter was CUNY's Deputy Chief Operating Officer, with whom I had worked since the late 1970s. Y.C. was a physicist at Hunter who worked with me in

1995 on the *New York City Collaborative for Excellence in Teacher Preparation*, the NSF funded project designed to improve the teaching of science, mathematics, and technology mentioned earlier. In finalizing the logistics, Y.C. and I decided to room together during parts of our stay in China. This turned out to be a great decision because besides being a pleasure to be with, Y.C. was from China and spoke the language fluently. He was also able to explain in some detail the places we saw, the people we met, and the discussions we had. Y.C. made my stay a cultural education.

I traveled with George Otte from New York to China. The eighteen-hour trip to Beijing included a layover in Detroit and we arrived in China on Friday afternoon on June 8th. Beijing International Airport was a sea of humanity with pushing and shoving being the rule. Fortunately, a guide from Shanxi who spoke English was there to meet us. She was able to help us get our luggage and a taxi to take us to the hotel where we would stay for two nights in Beijing before leaving on a six-hour van ride to Taiyuan, the capital of Shanxi. Y.C. had already arrived in Beijing and he and I met at the hotel.

I had one day in Beijing to do some sightseeing and confined myself to the Tiananmen Square area. The square is bounded by the Monument to the People's Heroes, the Great Hall of the People, the National Museum of China, and the Mausoleum of Mao Zedong. The Forbidden City is just across the street. Several of us decided to make quick visits to each rather than spend hours in any one of them. It was also my hope to spend more time in Beijing at the end of our visit to Shanxi. The large boulevard that passes right by the Square teemed with all means of transportation including cars, buses, bicycles, rickshaws, carts drawn by donkeys, mules, cattle and even a camel or two. Lane dividers were mere suggestions and the vehicles and animals formed one mass of motion moving in one direction or the other. The cross streets were particularly dangerous because everything and everybody including pedestrians inched to the center to get to the other side. In addition to the square, we also paid a visit to the main open market that went for as far the as the eye could see. Every type of produce, food, and small merchandize was available in this market which, by the way, was not there for the tourists but for the Chinese residents. The price of every item could be negotiated and the haggling was serious and at times loud. I was too intimidated to buy anything. George, Manfred, and I had dinner a in a Mongolian yurt that night and went back to our hotels early. The jet lag had sapped the energy out of me and most of my companions.

The next morning (Sunday, June 10th), we left Beijing in a small bus that held all 25 of us plus two interpreters and a member of the Communist Party who made sure we didn't have any problems with any local authorities throughout our stay in China. The six-hour trip started on a modern highway and ended on one-lane dirt roads. The Taiyuan University of Technology would be hosting us during our stay and a dormitory had been converted into our base of operations. We had communal meals and after dinner, at about 8:30 pm, we were free to do as we pleased. Several of us, including Y.C. Chen and myself would go out in the evening and walk in Taiyuan. We were warned to stay on the main streets and boulevards, which we did. Like Beijing, there was an extensive open-air market that sold almost anything. Y.C. explained everything we were seeing. Our sessions during the days included higher education administration, science, literature and humanities, English language teaching, and educational technology. George and I were the main presenters for the last of these. While our hosts were very interested in technology, it was obvious that they had done very little in this area particularly with regard to teaching and learning. The faculty were attentive but skeptical, a major issue being that their success as teachers depended upon their students passing standardized tests. As a result, much of their teaching was lecture style with an emphasis on memorization that prepped students to take the tests. In fact, every morning as early as 5:00 am, in the areas around our dormitory at Taiyuan University of Technology, it was common to see dozens and dozens of students with books open memorizing out loud their daily lessons. I attended several classes to see that the basic delivery style was lecture with minimal student interaction. We had excellent discussions about pedagogical practice with our Chinese colleagues, but I could tell it would be a leap for the faculty to engage their students with free-form discussions, Socratic methods, active learning, and instructional technology. My most memorable presentation was at one of the normal colleges where the president, Sidian Li, asked two of us to address his faculty and students on an evening after our regularly scheduled day's events. President Li had done his graduate work in London, was fluent in English, and acted as our interpreter. I was the second speaker and I was supposed to do a thirty-minute presentation that turned into almost ninety minutes because of all of the questions. President Li encouraged me to keep talking. The auditorium where I was speaking was packed and a second auditorium was receiving a video feed. Most of the students understood everything I was saying because China had adopted English as a required language in the primary and secondary schools about fifteen years earlier. All of the older faculty had to wait for President Li's translation. Whenever I made a humorous comment, the students would smile and laugh immediately while the faculty waited for Li's delayed translation then laughed after the students. The students were incredibly interested to know everything about American higher education. The majority of their questions related to the nature of American colleges and universities; how many students enrolled in higher education; what the popular majors were, etc. They had difficulty understanding that many of our colleges were open-admissions institutions, since in China, there was a rigorous national examination system that determined which students advanced to college. During our stay, it was mentioned several times that approximately 17 percent of the population went on to college, but that the government had recently initiated a ten-year plan to provide a higher education for 25 percent of the population. All in all, it was quite an evening. We had dinner with President Li that night. It can only be described as a feast. We got back to our rooms about midnight.

On the Friday, Saturday, and Sunday, of our visit, the entire American contingent was treated to a tour of Shanxi and points north and west. The highlight of the tour was Mount Wutai, a mountain range also known by its Chinese name Wutaishan. The north peak (Beitai Ding) is the highest point in northern China at 10,043 feet. Mount Wutai is one of the holiest places in Buddhism and home to more than fifty temples of various designs and significance. On this one weekend, we visited a number of sacred temples and monasteries including:

The Hanging Monastery or Xuankong Temple built into a cliff 246 ft above the ground.

The Sakyamuni Pagoda, also known as the Wooden Pagoda, was built in 1056 AD.

The Yungang Grottoes, also known as the Wuzhoushan Grottoes, ancient Chinese Buddhist temple grottoes near the city of Datong. There are hundreds of sandstone grottoes and niches each with carvings and paintings on the walls and ceilings.

The Great White Pagoda, also known as Tayuan Temple, an enormous white structure that can be seen for miles and built in 1302 AD.

When we returned to Taiyuan, we had another five days of meetings. After our suppers, Y.C., several other colleagues, and I would walk into the town and enjoy a drink at local establishments. Our hosts had set up a small make-shift bar in the main foyer of the dormitory and we would have a nightcap or two before going to our rooms. The discussions over drinks were incredible sessions, sharing what we had seen and learned that day. The bartender, who would come and ask what we wanted, was a young man who was always busily studying his books. One evening, Y.C. asked what he was studying. He told us that at the end of June he would be taking an exam for entry to the university. He said his sister was already a student here and he hoped to be admitted also. Y.C,. then asked him what he would do if he didn't pass the exam. He answered that he would probably become a coal miner like his father. High stakes testing indeed!

We returned to Beijing on Friday, June 15th. It was sad saying good-bye to our Shanxi hosts. Y.C., five colleagues, and I spent Saturday and Sunday in

Beijing where we toured a number of major attractions including The Great Wall, the Forbidden City, and the Summer Palace. On Monday, June 18th, Ron Spalter and I decided to take a side trip to Tokyo for two days before heading home to New York.

In return, CUNY hosted a delegation of colleagues from Shanxi Province for two weeks in 2005 and returned the hospitality we were shown during our visit. In 2006, I was invited to the last Sino-American Conference held in Taiyuan. It was every bit as interesting as the first visit but it was clear that China had modernized significantly. Beijing was a city being rebuilt for the Summer Olympic Games to be held in 2008. Only cars and buses were to be seen on the main thorough fares. Underpasses had been built for pedestrians to get across the large intersections. The large open-air markets were incredibly gone. The trip from Beijing to Taiyuan was entirely on a modern, four-lane highway. The Taiyuan University of Technology had doubled in student enrollment and rather than in a dorm, we stayed at a Communist Party recreation compound outside the city. We weren't allowed to leave the grounds after our day's activities. All of this changed in a short five years.

After our visit in Taiyuan, George, Manfred and I were invited to give a series of talks in Hong Kong. We visited three universities in three days. The differences between Hong Kong and Taiyuan were sharp. English was spoken every place in Hong Kong, and we didn't need an interpreter. There was also a very British feel at the universities. Our presentations were very well-received and many faculty related well since they were already using online technology for teaching and learning.

On September 11th, 2001, George Otte and I were scheduled to give a presentation at the CUNY Open Systems Laboratory. It was scheduled for 9:30 am. I had driven my car to the Westside of Manhattan and just as I was getting ready to park, I heard on the radio that a plane had crashed into the North Tower of the World Trade Center, about fifty city blocks from where I was. I assumed it was a small plane that was accidently involved in the crash and I hoped that no one was hurt. As I walked to the building on 11ᵗʰ Avenue housing the Open Systems Laboratory, I could see wisps of smoke coming out of the World Trade Center. When I got to the Lab, the entire staff of the CUNY Central Computer Center was in the Open System Lab looking at the television feed of what turned out to be the terrorist attack on the Tower. At 9:03, a second plane hit the South Tower and it collapsed at 9:59 am. When it did, we all went to the windows where we could see the huge billows of smoke and dust. At approximately 10:00 am, I received an email from Sidian Li in Taiyuan asking me if I was safe. It was the first of many I would receive that day from family, friends and colleagues around the country. The North Tower collapsed at 10:28 am. 2,192 civilians, 343 firefighters, and 71 law enforcement officers died as well as all the passengers and crew on the airplanes, including 147 civilians and the ten hijackers.

In March 2002, I visited and gave a presentation at Ludwig Maximilian University in Munich, Germany. I had been invited by Franz Gramlinger who was a professor at Johannes Kepler University in Graz, Austria. Franz had visited New York several times and was invited by Colette Wagner to attend sessions in our Open Systems Laboratory. He saw technology as the future for colleges and universities in Europe.

Having never been in Munich, I arrived two days early to do sightseeing. Munich is a very old German city and prides itself on the restoration it did after World War II. I went to several museums including The Deutsches Museum, the world's largest museum of science and technology with over 28,000 exhibits. Marienplatz or St. Mary's Square is the city center of Munich. The buildings are of the old Bavarian style with the famous Glockenspiel clock tower. People start lining up in the square about ten minutes before the hour to see the figures revolve and do their little dance. However, the most unforgettable part of my visit was my time at the Dachau Concentration Camp Memorial Site, about fifteen miles outside of Munich. I thought I would spend about an hour, but instead stayed almost three hours trying to take in the horrors that occurred there. Dachau was the first Nazi concentra-

tion camp and was built in 1933 shortly after Hitler came to power. It is difficult to comprehend the extent of man's inhumanity, but a visit here leaves an
impression that lasts a lifetime. Every means of torture and death including
a crematorium were used to imprison and kill people there during the Holo-
caust. At its height, more than 32,000 people were held here, most of whom
were doomed. The Jewish Memorial on the grounds is a cave-like structure
of basaltic stones that is completely dark except for a small opening in the
ceiling that allows a narrow ray of sunlight to stream through.

Following my presentation, Franz drove us almost the whole length of
the Autobahn to the University of Hamburg where he had a visiting professorship. I gave several informal talks to his colleagues and other faculty, all
of whom were most interested in what I had to say. In October 2003, I was
invited back to the University of Hamburg to be part of a panel at a Campus
Innovation Conference. I stayed with Franz and his wife, Sigrid, who couldn't
have been more hospitable.

In 2002, my ADSUP colleagues (Janet Patti, Marcia Knoll) and I were
the recipients of a $3.3 million grant from the U.S. Department of Education
to design and implement customized leadership programs in several of the
poorest community school districts in New York City. It was a collaborative
project with the New York City Department of Education, New Visions for
New Schools, and New Leaders for New Schools. The major focus was to
work with school leaders in poor areas such as East Harlem, the South Bronx,
Central Brooklyn and Jamaica, Queens, to identify exceptional teachers and
to train them to become assistant principals. Janet and I were co-principal
investigators but it was Janet who did most of the heavy lifting with the grant.
Once again, I was treated to one of those important learning experiences that
helped broaden my knowledge and understanding of the myriad needs of
the public schools of New York City. The grant also elevated the reputation
of the ADSUP program throughout the City.

51

A s the world proceeded into the new millennium, my online teaching was progressing as well, but I had decided to make a change in my ADSUP research methods course. While there was no problem teaching much of this course online, the "hands-on" statistics module was problematic and both my students and I struggled with it. I decided to move this module to one intensive face-to-face weekend meeting for six hours on a Saturday and Sunday. The course worked much better. In sharing my work with several colleagues in the ADSUP program, I discovered that they too preferred this mixed approach rather than teaching a course entirely online. Since Hunter was a commuter college in a city with an extensive public transportation system, it wasn't difficult to ask students to come to face-to-face classes several times during the semester.

In 2005, my colleagues in the ADSUP program at Hunter College and I requested and were approved to offer the first academic program in CUNY that would have online components integrated in every course. In fact, ADSUP was the first program in CUNY to have the formal designation of a "blended program" approved by the New York State Education Department.

In November 2002, a small group of colleagues and I who were attending the Sloan-C International Conference on Online Learning in Orlando, Florida, had a discussion about this new mixed teaching phenomenon. College faculty were blending and matching face-to-face and online learning techniques and materials in their courses. This group of colleagues represented institutions such as the University of Illinois, the University of Central Florida, University of Maryland University College, the University of Wisconsin–Milwaukee, and the City University of New York. As the discussion went on, a consensus emerged; we were witnessing a new approach to teaching and learning that was different from either of its basic components. Face-to-face instruction had been around for centuries and fully online instruction had blossomed in the 1990s with the development and ubiquity of the Internet. We observed that there appeared to be no single pattern or model for blending these approaches. Some faculty taught basically a face-to-face course with a small portion of online activities. Others taught essentially online courses with a face-to-face component. Further, developing online components, various technologies such as interactive and non-interactive media, asynchronous discussion boards and blogs, as well as synchronous conferencing were being utilized to meet specific pedagogical goals and objectives. There were also distinctions in the development and scheduling of face-to-face components, some meeting once a week, others every other week, and still others once a month. This discussion resulted in the idea that a group of knowledgeable individuals from around the country should be assembled to discuss "blended learning" and its implications for education. Funded by the Alfred P. Sloan Foundation, an invitation-only workshop was held in April 2003 and coordinated by Mary Niemiec at the University of Illinois-Chicago. About thirty individuals met for two days and while many ideas were floated and discussion at times was unwieldy, this group concluded that blended learning was important, needed further investigation, and would likely have significant pedagogical, administrative, and institutional ramifications. A community of professionals was born. This community, under the auspices of the Sloan Consortium, held annual workshops which in 2012 attracted 665 participants. It would evolve into the Sloan Consortium's INNOVATE Conference which attracts about 2,000 onsite and virtual attendees a year.

52

n November 2002, I received a phone call from George Otte asking me if I would come to a meeting with the new CUNY Vice Chancellor for Academic Affairs, Selma Botman. George indicated that the Vice Chancellor wanted to develop fully online programs at CUNY, and she wanted to discuss this with several of the faculty who had been doing online instruction. Since the late 1990s, more and more faculty had been teaching online, especially in blended formats, but there weren't any fully online academic programs. CUNY was prime to develop completely online programs especially given the breadth of its graduate programs in professional areas such as business, education, health science, and social work.

At the meeting. Vice Chancellor Botman made her case for developing online programs. In response several of us indicated that many of the faculty were actively engaged with online learning but a move to full programs would require an investment in advisement, library and other student services since there was no support infrastructure for fully online programs. In addition, the Professional Staff Congress (PSC) had issued statements that any development of online programs at CUNY couldn't compete with existing face-to-face programs. She indicated that she understood the issues and was ready to develop a new school of professional studies that, among other things, would be chartered to offer fully online academic programs. John Mogulescu, a colleague of many years and a major developer of non-traditional academic programs, would be leading the new school. It would be John's responsibility to develop an infrastructure and deal with the politics of the PSC. The Vice Chancellor needed a core group of faculty to develop online programs. Besides George, there were six faculty who were being asked to participate in the program development activity. The most startling aspect of the meeting was a request from the Vice Chancellor to have a fully online baccalaureate program available for enrollment by September 2003.

The six of us looked at each other silently and were wondering how we got ourselves involved with this.

I congratulated George for taking on the leadership of this effort, but there were a lot of concerns to be resolved. We subsequently had several meetings, some of which were held as early as 6:00 am in hopes of meeting the deadline. In need of additional expertise, we also quickly expanded our committee to twelve members and agreed on several major principles for the online BA program. First, it would have to be a generic major that might appeal to many students. Second, since CUNY as most open admissions public institutions, had thousands of students who had left college without earning degrees, earning a bachelor's degree was more important than study in a particular field. We would look to recruit many of these former students through a flexible policy in accepting their prior course work. Third, the requirement for a BA in New York State was a minimum of 120 credits. Half of these would meet the general education requirements. The remaining credits would be taken in a major, a minor, and electives. We would have to develop or identify courses to meet these requirements. Fourth, we would prevail upon other CUNY faculty who had already developed online courses in their home colleges to teach in our program or ask for permission to use their courses. This would be especially crucial for the general education requirements.

After approximately one month of meetings, our committee decided to develop a baccalaureate degree with a major in communication and culture. This was surely broad enough to appeal to large numbers of students and it wouldn't directly compete with any other CUNY face-to-face program, thus mitigating the issue raised by the PSC. The general education requirements remained a major hurdle for the committee. George and Rob Whitaker, an associate provost at Herbert Lehman College, did yeoman's work in identifying online courses that already existed at the CUNY colleges that could meet these requirements. I must say that Rob laid out a grid that was the clearest plan for general education that I had ever seen. Plugging in available online courses reduced our development work significantly. George was able to get the approval of most of the CUNY faculty who owned these courses to use them in the program. The rest of us took on assignments to develop courses that could be used in the major. I had no background in communication and culture, but it had been decided early on that research and data analysis would be a part of the major. I designed two online courses (Research Methods I and Research Methods II) patterned a bit after the course I taught in the ADSUP program at Hunter College. By July 2003, we had a plan for offering a fully online BA degree in communication and culture.

While our committee was busy doing the academic program development, Brian Petersen, who was a long-time associate of John Mogulescu, was hired as the Associate Dean for Administrative Services. He put together a first-rate group of administrators to handle student services, admissions, registration, financial aid, academic advisement and counseling. He arranged with Baruch College to use their fully online library system. As a result, we were ready to admit our first students in the School of Professional Studies (SPS) in September 2003. Many more online undergraduate, graduate and certificate programs would follow. At the time of this writing (2021), *U.S. News & World Report* ranked the CUNY SPS as the best online bachelor's degree program in New York State and also ranked it in the top two percent nationwide.

I taught in the new program for one year and served on several committees that developed policies regarding faculty compensation, course ownership, faculty course evaluation, and student progress to degree. I continued to serve on the SPS governing board until 2010.

In August 2005, I was saddened by the news that Mike Ribaudo had died suddenly of a heart attack. He was a fine colleague who had spent his life doing good things for CUNY. He was incredibly generous with me and provided opportunities that surely advanced my career. When I went to Mike's wake, I was a bit early and the only other person in the funeral home was Bill Kelly, who was the provost at the CUNY Graduate Center. I didn't know him, but we struck up a good conversation about Mike, and we were of a like mind regarding his contributions to our university.

Later in 2007, I was honored to be the co-recipient with the other faculty who developed the BA degree in communication and culture, of The Annual Mike Ribaudo Award for Excellence in Information Technology.

53

One of the significant research activities that the Sloan Consortium sponsored was the annual studies of the extent of online learning in American higher education. Elaine Allen and Jeff Seaman conducted these studies each year starting in 2003. They were based on surveys sent to a national sample of chief academic officers and continued until 2017. These studies were exceptionally well-done and were followed nationally by the higher education community. No other organization including the U.S. Department of Education was collecting these data. In 2004, I had an idea that it was time to do something similar for the K-12 community. There was a dearth of research of any sort on online learning in primary or secondary education. I approached Frank Mayadas about funding studies in K-12 similar to those conducted by Allen & Seaman, but he was reluctant to do so, since the Sloan Foundation as a matter of policy, didn't fund grants for the K-12 community. I had several long discussions with Jeff Seaman, and he was all for doing this research. We approached several other foundations without success, and I decided to go back to Frank. I used the argument that a lot of the colleges had begun offering online credit-bearing courses to high school students and that it would be beneficial to start studying this population. In 2005, Frank relented and agreed to fund Jeff Seaman and me to conduct several studies on the extent and nature of online learning in K-12 schools.

A few years later, in 2008, the Alfred P. Sloan Foundation would announce the end of all funding to the Consortium by 2013, which meant that if it was to continue to exist it had to generate enough revenue to pay its expenditures. The potential of the Sloan Consortium as an organization capable of generating its own funds through dues-paying membership and other revenue-generating activities was questionable. It is important to keep in mind that the beginnings of a community preceded the formal Consortium. Community-building activities such as the summer workshops and the annual meetings emerged in part from grants made to individuals and colleges such as the University of Illinois, State University of New York, and the University of Central Florida. Without a doubt, the Consortium provided important services to facilitate these activities, but much of the effort including planning were performed by individuals not directly connected to the Consortium. As an example, annual meetings that evolved into the Sloan Consortium Annual ALN Conference had a history of being organized, planned, and implemented by the University of Central Florida in concert with a voluntary planning committee of Sloan Foundation grantees. Patrick Wagner (UCF) was most instrumental in helping this conference grow into a major annual event. In 2001, the same year as 9/11 and the anthrax scare in Central Florida, the first broad-based Sloan ALN International Conference was held in Orlando attracting 366 attendees. It has been held every year since and now attracts thousands of on-site and virtual participants each year. Other individuals (Gary Miller, Meg Benke, Jacquie Moloney, Eric Fredericksen, Peter Shea, Karen Swan) involved with planning the conferences continued to serve and work for the Consortium without compensation in their roles as members of the Board of Directors. The Sloan Consortium formalized and incorporated as a private, non-profit organization in 2008. However, in order to survive, the Consortium would need to hire full-time staff and develop more revenue-generating activities such as webinars, consulting services and paid memberships. In 2014, the Sloan Consortium formally changed its name to the Online Learning Consortium (OLC). By 2021, OLC had 653 dues-paying member colleges and organizations and employed 23 full-time staff members, generating approximately $5 million in revenue each year.

PART VIII

CUNY Graduate Center
New York, New York
2007-2018

54

In June 2007, I received a telephone call from Bill Kelly, the President of the CUNY Graduate (GC), whom I had met at Mike Ribaudo's wake in 2005. He wanted to know if I might be interested in being the Interim Executive Officer for the PhD Program in Urban Education. The program's Executive Officer Phil Anderson was taking a one-semester sabbatical and several of the faculty at the GC had recommended me. This was a complete surprise and I told President Kelly that I needed to think about it for a couple of days.

The GC was founded in 1968 and at that time was designated as the doctoral-granting center for all of CUNY. It was developed on a consortial model to draw faculty from all the CUNY colleges. The GC would also have its own small full-time faculty who would be assigned to the various doctoral programs, of which there were thirty-two in 2007. The decision to house the doctoral programs at the Graduate Center was made because CUNY didn't have the resources to develop these programs at the colleges, and it made sense to pool resources and faculty talent into a central operation. It was also politically smart to provide doctoral program participation options to faculty in all the senior colleges. In the years following its creation, there was still some resistance and resentment among faculty at the older senior colleges over the status that the Graduate Center had been given. More information about CUNY's decision to create the Graduate Center can be found in Picciano and Jordan (2018.)

The PhD Program in Urban Education was designed in the late 1990s and although I was on the development committee, I didn't participate as much as I would have liked because of other commitments. Jay Lemke, a professor at Brooklyn College, did a good job of chairing the committee although I was disappointed that the "leadership" designation was eliminated in the proposed *Policy Studies and Leadership* strand. The program had three strands: Arts, Humanities and the Social Studies; Science, Mathematics and Technology; and Policy Studies. The first students were admitted in 2001. Following the approval of the program, I taught two courses in the program and I thought the students were excellent and committed to their studies.

The program itself had several features which I fully supported. First, it was an interdisciplinary program in which students were encouraged to take courses in other doctoral programs either at the GC or other universities in New York. CUNY along with Columbia, New York University and Fordham University had an agreement that doctoral students could take courses at any of the institutions at the tuition rate of the home college. This provided an excellent opportunity for our students to broaden their experiences. Second, it wasn't a heavily prescribed program and had only six required courses plus two colloquia. It was my opinion that these could easily be reduced further. Third, there was a genuine commitment to diversity among students and faculty. Forty-five percent of the students were black or Latina/o, as were the twenty-seven graduates of the program at the time Kelly had called me. While the students in the program represented a diverse population in terms of race and ethnicity, the three full-time GC faculty were white and the vast majority of the faculty from the CUNY colleges who taught in the program were white. The full-time faculty were Jean Anyon, Ken Tobin, and Nick Michelli. Steve Brier, a historian, was also on the full-time faculty and split his time with other programs. Jean considered herself a political economist who devoted her scholarship to broader societal issues and its effects on education. Ken was a prolific scholar in our program and wrote on education issues related to science, mathematics, and technology. Nick had an extensive administrative career in teacher education. Christine Saieh was the assistant program officer and took care of many of the administrative details that kept the program running smoothly. She had a great personality and welcomed everyone who came to our offices with open arms. The students loved her like an older sister. In 2007, there were 120 students in the program, having just admitted 33 students in fall 2007.

I discussed the offer with my wife and we both thought it would be a good change of pace, so I contacted President Kelly and told him I'd accept. I had been completely enmeshed for eleven years in teaching, doing professional development, and conducting research in online learning so a little short break with a chance to involve myself in a new environment was appealing. I also thought being involved with different issues, colleagues, and students would recharge my thinking a bit.

For the fall semester, I was to teach one course at the GC that was a colloquium or orientation to doctoral study. This didn't require extensive preparation since it was a group advisement class where the new students became acclimated to our program. I invited speakers, many of whom were faculty at CUNY, to share their scholarship and to give their perspectives on issues important to urban education. As the Interim Executive Officer, I saw my role as a caretaker of the program for a semester. My main focus was to make sure that there wouldn't be any major disruptions or other issues during that time.

By October 2017, I had gotten a good feel for the program. The faculty were most cooperative. The students seemed fully engaged. Christine handled the procedural and process issues that arose. I also was enjoying the administrative and collegial interactions at the GC. President Kelly was a good leader and very accessible since the GC had a very flat administrative organization. The Executive Officers of the thirty-two PhD programs all are appointed by the president for three-year terms and serve at his pleasure. This is unlike the CUNY colleges where the academic departments have chairpersons elected by the faculty, and there is usually a robust structure of academic deans between the chairs and the president. The GC executive officers met once a month. President Kelly chaired these meetings and provided information about the budget, CUNY policy issues, and new initiatives. There were several other meetings that I was required to attend each month but none of them were onerous or lengthy. I chaired four committees within the program, only one of which (Executive Committee) met regularly. The other committees (Admissions, Curriculum, Faculty Personnel) met as needed. Teaching only one course and carrying a moderate administrative load allowed me to spend a good deal of time on my writing and scholarship.

References

Picciano, A.G. & Jordan, C. (2018). *CUNY's first fifty years: Triumphs and ordeals of a people's university*. New York: Routledge/Taylor & Francis, Publishers.

55

Just before I assumed my position at the Graduate Center, Frank Mayadas had awarded Jeff Seaman and me a grant to conduct a survey of K-12 school district administrators to determine the extent and nature of online learning in their schools. While the research and scholarship of online learning in higher education was growing extensively, this was the first survey of its kind in primary and secondary schools. The key findings of this study published in 2007 were:

1. Almost two-thirds of the responding public-school districts are offering online courses:

> 63.1% had one or more students enrolled in a fully online or blended course.
> 57.9% had one or more students enrolled in a fully online course.
> 32.4% had one or more students enrolled in a blended course.

2. Over 60% of school districts with students enrolled in online courses anticipate their online enrollments will grow. Over the next two years districts predict online enrollments will increase by 18.6% and blended enrollments by 22.9%.

3. The overall number of K-12 students engaged in online courses in 2005-2006, is estimated at 700,000.

4. Respondents report that online learning is meeting the specific needs of a range of students, from those who need extra help to those who want to take more advanced courses and whose districts do not have enough teachers to offer certain subjects.

5. School districts typically depend on multiple online learning providers, including postsecondary institutions, independent

vendors and state virtual schools as well as developing and providing their own online courses.

6.   Perhaps the voices heard most clearly in this survey were those of respondents representing small rural school districts. For them, the availability of online learning is most important in order to provide students with course choices and in some cases, the basic courses that should be part of every curriculum. These rural districts might be providing models and lessons for other districts facing teacher shortages in high-need subject areas such as science and mathematics.

7.   While concerns about the quality of online courses, funding, and teacher development were expressed, it appears that many of these issues were gradually being resolved. (Picciano & Seaman, 2007)

The report was well-received and long overdue. Jeff and I had requests from professional as well as general publications to comment on the findings. News outlets such as *Bloomberg News*, *Forbes*, *Education World*, *Science and Society*, and *The Associated Press* reported on our work. Jeff and I had invitations for interviews from all over the world and were invited to present a paper at UNESCO Headquarters in Paris, France.

In October 2007 and again in 2008, Jeff and I applied for and received funding from the Sloan Foundation for two more national studies of K-12 education. The second study (Picciano & Seaman, 2009) was conducted in 2008 and published in 2009. The key findings of this study were:

1.   Three quarters of the responding public school districts are offering online or blended courses:

> 75% had one or more students enrolled in a fully online or blended course.
> 70% had one or more students enrolled in a fully online course.
> 41% had one or more students enrolled in a blended course

These percentages represent an increase of approximately 10% since 2005-2006.

2.   66% of school districts with students enrolled in online or blended courses anticipate their online enrollments will grow.

3.   The overall number of K-12 students engaged in online courses in 2007-2008, is estimated at 1,030,000. This represents a 47% increase since 2005-2006.

4.   Respondents report that online learning is meeting the specific needs of a range of students, from those who need extra help and credit recovery to those who want to take Advanced Placement and college-level courses.

5.   School districts typically depend on multiple online learning providers, including postsecondary institutions, state virtual schools and independent providers as well as developing and providing their own online courses.

6.   Perhaps the voices heard most clearly in this survey were those of respondents representing small rural school districts. For them, the availability of online learning is a lifeline and enables them to provide students with course choices and in some cases, the basic courses that should be part of every curriculum. (Picciano & Seaman, 2009)

Of the three studies, this one has been the one most often referenced in scholarly journals.

Our third study, conducted in 2009 and published in 2010 (Picciano & Seaman, 2010), examined specifically online learning in secondary schools. I thought this was the best of the three studies containing a lot more analysis of key issues such as credit-recovery programs. A summary of our findings follows.

Improving Graduation Rates and Credit Recovery

Credit recovery has evolved into the most popular type of online course being offered at the secondary level. Students needing such courses make up a significant portion of the high school student population that subsequently drops out or is late in graduating.

Urban high schools, which historically have the lowest graduation rates of any schools in the country, appear to be embracing online credit recovery as a basic part of their academic offerings. While employing online courses for credit recovery, high school administrators still have concerns about their quality and indicate that students need maturity, self-discipline, and a certain command of basic skills (reading and mathematics) in order to succeed.

Building Bridges to College Careers

Online and blended learning courses are increasingly being used to overcome logistical issues in programs to bridge the high school and college experiences. These courses have allowed high schools to expand the opportunities for their students to start their college careers while still in high school high.

High school administrators consider online elective college-level courses as an effective means for some of the more able students to begin their college careers.

Differentiating Instruction

High school administrators see online learning as meeting the diverse needs of their students whether through advanced placement, elective college courses, or credit recovery.

The major reason high school administrators cite for online and blended offerings is to provide courses that otherwise would not be available. This strongly supports the concept that online technology can provide differentiating instruction and more choices for high school administrators in developing their academic programs.

Financial and Policy Issues

Survey respondents report that offering online and blended courses makes financial sense when trying to meet specific needs for small groups of students. This allows schools to maximize their full-time faculty resources in required and other popular courses and to minimize offering courses in face-to-face mode for small numbers of students.

Respondents also see costs and funding formulae as barriers to expanding and implementing online and blended courses. State and local education policies that follow strict attendance-based funding formulae do not easily accommodate students taking online or blended courses.

The Pedagogy of Online Learning

Educators express concerns that online learning is not as effective as face-to-face instruction. Specific concerns include the need for motivation and maturity levels, study habits and organizational skills, and adequate academic preparedness for online students to succeed.

High school administrators see benefits to online learning programs that overshadow concerns about pedagogical value — the vast majority of their schools are moving forward with their programs and looking to expand them in the future.

Online learning is seen as a means to broaden and expand student experiences. It allows students looking for more advanced work to test and challenge their skills by taking more demanding instructional material. It also allows students who might be at risk to make up coursework that they have missed in order to graduate.

Rural Schools in the Vanguard

Rural schools are in the vanguard in offering online and blended learning programs to their students— using online courses to overcome significant problems in funding, teacher certification, and small enrollments.

High schools in all locales are facing serious challenges, but rural schools probably have the most difficult. Online and blended learning are a critical part of the strategy they are employing to deal with limited tax bases, low enrollments, and difficulty in attracting and keeping certified teachers. (Picciano & Seaman, 2010)

Throughout the period of these studies (2007-2010), our work was the only research that examined the extent and nature of online learning in K-12 education using national samples. These studies were cited and referenced extensively by researchers, K-12 practitioners, and education policymakers throughout the country and beyond. In 2011, the United States Department of Education started collecting similar data on a regular basis.

In 2010, in recognition of my K-12 research and other scholarship, I was honored to be the recipient of the Sloan Consortium's National Award for Outstanding Achievement in Online Education by an Individual.

References

Picciano, A.G. & Seaman, J. (2010). *Class Connections: High School Reform and the Role of Online Learning.* Boston: Babson College Survey Research Group.

https://www.onlinelearningsurvey.com/reports/class-connections.pdf

Picciano, A.G. & Seaman, J. (2009). *K–12 Online Learning: A 2008 Follow-Up of the Survey of U.S. School District Administrators.* Needham, MA: The Sloan Consortium.

http://www.sloan-c.org/publications/survey/
pdf/K-12_Online_Learning.pdf

Picciano, A.G. & Seaman, J. (2007). *K–12 Online Learning: A Survey of U.S. School District Administrators* Needham, MA: The Sloan Consortium. Needham, MA: The Sloan Consortium.

https://www.onlinelearningsurvey.com/reports/k-12-online-learning.pdf

56

In December 2007 I was having lunch with one of the Urban Education faculty, Ken Tobin, when he told me that Phil Anderson would be extending his leave into spring 2008. The following week I received a phone call from President Kelly to tell me the same thing and suggested that we meet to discuss my staying on as the Executive Officer for another semester. I hadn't planned on this and had started making plans to return to Hunter College. In fact, I had already discussed my teaching schedule for the spring with Migdalia Romero, the chair in the Curriculum & Teaching Department. I met with President Kelly who told me that he was pleased with my work and would like me to continue in Phil's absence. Then came a blockbuster surprise. If I was amenable, he would like to appoint me to a three-year term as the Executive Officer starting in fall 2008 since Phil Anderson's three-year term was coming to an end in June 2008. I told him that I had to think about it and would get back to him shortly. The Graduate Center had a policy of not offering courses during the summer. This freed faculty, including executive officers, to focus for three months on writing and research. I found myself weighing the time commitments of my workload at the two institutions. I had several ideas for book projects and came to the conclusion that the Graduate Center would offer me greater time flexibility than Hunter College. In addition to the difference in teaching load, the teacher education programs at colleges throughout the state, including ADSUP at Hunter, were being subjected to increasing reviews, assessments, and recertifications by the New York State Department of Education and external accrediting agencies. These required an extraordinary amount of committee work and report writing which, to be quite honest, I resented. So, I called President Kelly and accepted his offer to be the Executive Officer until June 2011. The next day I received an email from the provost congratulating me. She also informed me that the PhD Program in Urban Education was due for its first external review. In preparation, a self-study of the program would have to be completed by June 2009. Ugh!

The word got out quickly that I would be continuing on at the Graduate Center and I received congratulations from faculty and students at the Graduate Center and throughout CUNY. I was sad to leave my colleagues at Hunter.

In April 2008, I heard from Dr. Roscoe Brown, the retired President of Bronx Community College, who was an icon at CUNY having served in World War II as one of the Tuskegee Airmen, an all-black team of pilots who flew combat missions over Europe (see note at the end of this chapter). During the CUNY fiscal crisis of the late 1970s, Dr. Brown's contacts in state and local politics benefitted CUNY significantly. Although he did not teach any courses, Dr. Brown was on the Urban Education faculty and maintained an office at the Graduate Center. He asked if I would have lunch with him and several of his colleagues. After congratulating me on assuming the leadership of the PhD Program, he and his colleagues asked if I could help provide a career path for minority administrators at CUNY. Dr. Brown believed that there were a number of excellent, black, mid-level administrators who had reached a ceiling in their advancement because they didn't have doctoral degrees. I was sympathetic to his request and promised that I would do what I could to assist these individuals. As a result, and starting in 2009, I carefully reviewed each year's applicant pool to locate mid-level administrators (black or white) working in CUNY who might benefit from earning a PhD. In each cycle thereafter, I encouraged my colleagues on the Admissions Committee to consider these candidates as our special contribution to CUNY without lowering any of our standards. This became an important point of reference, because within a couple of years, admission into our program would become very competitive. Even so, a small number of CUNY administrators, half of whom were men or women of color began to be admitted to our program in each cycle. The vast majority of them including Maureen Samedy, Ferdinand Verley, Manny Lopez, Naomi Nwosu, and Fenix Arias graduated from our program and advanced their careers at CUNY.

Note: Roscoe Brown

During World War II, Roscoe Brown flew 68 combat missions, downing a German jet outside Berlin during an escort mission in 1945. As a part of the Tuskegee Airmen's bomber-escort missions in the 99th Fighter Squadron, he was one of three Red Tailed Angels. In 2007, Brown and five other Tuskegee airmen accepted the Congressional Gold Medal on behalf of the nearly 1,000 black men who went through the Tuskegee Airmen program between 1941 and 1945. Brown also earned the Distinguished Flying Cross for his bravery and skill.

In an oral history, Brown said: "Many of the bomber pilots [we escorted] said, 'We saw the Red Tail P-51s and they were our saviors… Many of them did not know—most of them did not know—[we] were African Americans.

After the war, Brown became an educator, social activist and one of the most prominent caretakers of the Tuskegee Airmen legacy until his death at age 94. Accessed at: https://www.history.com/news/6-renowned-tuskegee-airmen-davis-brown-mcgee

57

At the end of fall 2007, I had received the news that a long-standing request to add a full-time faculty member to our program had been approved by the CUNY Central Office. We began a search and by late spring 2008, we made an offer to Ofelia Garcia, an English language learning specialist who was on the faculty at Columbia Teachers College. She fit right in and was one of the best hires I made in my career. She was one of our most productive faculty members in terms of scholarship, teaching, and student advisement. Ofelia also was instrumental in acquiring a multimillion-dollar grant, the CUNY- New York State Initiative on Emergent Bilinguals, that focused on research and best practices in teaching English Language Learners. This grant provided significant funding for our students to conduct research in this area and to be part of a community of practice. At the same time as we were hiring Ofelia, President Kelly met with me to discuss a personnel issue he was having with a black professor who was unhappy in the Psychology Program and was wondering if I could envision a position for him in Urban Education. I said I was amenable, but I would have to discuss it with my colleagues. Martin Ruck joined our program in fall 2008, bringing the total number of faculty to seven, including Steve Brier's shared responsibilities and myself.

In spring 2008, I devoted a lot of my time at the Graduate Center to developing the self-study in preparation for a site visit in spring 2009 by the external evaluators. I reviewed the entire program (students, faculty, advisement, curriculum, and quality of the dissertations) and developed an extensive schedule of meetings and forums so that all involved would have input into the self-study. Christine Saieh produced the data that we would need to describe the program and support our recommendations for further study and review. I drafted a self-study in June 2008 and sent it to the Provost with the understanding that the students and faculty would do one more review in fall 2008. The study identified a number of issues to be examined by the external review team related to the size of the program, the names of the three strands, whether we needed strands at all, the core requirements, the need to expand the research methods courses, space for the program, the relationship of Graduate Center faculty, and the relationship between college/campus-based faculty.

In fall 2008, we held another series of meetings within the community, provided additional data on student outcomes, and modified the self-study accordingly. All of the changes requested were modest. In spring 2009, the site visit by the external evaluation team went quite well. They issued a report in April 2009 that identified sixteen recommendations, most of which were just fine as far as I was concerned. There were recommendations to enhance student advisement, reduce the number of student admissions each year, examine the content and need for the present core courses, and evaluate the naming and need for the three strands. The Urban Education Program's Executive and other committees were able to address most of the recommendations and implement changes within twelve to eighteen months. The only recommendation that required more time to implement was renaming of the Science, Mathematics, and Technology Education strand to Learning Sciences. It took almost four years to reach agreement. The change that I was most happy about was the reduction of the core requirements from six courses and two colloquia to four courses and one colloquia, which could now be completed in one year.

In 2009, we hired Wendy Luttrell to our full-time faculty. She came to us from the Harvard University School of Education where her primary research focus was on gender, race, and class.

In 2009, I decided to develop a blog. Over the summer, a colleague of mine, Matt Gold, led an initiative to create a CUNY Commons that would evolve into a social networking site based at the Graduate Center. I was in the elevator with Matt one day and I asked him how the CUNY Commons was coming along. He said it was okay but that it could use more activity and he wondered if I might start a blog. I was skeptical to say the least, but I liked Matt and decided to give it a try. As a result, *Tony's Thoughts* was begun in November 2009. I blogged about technology and higher education. Today the blog represents my take on scholarly articles, stories, and issues that I read about during my daily review of newspapers, professional journals and social networking sites. In 2016, Jim Groom, a well-known blogger, visited *Tony's Thoughts* and wrote:

> "That fact pushed me to take a look back at the site archives, and I was quite impressed. There has been at least one post (and usually closer to 20 or 30!) every month since November of 2009. That's a blogging streak to brag about. And fall of 2009 is significant because that's when the Commons came online. So, effectively, *Tony's Thoughts* has (or have) been regular and active since the very beginning! What's more, the blog remains a tight, curated space wherein he shares what he's reading, thinking, and doing. A process that over time becomes a rich, open, and inviting archive/testament to his personal and professional presence at the Grad Center." (Jim Groom, 2016, https://apicciano.commons.gc.cuny.edu/)

In 2011, I started taking advantage of a software enhancement that was made to the CUNY Commons that allowed blog posts to be forwarded automatically to Twitter, Linkedin and Facebook. I have kept a counter on the blog and at the time of this writing, I am approaching 8,000,000 visits since its inception in 2009. I am rather pleased with that.

58

Ralph Gomory, the President of the Alfred P. Sloan Foundation had retired in 2007 and Frank Mayadas eventually followed him. Paul Joskow, an economist from MIT, followed Dr. Gomory as the President of the Foundation, and the *Anytime, Anyplace Learning Program* grant program came to an end. Before he left the Foundation in 2009, Frank gave me the last grant from the program and asked if I would document its work. For the next three years, I interviewed several dozen individuals who had been major grant recipients. Most of them were colleagues of mine at the Sloan Consortium. Frank also gave me summary copies of all of the grant's files to work from and I pieced together the history of the *Anytime, Anyplace Learning Program*. Here's the Executive Summary of my report that was issued in 2013:

Executive Summary

In 1992, the Alfred P. Sloan Foundation established the *Learning Outside the Classroom Program*. The name was changed soon after to the *Anytime, Anyplace Learning Program*, the purpose of which was to explore educational alternatives for people who wanted to pursue higher education but who couldn't easily attend regularly scheduled college classes. This exploration resulted in a promulgation of a major development in pedagogical practice commonly referred to as the asynchronous learning network or ALN. Using modern data communications technology, including the Internet and World Wide Web, ALNs allow teaching and learning to transcend time and space in order to provide access to a quality higher education. Twenty years later, ALN evolved into online learning to become a basic aspect of American higher education. (Allen & Seaman, 2013)

In June 2009, a project was conceived to examine and evaluate the *Anytime, Anyplace Learning Program*. The purpose of this project was twofold: first, to analyze the role of the *Anytime, Anyplace Learning Program* in nurturing online learning enabling it to evolve into a major vehicle for providing higher education opportunities to millions of students; and second, to examine the historical record and to begin the process of documenting and preserving the stories of the individuals, colleges, universities and organizations that were critical players in the *Anytime, Anyplace Learning Program*. This report documents the processes, findings and conclusions of this project.

It is the opinion of these researchers that the Alfred P. Sloan Foundation had an important role in fueling the development of online learning in American higher education via its *Anytime, Anyplace Learning Program*. The Foundation's timing was critical by beginning this program just before the Internet was evolving as a major technological breakthrough. Starting in 1992, the Foundation funded 346 projects totaling $72 million, most of which were made to non-profit colleges and universities. Major distance and adult learning providers such as the University of Maryland University College and the Penn State World Campus were early grantees. Following on the heels of these institutions, large mainstream public university systems such as the University of Illinois, the State University of New York, the University of Massachusetts, and the University of Central Florida developed substantial online learning programs. In the early 2000s, large urban universities in New York, Chicago and Milwaukee were funded to develop and expand blended learning environments. Perhaps the most significant initiative of the grant program was the establishment of the Sloan Consortium of Colleges and Universities (Sloan-C). Originally an informal organization of Foundation grantees, the Consortium incorporated in 2008 as a non-profit, 501 (c) (3) organization. Sloan-C became the largest recipient of funding from the *Anytime, Anyplace, Learning Program*, receiving in excess of $15 million over the course of the grant program.

Summary of Findings

First, the public sector of higher education was integral to the success of the *Anytime, Anyplace Learning Program.* The vast majority of the grants awarded as part of this program went to large public university systems including community colleges. This was not an accident but by design.

Second, most individuals from institutions that have major online learning programs who were not *Anytime, Anyplace, Learning Program* grantees (public, private non-profit, private for-profit) , are not aware of the contribution of the Foundation. The awareness among this group that does exist comes more from their involvement with the Sloan Consortium.

Third, among individuals in private, for-profit institutions, awareness of the Foundation's contribution to online learning is modest at best and somewhat lower than for other non-grantee institutions. And again, the awareness that does exist comes from their association with the Sloan Consortium.

Fourth, the Sloan Consortium has made its presence known to the majority of all major online learning providers regardless of whether they are public, private, non-profit or for-profit. It is likely that the legacy of the *Anytime, Anyplace Learning Program* rests with the success of the Consortium.

In sum, a mix of online technology and pedagogical practice is rapidly reshaping instruction in our colleges and universities. The Alfred P. Sloan Foundation was at the forefront of and served as a catalyst for this movement. It will continue to grow for years to come. (Picciano, 2013)

The entire report, as well as interviews with Ralph Gomory, Frank Mayadas and a number of grant recipients can be found at: http://aalp-sloan-report.gc.cuny.edu/

It was the end of an important era in the history of online learning development. In 2009, Paul Joskow informed the Board of Directors of the Sloan Consortium that all funding from the Sloan Foundation for its operations would cease in 2013. Furthermore, the Consortium would have to re-incorporate under a new name that didn't include any reference to the Sloan Foundation. In 2014, the Alfred P. Sloan Consortium became the Online Learning Consortium (OLC).

By 2010, online learning was mushrooming in our country and across the globe. The annual Allen & Seaman studies on student enrollments in American higher education reported twenty percent increases. approaching a total of five million students. Accurate data on students enrolled in blended learning wasn't known because of problems with definitions and the failure of most colleges and universities to keep accurate data. At least once or twice a month I was being asked to give talks and present papers at national and regional conferences.

Interest in the entire online learning movement received a significant boost around this time with the development of massive open online courses or MOOCs. The term "MOOC" was coined in 2008 by Dave Cormier and Bryan Alexander to describe an online course led by George Siemens of Athabasca University and Stephen Downes of the National Research Council. The course enrolled more than 2,000 students. In 2011, Stanford University offered several MOOCs--one of which, led by Sebastian Thrun and Peter Norvig,-- enrolled more than 160,000 students. Shortly thereafter, Thrun started a MOOC company called Udacity, and a few months later, Andrew Ng and Daphne Koller, also from Stanford University, launched Coursera, another MOOC provider. The MOOC model was grounded in improving student access to higher education and cost effectiveness, with emphasis on "massive" enrollments." Venture capital from private investors and philan-thropies flowed into MOOC development.

The major interest in MOOC technology wasn't its pedagogical benefits but the possibility of increased access to higher education, and courses that were enrolling hundreds of thousands of students attracted deserved atten-tion. In addition, faculty from major institutions such as Stanford University, Harvard, and the Massachusetts Institute of Technology became associated with the MOOC phenomenon. MOOCs were glamorized by their founders at companies such as Udacity, Coursera, and edX as a technological innovation that would revolutionize higher education. The media went into a frenzy. The *New York Times* declared 2012 as "The Year of the MOOC" (Pappano, 2012). Education policymakers and university trustees took notice and thought they had found a solution to their education funding woes. Major new MOOC initiatives were being mounted at the California State University System, the University of Rochester, and the University of Virginia.

As the MOOC phenomenon took off, those of us who had been devel-oping and promoting online learning took a closer look at their design. I enrolled in two MOOC courses and observed weakness in their pedagogical basis. The mechanistic style of these MOOCs, based on "read, watch, listen and repeat" course materials, was questionable. Those of us who preferred more socially constructed pedagogical approaches emphasizing extensive interaction among students and faculty were a bit dismayed. In addition, the high student dropout rates, reaching 90 percent in some MOOC courses, couldn't be easily explained away. Educational leaders and faculty around the country began to question the use of MOOC course materials developed at Harvard, MIT, Stanford and other highly selective universities since some saw this as elitism and arrogance on the part of the MOOC providers.

By the end of 2013, the media's infatuation with the overhyped MOOCs receded. In November 2013, I was with Daphne Koller, a founder of Cour-sera, at the Sloan Consortium International Conference on Online Learning where she was giving a keynote address. Koller admitted that MOOC companies might have to consider the development of more pedagogically sound course materials that could be used in blended online formats rather than fully online formats. In a sense, Coursera and other MOOC providers might need to rebrand themselves as producers of high-quality content that faculty would use to their best advantage. I was heartened to see pedagogy returning to the forefront of online learning development once again.

References

Picciano, A.G. (2013). *Pioneering Higher Education's Digital Future: Twenty Years (1992-2012) of the Alfred P. Sloan Foundation's Anytime, Anyplace Learning Program.* This website documents the Alfred P. Sloan Foundation's grant program and contains a plethora of material including an evaluation report and video commentary. http://aalp-sloan-report.gc.cuny.edu/

59

On April 12, 2013, CUNY Chancellor Matt Goldstein announced his plans to retire. He would step down on July 1, 2013, after having been CUNY's longest serving chancellor. He was appointed in 1999 and led a number of major changes at the University. During his tenure he established the CUNY School of Public Health at Hunter College, the CUNY School of Pharmacy at York College, the William E. Macaulay Honors College, the CUNY Graduate School of Journalism, the CUNY School of Professional Studies, and Guttman Community College based on the widely-regarded Accelerated Study in Associate Programs (ASAP). Goldstein was also credited with securing the funding for 2,000 new faculty lines and increasing student enrollment to its highest levels ever at almost 270,000 students in credit-bearing programs and 226,000 in adult and continuing education. His time as Chancellor wasn't without conflict, as was common in our large, diverse, urban university. He inherited a Board of Trustees' decision that limited students needing remediation to the community colleges, reversing the open admissions policy that was passed in 1969. The sharpest conflict of his tenure came when he proposed and implemented the Pathways Initiative which imposed CUNY-wide rules on general education and transfer programs, previously under the purview of the faculty at the individual colleges. The Pathways Initiative was seen as part of the Chancellor's move to secure substantial decision-making and control for the Central Office at the expense of the colleges. I had been in the Chancellor's company on several occasions as part of my work with Mike Ribaudo and he even sat in on one of my professional development presentations. My assessment was that he did a fine job overall as chancellor and moved the University in a positive direction.

Chancellor Goldstein's retirement would have ramifications for the Graduate Center. President Bill Kelly was named the Interim Chancellor by the CUNY Board of Trustees to start on July 1st. Kelly had served at CUNY for over forty years, had extensive knowledge of the University, and had a good working relationship with Chancellor Goldstein, all of which had benefitted the Graduate Center. Bill Kelly was a finalist for the Chancellor's position and many of us who knew him were hoping he would get the position. The CUNY Board of Trustees instead selected James B. Milliken, the former head of the University of Nebraska, as chancellor. The Trustees also announced that Interim Chancellor Kelly would be leaving CUNY. He would go on to be named The New York Public Library's Andrew W. Mellon Director of the Research Libraries starting in December 2015.

In July 2013, I received a phone call from Jean Anyon saying that she might not be able to teach a full load in the fall and asked if I would make an accommodation. Jean had been quietly battling cancer for two years. I assured her we could do something and that she should take care of herself. In August, Jean called me again to say she didn't think that she would be able to teach at all in the fall. We had a good conversation about a lot of different things. On September 7th, Jean passed away and our entire community was saddened. Jean was a fine colleague who was well loved by everyone and adored by her students.

I would especially miss her. She deeply understood education policy and social issues, and was completely devoted to her students and their research. I never once had to be concerned about the quality of a dissertation that she advised. At meetings, she and I played this game where we would bet a martini lunch on predicting the outcome of some matter or other. She invariably won. We also had dinner at the end of each semester to review how things went in the program and what we should be thinking about for the next semester. I took her advice seriously and planned accordingly. One of the great honors in my career was consulting with Jean on an article on education policy that she had been invited to publish in the *Harvard Education Review's* special 75th Anniversary issue. This issue had only five invited articles by several of the most important people in the field of education policy. She concluded her article with "I would like to thank my colleague

Tony Picciano for his thoughts." She didn't have to include this small attribution, but I always cherished it.

In the Fall 2013 semester, we had several tributes to her in our small community room giving the students and faculty a chance to express their sorrow. We had a more extensive memorial service for her at the end of the semester. It was a sad affair even as we celebrated her life. As I look back on my career, she was one of my favorite colleagues.

May she rest in peace!

60

In August 2013, I received an email from Seugnet Blignaut, a researcher from the Faculty of Education Sciences, North-West University (NWU), Potchefstroom, South Africa. She asked whether it would be possible for me to visit NWU for two weeks in May 2014, to deliver a series of seminars and workshops on online and blended learning. I thought long and hard before accepting this invitation since I had to re-arrange my schedule at the Graduate Center a bit. I was to arrive on May 2nd and leave on May 15th. My itinerary (see below) for the visit was packed and every day and night included some activity. I met with the president, most of the administrators, faculty and students. And not on the itinerary, every evening I had dinner with one or more members of the NWU community during which we discussed technology and education. A major reason I had been asked to visit was that the Education Ministry of South Africa had initiated a program to expand higher education to new segments of its population, particularly students who didn't live in the major urban areas such as Johannesburg, Cape Town and Durban. In order to move quickly and to defer the cost of building new campuses and facilities, the public universities were being asked to increase significantly their online and blended learning offerings. To be quite honest, it was an exhausting but exhilarating trip.

Seugnet arranged for me to have an assistant, Verona Leendertz, who kept my schedule each day and provided my transportation to the different locations. NWU had three campuses although all of my activities would be at two of them. Most of the time, I stayed at a small inn or guest house. The Little Eden Guest House near the Vaal Triangle Campus served as my base accommodation. Verona was a godsend for her organization, pleasant personality, and attention to details. She also spoke several of the eleven official languages of South Africa which came in handy throughout my stay.

Seugnet was very knowledgeable about instructional technology and was familiar with much of my scholarship. The administrators with whom I met understood the tasks before them and were rightfully concerned about implementing the Education Ministry initiative. Their basic issues included access to technology, wifi connectivity, and in some rural areas, reliable electrical service, and my meetings with them were essentially about strategic planning. I was sympathetic. Their task was difficult. My focus with faculty and students was on pedagogical issues related to design and development of academic programs and courses using online instruction. At every session there were enthusiastic participants who were well-prepared and had read much of my work. The free, open-access Sloan Consortium *Journal of Asynchronous Learning Networks* (JALN) made it easy for them to gain access to my articles.

The presentation technology available to me at the campuses was very reliable and well designed. Many of my presentations at the Vaal Triangle campus were in a library lecture room. The library itself appeared to be well-stocked with books and technology services and was busy with students. The library lecture room was well-lit with wall-to-wall windows that overlooked a little plain where small antelope and baboons grazed and sauntered around. An extraordinary sight to a New Yorker like me.

In addition to my seminars, workshops, and dinners, with my NWU colleagues, I was also treated to a number of tours and mini excursions to game parks, museums and important sites in and around Johannesburg. One of the most memorable was a weekend on Esmarie Strydom's 900-acre farm. Esmarie was one of the deans at NWU and couldn't have been a more gracious host. We had wonderful meals and stayed up late into the evening drinking wine, listening to the sounds of wildlife, and taking in the incredible African sunsets that seemed to last and last.

This visit was also important to me, since it exposed me to an entirely different culture. For instance, which language one spoke (Afrikaans, English,

Venda, Zulu, etc.) immediately said something about who you were beyond black and white. It reflected background, geography, tribe, customs and traditions, all of which were respected. The two weeks I spent in South Africa went by rapidly and I enjoyed every minute. It was good to see some of the people with whom I met on several later occasions at our Sloan Consortium conferences. They always went out of their way to say hello and spend some time with me.

Itinerary of the Visit of Dr Anthony Picciano to North-West University

2 May – 15 May 2014

Day	Event	Detail
1 May Thursday	Departure from JFK to Johannesburg, South Africa	Seugnet issued tickets
3 May Saturday	• Dr Picciano arrives at JHB airport: 08:05 • Transfer to Vaal Triangle Campus (VTC) • Settling in at Little Eden Guest House: http://www.safarinow.com/go/LittleEdenGuestLodgeVanderbijlpark/	• Little Eden Guest House transfer from airport to VTC (Helei Jooste) • Overnight at Little Eden Guest House (Helei Jooste)
4 May Sunday	Visit to the Lion Park at Krugersdorp http://www.lion-park.com/ or Visit to the Hector Pieterson Museum, Johannesburg http://www.gauteng.net/attractions/entry/hector_pieterson_memorial_and_museum/	• Seugnet • Transfer with Dr Verona Leendertz • Overnight at Little Eden Guest House (Helei Jooste)
5 May Monday	Technology Enhanced Learning in Higher Education (TELHE) research workshop Day 1 at VTC (09:00-16:00)	• Seugnet • Overnight at Little Eden Guest House (Helei Jooste) • Transfers with Verona to VTC • Workshop at Building 13, SL224, Research Wing Seminar Room, Split Level 2

6 May Tuesday	TELHE research workshop Day 2 at VTC (09:00-16:00)	• Seugnet • Overnight at Little Eden Guest House (Helei Jooste) • Transfers with Verona to VTC • Workshop at SL224, Research Wing Seminar Room, Split Level 2
7 May Wednesday	• South African Election day (Public holiday) • Visit to the home of Dr Gerhard de Plessis for informal meetings with various role players	• Transfer to Potchefstroom with Verona • Visit to Gerhard's home for workshop planning and informal discussion • Transfer with Verona to Vanderbijlpark • Overnight at Little Eden Guest House (Helei Jooste)
8 May Thursday	• Prestige lecture at VTC: *Blended Learning Meets MOOCs: Higher Education's Digital Future!* (09:00-11:00) • Lunch at VTC • Afternoon discussions with Seugnet (and other interested staff members) on TELHE research models	• Seugnet • Building 24, Boardroom, VTC • Transfer with Dr Verona Leendertz to Potchefstroom late afternoon • Overnight in guesthouse Ma Cachette guesthouse (Dr Gerhard du Plessis)
9 May Friday	Day 1: Intensive BL Workshop/ Integration of technology: ADS Staff members at Potchefstroom Campus, including round-table discussions of with faculty leadership (school chairs, programme managers) on the implications of blended learning integration (09:00-16:00)	• Dr Gerhard du Plessis • Transfer to campus with Verona • Building C1, Conference Room 250 • Transfer with Dr Verona Leendertz after the workshop to farm (plus Gerhard)
10 May Saturday 11 May Sunday	Farm visit Visit to the Vredefort Dome Heritage Site: http://www.southafrica.net/za/en/articles/entry/article-southafrica.net-vredefort-dome	• Esmarie, Seugnet, Verona, Gerhard • Transfer to Vanderbijlpark with Verona via Potchefstroom to drop off Gerhard) • Overnight in guesthouse Little Eden Guest House (Helei Jooste)

12 May Monday	Day 2: Intensive BL Workshop/ Integration of technology: ADS Staff members at Vaal Triangle Campus (09:00-16:00)	• Dr Esmarie Strydom and Marieta Janse van Vuuren • Building 13: Learning and Research Commons, Split level 3, Room 329 • Transfer with Verona to Potchefstroom late afternoon • Overnight in guesthouse Ma Cachette (Ms Vivian Claasen)
13 May Tuesday	Workshop for Faculty of Education Sciences, Potchefstroom Campus	• Overnight in guesthouse Ma Cachette (Ms Vivian Claasen) • Transfers to campus and dinner with Prof Robert Balfour with Verona
14 May Wednesday	Workshop for Faculty of Education Sciences, Potchefstroom Campus	• Guest of Ms Vivian Claasen • Transfer to campus with Verona • Transfer with Verona to Vanderbijlpark • Overnight at Little Eden Guest House (Helei Jooste)
15 May Thursday	Round-table discussions of learning experience and strategic planning forward with focus on the VTC experience and expectation Joint ADS from VTC and Potchefstroom	• Dr Esmarie and Dr Marieta Janse van Vuuren • Transfers with Verona • Overnight at Little Eden Guest House (Helei Jooste)
16 May Friday	• Intensive BL Workshop: ADS Staff members at Potchefstroom Campus: *Redesigning North West University for Blended Learning: Elements of a Comprehensive Strategy* • Lunch at Quest • Depart to JFK, New York at 20:25	• Guest of Prof Martin Oosthuizen • Workshop at Quest Conference Venue • Transfer to Quest and guesthouse with Verona • Little Eden Guest House transfer to airport at about 4:30pm (Helei Jooste)

References

Pappano, L. (2012, November 2). *The year of the MOOC*. New York Times. Retrieved from:

http://www.nytimes.com/2012/11/04/education/
edlife/massive-open-online-courses-are-

multiplying-at-a-rapid-pace.html?pagewanted=all&_
r=0 Accessed: January 23, 2021.

61

In July 2013, Chase Robinson, had been named interim president of the Graduate Center, replacing Bill Kelly. He had come to the GC as the provost in 2008 after spending most of his career at Oxford University. Following a year as interim president, the CUNY Board of Trustees appointed him President of the Graduate Center effective July 1, 2014.

In fall 2014, I met with President Robinson and we agreed that I would leave as the Executive Officer of the PhD Program in Urban Education in 2017. After that, I would also stay on for one more year as full-time faculty at the Graduate Center to help smooth the way for the new Executive Officer. I would be seventy years old in 2017 and my interest in doing administrative work was waning. Having served as Interim Executive Officer, followed by three terms as the Executive Officer, I was quite proud of the PhD Program and based on our student outcomes, was confident that it had evolved into one of the best doctoral programs in CUNY. Demand for the program was soaring and applications were hovering around 150 per year from which we would select twelve to fourteen new students, all of whom received some form of financial aid. We continued our commitment to diversity with 40-45 percent of new admissions black or Latina/o. These same percentages continued to hold true for our graduates. In 2018 when I would leave, the program had a cumulative total of 156 graduates, all of whom were gainfully employed. Seventy percent of these students were working as faculty at colleges and universities all over the world. CUNY teacher education programs had hired thirty of our graduates while others worked in institutions such as Harvard, McGill, Penn, and NYU. Our graduates could also be found in South Africa, Luxembourg, and Rwanda. Of those who didn't pursue faculty positions, most were employed as administrators or policy analysts in the New York City public school system, at CUNY or other colleges, or at professional education organizations.

One of the major reasons I had accepted the position as the Executive Officer at the Graduate Center was that I would be able devote more time to writing and scholarship. By 2018 when I would return to Hunter College, I had authored or co-authored seven books, edited or co-edited ten issues of professional journals, and written twenty-one articles or chapters in peer-reviewed publications (see Appendix C). While most of these publications focused on technology, I also started writing on education policy. I was most pleased that I began to publish with several colleagues from the Graduate Center and around the country. Chuck Dziuban, professor and Director of the Research Initiative for Teaching Effectiveness at the University of Central Florida and I published four books together and have given innumerable presentations on panels at national and regional conferences. We have become good friends and always are able to share a laugh about the world around us. Charles Graham, a former dean and professor at Brigham Young University, likewise became a fine colleague. I published three books with him and also have been on a number of panels with him at conferences. Our backgrounds couldn't have been more different but we always had time to share what was going on with our families. Patsy Moskal, Chuck's assistant at the Research Initiative for Teaching Effectiveness at the University of Central Florida, and I have published two books together and have co-edited three special editions of the *Online Learning Journal*. She is a consummate professional who puts in twice the effort as everyone else in everything we do. She also has deep concern for our society, especially during difficult times such as the coronavirus pandemic of 2020-2021. Rob Steiner was a good colleague for many years and our paths kept crossing in a number of different venues in New York City. Rob was the Project Director, for the American Museum of Natural History's (AMNH) Seminars on Science Series, that utilized multimedia material from the AMNH Archives. In 2008, we co-authored an article entitled, *Bringing the real world of science to children: A partnership of the American Museum of Natural History and the City University of New York*. This article was selected to be part of a website dedicated to the United

Nations commemorating 2008 as the "Year of the Child". See: http://www. distanceandaccesstoeducation.org/Results.aspx?searchMode=3&criteria=en

I also have been blessed to collaborate with a number of other colleagues on special editions and articles including Karen Swan, Peter Shea, Eric Fredericksen, Laurie Dringus, Paige McDonald, Jill Buban, Liz Ciabocchi, Amy Ginzberg, Norman Vaughan and Karen Vignare.

At the Graduate Center, I cherished my collaboration with Joel Spring who is a prolific author of books on education policy and American politics. His seminal work, *American Education*, is in its 19th edition, and is a must read for every educator. I invited Joel, a professor at Queens College, to teach one of the core courses in the PhD Program in Urban Education. It was a great decision. The students loved him and he brought a plethora of experience and knowledge to the program. Joel suggested we co-author a book on *The Great American Education Industrial Complex* that would expand on an article I had published in 1994. It was an exhilarating experience for many reasons, but especially because our writing styles were so different. While Joel hammers away like a machine gun on an issue, I tend to draw it out slowly before reaching a final conclusion. Even though Joel is now retired, he and I keep in touch. We see each other regularly along with our wives, who have become fast friends.

I also published several books and articles on my own. In 2014, my article, *Big data and learning analytics in blended learning environments: Benefits and concerns* was published in the *International Journal of Interactive Multimedia and Artificial Intelligence*. This article was a critical examination of the emergence of big data and learning analytics software in education. The article drew on concepts associated with data-driven decision making and how it evolved into big data techniques and analytics. See: https://www.ijimai. org/journal/sites/default/files/journals/IJIMAI20142_7.pdf

In 2015, *Planning for online education: A systems model* was published in *Online Learning*. While not meant to be an exhaustive treatment of the topic, this article was timely because many colleges and universities were considering the development and expansion of online education as part of their strategic planning activities. The article argued that purposeful planning was key to the successful implementation of online education as opposed to disruption or radical transformation that may be damaging to an institution's culture. See: https://olj.onlinelearningconsortium.org/index.php/olj/issue/view/47

In 2017, *Theories and frameworks for online education: Seeking an integrated model* was published and was the most significant article I had ever published with respect to theory building. It examined a number of theoretical frameworks and models that focused on the pedagogical aspects of online education. It built on the work of Terry Anderson, one of the foremost distance education theorists in Canada. He and I exchanged ideas as I developed this article which took more than three years to write. After a review of learning theory as applied to online education, I proposed an integrated *Multimodal Model for Online Education* (see Figure 61.1) based on pedagogical purpose. This model has become especially important as blended learning evolves into the instructional modality of choice and because, as some would say, the "new normal." See: https://olj.onlinelearningconsortium.org/index.php/olj/article/view/1225

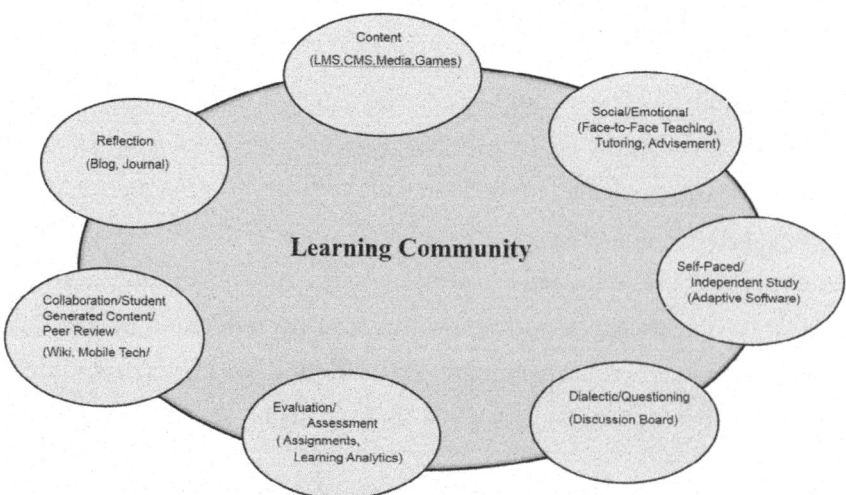

Figure 61.1 Multimodal Model for Online Education

In November 2016, Donald Trump was elected president in an upset victory over Hillary Clinton. This followed a year of bitter campaigning that saw Mr. Trump say and do anything to impassion the Republican base of voters. Having come from New York City, Trump was well-known as a huckster and bloviating egotist. Former Mayor Michael Bloomberg during the Democratic National Convention said it well when in front of national audience. "I am a New Yorker. I know a con artist when I see one!" I feel confident that I speak for the majority of faculty and students at the GC in saying we were appalled at the election of a man with no respect for facts or the dignity of others and no interest in intellectual endeavors of any kind. Trump went on to exhibit all of our worst fears during his four years as president.

Despite the many disturbing national trends that accompanied the election of 2016, the truly precious aspects of teaching in a PhD program continued to uplift me. The opportunity to develop deep relationships with students as they pursued their studies was my most rewarding experience at the Graduate Center. Working with students on their dissertations, which in most cases meant a two to four-year commitment, is different from teaching at any other level. You become a close adviser and colleague, involved with their research and their lives. A well-done dissertation exhausts so much time that it impacts everything else in a student's life. I was blessed with chairing or serving on over sixty dissertation committees. I cannot review everyone one of them here but let me say that I learned a great deal from these students and will always be grateful to them. I would like to mention several who represent a cross-section of the students with whom I was fortunate enough to work.

Chet Jordan was an instructor at Guttman Community College whose background was in literature. He wasn't sure what he wanted to focus on for his dissertation, but he took a course on higher education which I team-taught with Matt Goldstein, the CUNY Chancellor. He was hooked on studying higher education policy especially related to community colleges. He did a fine dissertation and we developed a close relationship. He is now the

Dean of Social Sciences and Professional Studies at Greenfield Community College in Massachusetts. He and I would co-author two books, one a history of CUNY, and the other an examination of community college policies in the post-2008 recession. He remains a good colleague and good friend of mine.

Deborah Greenblatt showed up at my office door one evening without an appointment and asked to speak to me about the PhD program. She had been a student of mine at Hunter College in the Administration & Supervision Program. We spoke for several minutes and she sold me that she had a lot to offer and would benefit from being in our program. She was absolutely right in her own self-assessment. She evolved into a first-rate researcher and is now an assistant professor at Medgar Evers College.

Joseph Nelson was in our program and was proceeding nicely when his chair and a member of his dissertation committee dropped him suddenly over an Institutional Review Board (IRB) issue. A question had arisen about whether he needed approval from CUNY if the project he was writing about was funded and already approved by the IRB at New York University. He came to see me and was ready to withdraw from the program. I suggested we try to work this bureaucratic issue out and I became his chair. He did an incredible dissertation on black boys' identity in a single-sex school for boys of color. He graduated and now teaches at Swarthmore College.

Eric Fuchs was a mathematician who worked in corporate finance on Wall Street. He was in Lower Manhattan at his office not very far from the Twin Towers when they were attacked and collapsed on 9/11. He could never face working again south of 14th Street and decided to change his career. He came to our program and focused his research on remedial mathematics education in community colleges. He completed his dissertation and is an assistant professor at Metropolitan College of New York where he coordinates its secondary education mathematics program.

Zoila Taisi was a principal at a small public early childhood school in Ossining, New York. Her dissertation was based on a grant program her school received to follow pre-K English Language Learners. She had never done quantitative research, but for her dissertation she did a time-series longitudinal study following students for three years. She graduated and gave up a sizeable principal's salary to be an associate professor at Mercy College.

Lee Gabay was a teacher at Passages Academy, a high school for incarcerated youth awaiting disposition of their criminal charges. His dissertation was based on his and his fellow teachers' experiences working with students whom they see for only a few months. The fortunate ones have their charges dismissed and go home; the unfortunate ones are sent to long-term youth correctional facilities in upstate New York. Lee graduated and continues to work as a high school teacher in New York City.

Liza Pappas was an activist student in our program. She was a student representative on several of our committees and was most helpful in moving along initiatives and activities that would benefit students and the program in general. In 2011, she regularly led cadres of students down to the Occupy Wall Street Movement. She and I had lunches and dinners together and even met once in Seattle when my wife and I were visiting our daughter. Upon graduation, she became a researcher with the New York City Independent Budget Office studying issues related to homeless students in the New York City public school system. Her studies received a good deal attention in the local press. Presently, she is the Executive Director of the *Grown Your Own* organization that seeks to attract minority students in Chicago to teach in the public schools.

Mark Dunetz and Danny Voloch were fine students in the program who had incredibly busy life and work schedules and were concerned about ever finishing our program. Danny, in particular, came to my office several times thinking he should withdraw from the program. I encouraged both to persevere and to stay the course. They both finished the program and today, Mark Dunetz is the president of New Visions for New Schools (NVNS) and

Danny is his vice president. NVNS is a major organization that develops and administers school reform initiatives for K-12 education.

Megan Moore-Wilk was a mother of two young children who was doing very demanding facilities planning work at CUNY Central. I don't know how she found the time to do her dissertation which was almost 600 pages long and examined the erosion of funding in state public higher education systems. It was a masterful piece of higher education policy research. She is now the Chief of Staff for the President of Queens College. She also recommended Ferdinand Verley, a colleague of hers, to our program. He completed his dissertation in 2020 and is now the Deputy University Capital Budget Director at City University of New York.

Patrick O'Reilly was an administrator in one of the school districts on Long Island. He asked to meet with me in 2012 with the expressed purpose of withdrawing from the program, having only the dissertation to complete. It was another of those situations where a talented student just has so many responsibilities that school seems impossible. I told him that I would not accept his withdrawal. Although I wasn't the chair of his dissertation committee, I told him he had all the ability in the world to finish, and I offered to help him through every stage until graduation. He defended his dissertation in January 2014 and went on to have a fine career as a school administrator.

Ashleigh Thompson worked primarily with my colleague Nick Michelli. She did a very insightful dissertation examining college students with disabilities and used CUNY as her case study. It was an eye-opening study and gained a good deal of attention. She currently is the Dean for Teacher Education for the entire CUNY system.

Annamarie Bianco worked as an assistant registrar at the College of Staten Island and worked for my wife. When she came to our program she was the CUNY University Registrar and was leading a multimillion-dollar system called CUNYFirst that would establish common administrative systems for the entire University. She left our program when she was offered the position of Associate Vice President & University Registrar at Georgetown University. She took a leave from our program and keeps in touch with me hoping one day to finish the PhD.

Roberto Martinez had been in our program for almost eight years and had exhausted his satisfactory progress options and was on the verge of withdrawing from the program. He had a demanding full-time position and workload as the Assistant Director of Graduate Advising & Student Services at New York University. He and I met and I encouraged him to stay the course. I offered to help him with his dissertation which focused on Mexican immigrant youth in New York City. He persisted, rededicated himself, graduated and is currently an assistant professor and program manager for the New York City Teaching Fellows Program at Brooklyn College.

Maryann Polesinelli was a student of mine in the Administration & Supervision Program at Hunter College in the early 2000s. She worked full-time at the New York City Department of Education and would bring her young daughter, Francesca, to classes on a regular basis. Francesca would sit in the front row and do her homework, and every once in a while would look up at me and give me a big smile. In fall 2016, Maryann was admitted to our PhD program. By that time, her daughter, Francesca, was already studying in another GC doctoral program in psychology. At the time of this writing, Maryann was finishing up her dissertation while working in a senior-level administrative position at the New York City Department of Education.

Kevin Froner who until 2008 worked at the American Stock Exchange when he decided he wanted to become an educator. Kevin approached me to assist him with his dissertation research, the purpose of which was "to deconstruct the dominant discourses shaping public education in America and to understand the ontological and genealogical roots of public education." I thought his topic was too broad and worked with him to focus and simplify his research objectives which he did and ended up doing a masterful dissertation. He currently is the principal of Manhattan Hunter Science High School and the Founding Director of the Gray Fellowship for Principal Excellence.

I inherited Chrystina Russell from another faculty member who didn't feel that Chrystina's research on blended learning fit his expertise. Most unusual about her research was that it involved the development and evaluation of higher education programs using blended learning at Kepler University in Kigali, Rwanda. She graduated and currently is the Executive Director of the Southern New Hampshire University's Global Education Movement working with higher education organizations in Africa.

Maureen Samedy was an academic adviser at the Marxe School of Public and International Affairs, Baruch College, when she came to our program. It took her more than four years to complete her dissertation. er topic Her topic was the legal issues involved in curriculum decisions at the University of Maryland. She specifically was going to compare major decisions at the historically black colleges to other colleges in the system. To collect her data, she interviewed several presidents over a summer and got their permission to survey faculty. When she distributed her survey, a directive came down from the University of Maryland Central Office prohibiting faculty and other personnel from participating in her data collection. She had to redo her research questions and change the nature of her study. She persevered, completed her dissertation and graduated in 2020. She is now the Associate Director of Academic Advisement at Marxe School of Public and International Affairs.

Derrick Griffith was a student in our program as well the Acting Dean of Student Affairs and Enrollment Management at Medgar Evers College. He and I developed a close relationship by virtue of our colleague, John Mogulescu, Derrick was completing the PhD in our program in order to cement a permanent appointment as the Dean at Medgar Evers College. He successfully defended his dissertation in February 2015 and was scheduled to receive his degree at the end of May. On May 13, 2015, he was one of eight passengers killed in an Amtrak train accident while coming back to New York from Washington, D.C. When I heard the news, I was among the many who were stunned and saddened. At his wake, funeral, and graduation in absentia, the tears flowed from family, friends and especially his students at Medgar Evers College.

I could go on to write blurbs about more than a hundred of my favorite students, but I hope that those I have highlighted provide some insight into how lucky I was to have worked and learned at the Graduate Center.

PART IX

CUNY Hunter College
New York, New York
2018-2021

62

In spring 2018, I met with Michael Middleton, the Dean of the School of Education at Hunter College, to work out a teaching schedule for the next year. We agreed that I would teach in the new EdD Program in Instructional Leadership, and the Administration and Supervision Program (ADSUP). As a result, I was assigned to teach two courses in the fall 2018: one, an education policy course in the EdD program, and the other was the ADSUP research methods course that I had taught for many years. I also was working with several doctoral students at the Graduate Center to round out my schedule.

I had several meetings with the previous Dean of Education, David Steiner, about the EdD program, and I had a number of reservations. The program was very prescriptive and had too many required courses and few electives. In fact, it was the exact opposite of the program my colleagues and I had designed for the PhD Program in Urban Education at the Graduate Center. The EdD program followed the Carnegie Project on the Education Doctorate (CPED) model and was designed to be very applied. Never-the-less, Dean Middleton wanted me to be involved with the EdD Program and to add my experience from my work at the Graduate Center. The coordinator of the program was Marshall George, who was very capable and adept at leading the CPED model. The faculty who taught in the program also taught in other teacher education programs at Hunter.

The students in my education policy course were in the third cohort of the program. I had nine students in the class who appeared capable of the work and interested in their doctoral studies. They were either school administrators or teachers working in traditional public schools or charter schools, and one at the college level. Their writing was up to par, which for me has always been an indicator of how well students would do in graduate study. During the course of the semester, I came to know them better, and found the majority of them to be excellent students and comparable to those in the PhD Program at the Graduate Center. One of them, Justin Gerald, was among the best students I have ever had in any program. He was completely passionate about his focus on race and English language teachers. Over the next year or so, he would write several papers, one of which was accepted for publication in a peer-reviewed journal.

I was welcomed back to the ADSUP by my colleagues, Janet Patti and Marcia Knoll. There were also two new faculty, Ben Shuldiner and Nell Panero. Ben and Nell were young, knowledgeable, and able colleagues. Ben was the coordinator for the program and appeared to me to be doing an excellent job. The program was doing very well and had over 250 students enrolled. Structurally, ADSUP was the same blended program that I had helped design back in 2005, but substantive changes had been made to update the content in several of the courses.

The ADSUP research methods course I would be teaching was the last course in the program and was paired with the internship/field experience course that was quite demanding in terms of student time. The majority of the students were teachers or beginning administrators without the formal title of assistant principal. This was especially the case for those working in charter schools. I would take this information into consideration as I reviewed and updated my syllabus especially the assignments. When teaching this course in the past, I had always set aside a three-week, hands-on module to review basic statistical concepts and data analysis using SPSS. I was pleasantly surprised to see that things had changed during my ten-year absence. Most of these students didn't need this module. They were familiar with and in some cases very knowledgeable about descriptive statistics. I asked where they developed their familiarity with data analysis and statistics, but I couldn't discern any specific pattern. It just seemed that their teacher education training as well as some of the work they were doing in their schools was exposing them to more quantitative analysis. I found this to be a very heartening development.

For both my courses, I set aside a number of sessions that would be taught online using threaded lists and/or Zoom software. I used the Blackboard course management system as the depository for readings and for its Discussion Board feature. One thing I noticed in the Zoom sessions was that many of the students used mobile devices such as iPhones and tablets to participate in class. In sum, I enjoyed working with the students in both courses and felt acclimated again to Hunter College.

63

My first year back at Hunter was also the final year of a two-plus year project that I was part of, and that funded by the United States Department of Education Institute of Education (USDOE). In January 2017, I received an email from Sarah Costelloe of Abt Associates of Bethesda, Maryland, asking if I might be interested in working on a research project with her company related to online learning. I had never done any work with Abt before and knew nothing about the company. It appeared to be a modest-size, legitimate think tank that did consulting and research for companies and governments on social issues. I emailed Sarah back and told her I might be interested. We had a telephone conversation during which I was convinced that Abt was a solid operation that had just received a major grant to conduct a modified meta-analysis of best practices in online learning at the postsecondary level. The project would be supervised by the Institute of Education Sciences (IES), a research arm of the USDOE that focused on quantitative research. This project would fall under the auspices of its *What Works Clearinghouse* (WWC) whose goal is to provide educators with the information needed to make evidence-based decisions gleaned from high-quality research using experimental designs. Sarah was most convincing and I agreed to be part of the project.

Our first meeting was in May 2017 in Bethesda. The team included five higher education representatives from around the country, six staff associates from Abt, and two officers from IES as follows:

Higher Education Expert Panel:

Nada Dabbagh, George Mason University

Randy Bass, Georgetown University

MJ Bishop, University System of Maryland

Anthony G. Picciano, City University of New York

Jennifer Sparrow, Pennsylvania State University

Abt Staff:

Sarah Costelloe

Kristen Cummings

Brian Freeman

Michael Frye

Allan Porowski

Sandra Jo Wilson

IES Officers:

Felicia Sanders

Christopher Weiss

All of the members of the team were accomplished professionals within their areas of expertise. The higher education expert panel included three faculty, an administrative leader, and an instructional designer. The Abt staff were all experienced data analysts. The IES officers provided oversight for the project and were especially attuned to maintaining the standards of IES.

The focus of this project was to examine the promising uses of technologies associated with improving postsecondary student learning outcomes. The main goal was to provide higher education instructors, instructional designers, administrators, and other staff with specific recommendations for supporting learning through the effective use of technology.

The IES review protocol defined the following: the purpose of the practice guide; interventions, populations, and outcomes covered by eligible research; the evidence criteria to be defined in reviews; and procedures for conducting the literature search. The protocol specified that studies used as evidence will examine interventions that incorporate technology to support student learning in various ways. In addition, to be eligible for the review, a research study had to:

- use a comparison group design (e.g., a randomized control trial or a quasi-experimental design).

- involve college students in the United States.

- be published in 1997 or later; and

- report on one or more outcomes in the following domains: (1) academic achievement, (2) college attendance, (3) credit accumulation and persistence, (4) attainment of a degree, certificate, or credential, (5) post-college employment and income, or (6) student engagement and motivation.

A comprehensive literature search was conducted to identify all studies potentially relevant to the practice guide. The search focused on studies published between 1997 and 2017 that examined practices for using technology to support learning in postsecondary settings. The studies were primarily identified through keyword searches of several databases and supplemented with additional studies recommended by the expert panel. The literature search generated more than 50,000 studies. All studies were screened for eligibility for the practice guide, using the criteria defined in the review protocol above. Eligible studies were then reviewed by WWC-certified staff against the standards defined in the What Works Clearinghouse Procedures and Standards Handbook, Version 3.0.55. Once the review was complete, studies were assigned one of the following evidence ratings:

- Meets WWC Group Design Standards Without Reservations.

- Meets WWC Group Design Standards With Reservations; or

- Does Not Meet WWC Group Design Standards.

Studies that met WWC standards, either with or without reservations, were classified as having a positive or negative effect on student outcomes provided the findings were statistically significant. The number of studies that the WWC identified, screened, deemed eligible, and ultimately included as supporting evidence in the practice guide can be found in Figure 63.1.

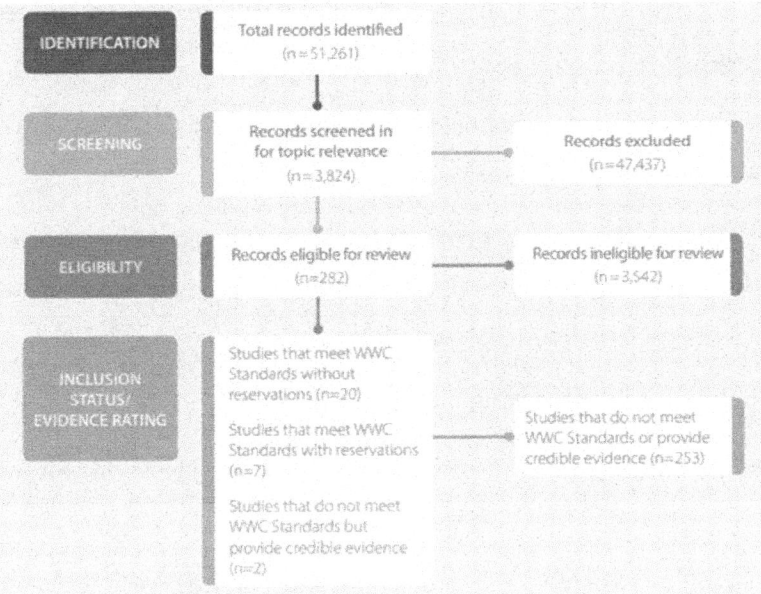

Figure 63.1 Studies Identified, Screened, and Reviewed for Inclusion in the Project

The work and effort that went into this project was enormous and I was impressed with the effort of the Abt staff. It took about eighteen months for the studies to be selected and reviewed for inclusion the project. The IES officers required strict adherence to its protocols throughout the process.

The major task of the higher education expert panel was to develop the set of recommendations that would go into the final report. There were close to a dozen meetings both in-person and via videoconferencing to reach agreement on the recommendations and their rank order. These sessions were intense, with a good deal of disagreement on the wording of the recommendations and their order. Through consensus, we generated a final list of recommendations as follows:

1. Use communication and collaboration tools to increase interaction among students and between students and instructors.

2. Use varied, personalized, and readily available digital resources to design and deliver instructional content.

3. Incorporate technology that models and fosters self-regulated learning strategies.

4. Use technology to provide timely and targeted feedback on student performance.

5. Use simulation technologies that help students engage in complex problem-solving.

Accompanying these recommendations were suggestions for how to design technology-based instruction to meet them.

Just at the end of my first year back at Hunter College, we finished writing and issuing the final report entitled, *Using Technology to Support Postsecondary Student Learning: A Practice Guide for College and University Administrators, Advisors, and Faculty,* in May 2019. It is available as a free download at: https://ies.ed.gov/ncee/wwc/PracticeGuide/25

I found the entire effort to be a worthwhile learning experience. The examination and synthesizing of the data were an education. The discussion among a group of very knowledgeable individuals was exhilarating and exhausting in a good way. Participating in a well-organized review and meta-analysis of the extensive online learning research was an unexpected opportunity. I'm glad I didn't pass it up.

64

I n 2018, I started writing a book that was about as different from the USDOE Abt report as can be imagined. The USDOE Abt report was a quantitative intense study of an important current topic that related to my professional interests in instructional technology. A year earlier, I had decided that I wanted to write a novel focusing on growing up in an old-time Italian neighborhood in the South Bronx in the 1950s and 1960s. I had never written fiction before and I am not a frequent reader of fiction, but as is the wont of many first-time novelists, my book would be based on my own experiences as a child and into early adulthood. I had gotten the idea for this book a good dozen or more years earlier while attending some informal reunion lunches with eight or nine friends of mine once or twice a year. Stories were told over and over again and I began to believe that I should document some of them. My wife asked several times who would ever read this book. My response was always the same: as long as you, our kids, grandkids and a few friends read it, I'll be happy.

I started outlining the book and organizing the stories in 2017. Then, in 2018, I actually started writing chapters until I had completed about 70,000 words. I edited, reedited and edited some more. I found writing fiction to be a real challenge and even thought about giving up on the project. I found writing dialogue to be particularly difficult. My previous seventeen books and numerous articles of non-fiction were no help at all. It took me a while to gain some control, but I never really mastered it. I also realized that I wanted the reader to be aware of the parts of the book that were true even though it was a work of fiction. I decided to use a convention that I came across while reading *The Shakespeare Conspiracy* by Ted Bacino. This novel, based on the theory that Shakespeare's plays were actually written by Christopher Marlowe, contained numerous facts. The author decided to include historical notes at the end of the book where he gave brief summaries of what was fact and what was fiction. I decided to do the same. Another challenging aspect of writing this novel was that I had to develop plots and subplots to keep the reader wanting to see how they would play out as they got deeper into the book. This kept me lying in bed at night thinking about what I would be writing in the next chapter.

In fall 2019, I gave a draft to my wife who edits all my work and is my severest critic. She also is completely devoted to fiction and averages at least a book a week. Depending upon what she said, I would decide to publish it or not. It took her about three weeks to edit but she liked it. She said she cried reading the sad parts and laughed at the funny parts. After receiving her edits, I went back and edited the book one more time. The only problem was I didn't have a title. One night while trying to fall asleep, I started thinking about my grandmother who is a major character in the book, and in whose house we lived in the South Bronx. *Our Bathtub Wasn't in the Kitchen Anymore* came to me. The title reflects that our bathtub was, in fact, in the kitchen and was the place where baths were taken, clothes were washed, and with the cover on it, food was prepared. Midway through the book my family moves to the North Bronx where we have two bathrooms, one of which has a bathtub and shower. And life is never the same.

I had one more decision to make before sending my book to a publisher, whether or not to use my real name or a pen name. I had spoken to a colleague of mine who used a pen name to separate his personal writing from his professional, discipline-based writing. I also recalled that the author Evan Hunter, whose name was Salvatore Lombino, took his pen name from two schools he attended: Evander Childs High School on Gun Hill Road in the North Bronx and Hunter College on the East Side of Manhattan. Many crime fiction enthusiasts would also know him as Ed McBain who wrote a series of novels about the 87th Police Precinct. I decided I too would use a pen name, but it had to have some significance. I decided on Gerade DeMichele. Gerade is my middle name, which was given to me by accident at birth. My mother wanted my middle name to be Gerard, but I was delivered by a midwife who misspelled Gerard on the document she filed with the Health Department. DeMichele is the maiden and married name of my grandmother who married her first cousin. So, for purposes of this novel, I decided on Gerade DeMichele, and a google search found no other.

When it came time to do the cover, I thought again about my grandmother. I had one old picture of her in my office. I decided she would be on the cover with a bathtub in a kitchen behind her (see Figure 64.1 below). My wife actually put together the cover and I was amazed at what a good job she did with my grandmother's photo since it was over sixty years old.

The book was published in April 2020. I bought a number of copies and sent them to friends from the old neighborhood and colleagues. The response was quite positive. My colleague, Joel Spring, a member of the Choctaw Nation who was raised on the West Coast, and whose background is quite different than mine, posted this blurb on Amazon.com:

A detailed and engrossing account of growing up in an Italian neighborhood in the South Bronx in the 1950's and 1960's. The 1955 movie *Blackboard Jungle* is based on the Bronx Vocational school located in the neighborhood. The neighborhood is a strong community linked by family ties, friendships and the local Catholic Church. Its destruction came with urban renewal upending the neighborhood and scattering families. In his high school years, the narrator retains his ties to the old neighborhood and helps establish a social club near his old home. Just a beautiful story. (J. Spring, 2020, https://www. amazon.com/gp/customer-reviews/R309I605Q8VQHO/ref=cm_ cr_dp_d_rvw_ttl?ie=UTF8&ASIN=1543999727)

I was elated when my novel won third place for urban fiction in the Readers Favorite Book Review and Awards Contest. A reviewer for the award wrote:

Our Bathtub Wasn't in the Kitchen Anymore is a work of fiction in the historical, coming of age and urban life sub-genres, and was penned by author Gerade DeMichele. Set in the 1950s and 1960s in the United States of America, this heartfelt tale follows its protagonist through the experiences of growing up in an Italian family in the South Bronx. From deeply entrenched Catholicism to street violence, hopeful dreams, and gentrification, the work explores how this young man and his wider community try to survive and stay together. What results is a very emotional and realistic work of fiction with plenty of cultural delights and true heart.

Author Gerade DeMichele has crafted a highly immersive and heartfelt novel that clearly comes from a true place deep in the author's heart. Readers who have experienced this life and culture are sure to find it an experience of pure nostalgia, but there's also plenty of trials and tribulations in the plot which keep it fresh and exciting. Despite its historical setting, the work has ties to its future and its place in the world, which makes this a highly accessible read for those who weren't around at the time but want to learn more about the heritage. One of the features which I enjoyed a great deal about the novel was its flair for dialogue, which really characterizes different figures uniquely, and delivers such a deep understanding of the culture and bone among people. Overall, I would highly recommend *Our Bathtub Wasn't in the Kitchen Anymore* to all historical urban fiction fans. (K.C. Finn, 2020, https://www.geradedemichele.com/)

I couldn't have been happier with my decision to write and publish this novel. And that comment about the dialog ? What a surprise!

Figure 64.1 Cover of *Our Bathtub Wasn't in the Kitchen Anymore!*

Over the course of my career, and especially during presentations, I would be asked questions from the audience regarding the future. In recent years, these questions have taken on a sense of concern on the part of educators as to the role technology will have on their practice. In 2017, I started developing a model (see Figure 64.2) on man-machine interfacing that I have used to explain where the technology is going and its effects on society and especially education. In 2019, I published an article entitled, *Artificial*

Intelligence and the Academia's Loss of Purpose, that speculates on the future of higher education as online technology, specifically adaptive learning and analytics as infused by artificial intelligence software, develops and matures. Online and adaptive learning have already advanced within the academy, but the most significant changes are yet to come. These evolving technologies have the potential to change the traditional roles in our colleges and universities to the point that many educators will reconsider their purposes as teachers, researchers, and administrators. I didn't choose this title to be provocative but because it represents my view based on fifty years of experience as to where higher education is heading in the not-too-distant future. The article is available at: https://olj.onlinelearningconsortium.org/index. php/olj/article/view/2023

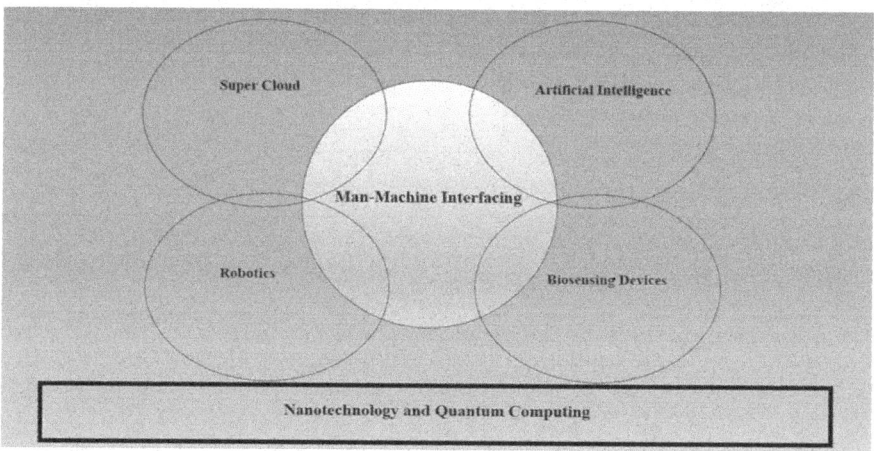

Figure 64.2 – Technology Forces Shaping the Future of Man-Machine Interfacing

A few years ago, a young associate professor approached me after I had given a talk about online education. Our discussion centered on the future of higher education and she asked if I thought that in ten years she would be out of a job. My answer to her was that she would not be displaced anytime soon, but that the way she teaches would change. I stand by that comment. Educators must be alert to new technologies, and adjust, change and adapt to those that may benefit their students. These changes are best implemented through carefully planned and developed projects, programs, and initiatives rather than by disruptive sudden upheavals. It is critical that colleges and universities be open to changing and adapting. Higher education will have no choice but to use technologies that are beneficial at the same time question those that are not. Most importantly, the technology cannot be ignored.

65

I am writing this chapter in spring 2021. The past twelve months have been as consequential a period as any for our country in the past fifty years. On January 30, 2020, the World Health Organization declared the coronavirus outbreak that started in Wuhan, China, a global health emergency. Here in the United States, we were becoming concerned about its spread, especially those of us who lived in and around large urban areas where international travel was common. By March 1st, our worst fears were being realized. Wearing masks, social distancing, closing restaurants and other retail establishments as well as other restrictions were implemented. Our schools and colleges were ordered to close and move to online or remote learning. At the time of this writing, the pandemic had infected over 100 million people worldwide with more than 2 million deaths. In the United States, there were 26 million cases and almost than 600,000 deaths.

On May 25, 2020, Minneapolis police officers arrested George Floyd, a 46-year-old black man, after a convenience store employee called 911 and told the police that Mr. Floyd had bought cigarettes with a counterfeit $20 bill. Seventeen minutes after the first squad car arrived at the scene, Mr. Floyd was unconscious and pinned beneath three police officers, showing no signs of life. Video showed one officer, Derek Chauvin, kneeling on top of Floyd's neck even as he and onlookers called out for help. Floyd suffocated and died. The next evening protests against police brutality erupted in Minneapolis and within days spread throughout the country and internationally. Here in New York, the protests were largely peaceful, although some violence and destruction occurred late at night. Floyd's death sparked months of demonstrations and rejuvenated the Black Lives Matter Movement that started in 2013. America had to look itself in the mirror and ask how we have let racial inequality and prejudice continue for so long. On April 19, 2021, Derek Chauvrin was found guilty on three counts of murder and manslaughter.

In the Summer of 2020, the presidential election picked up steam as Joe Biden and Kamala Harris emerged as the candidates for president and vice president for the Democratic Party. They would run against incumbent Republicans Donald Trump and Mike Pence, whose four years in office were controversial at best. While polls showed Biden and Harris winning by modest margins, the experience of the 2016 election when Trump defeated Hillary Clinton even though polls showed it would be otherwise, was still on people's minds. Although all of the television networks had called the election after two days, the 2020 election tally went on for almost a week beyond Election Day before Biden and Harris appeared to have taken an incontrovertible lead. Trump, however, refused to concede and claimed the election was "rigged." Most of his ardent supporters believed him and there were more than sixty legal challenges in a half dozen states, all of which were dismissed. On January 6th, 2021, an insurrection occurred following a rally for Trump during which he urged his followers to march to the Capitol Building and claim victory. The insurrection resulted in destruction and murder. Five people would die as a result including one police officer. Seeing the live television images of the desecration of one of our most treasured institutions reminded me of Friday, November 22, 1963, when John F. Kennedy was assassinated. These images, as the entire US government (with the exception of Trump) was forced to flee, haunted me and they haunt our nation to this day.

I have to admit that during 2020 and 2021, the subjects of my classes at times seemed less important and my students and I needed to have discussions with each other about more important national issues. Because of the pandemic, we were locked down in our homes and didn't have the normal opportunities to socialize, converse and share with colleagues. The faculty and I in the Administration and Supervision Program adjusted to teaching our courses online. However, the situation was difficult and in some cases impossible for many of my faculty colleagues as well as my students, almost all of whom were educators in New York City schools. They were thrust suddenly into teaching online and given a week or two to prepare. For those teachers who had never taught online, this was a completely new world. While some succeeded, many did not. There were major issues regarding access to wi-fi and computer technology and the ability of young students and those with special needs to understand what the new learning environment was about. Furthermore, no one envisioned in early 2020 this would be the new normal for another year and more. As the situation dragged on, national events further sapped our fortitude and resolve.

I conclude this chapter with hope as vaccines for coronavirus are now being distributed and millions of people are being inoculated. President Joe Biden and Vice President Kamala Harris are beginning to steady the ship that is our nation; other issues related to race, partisanship, violence, and respect for our democratic institutions still need the good will of all if we are to heal.

APPENDIX A

Developing an Asynchronous Course Model at a Large, Urban University appeared in Volume 2, Issue 1 of the *Journal of Asynchronous Learning Networks* (JALN in 1998). This was the first article I wrote on online learning. It was used extensively at professional development workshops and presentations in the late 1990s and early 2000s.

Developing an Asynchronous Course Model at a Large, Urban University

Anthony G. Picciano

Professor, Division of Programs in Education, Department of Curriculum and Teaching,

Hunter College of the City University of New York, 695 Park Avenue, New York, NY 10021 e-mail : antho13926@aol.com

Abstract

In Spring 1997, Hunter College offered the first asynchronous learning course in the City University of New York (CUNY), the largest urban university system in the United States enrolling 200,000 students in undergraduate and graduate programs. This graduate course, entitled <u>Administration and Supervision of the Public Schools - The Principalship</u>, was offered in the Division of Programs in Education. Funded by the Alfred P. Sloan Foundation, this course was intended to serve as a model for other courses at Hunter College and CUNY.

While many colleges have begun to offer asynchronous learning courses, the model presented here may be of special interest since it takes into consideration several variables of importance in large urban environments. First, all of the students in this course were adult, part-time students who delicately balance studies, careers, and families in their daily lives. In this respect, they represented a typical urban commuter population that would benefit from the convenience of asynchronous learning. Second, all of the students were commuter students who participated in the course via equipment located in their homes and offices. As a result, the model had to accept a wide variety of on-line services as the means of participation. Third, these students did not possess extensive technical skills and in terms of expertise could be classified as new to intermediate. This required that the model employ simple software interfaces that would minimize student frustration due to technical difficulties. Lastly, all of these students already had earned master's degrees and were teachers in the New York City metropolitan area. As experienced teachers, they are attuned to pedagogy and could provide valuable insight into an evaluation of the instructional components of the model.

The purpose of this paper is to share the results of a student evaluation of the instructional components of an asynchronous model that might be beneficial to others who are considering using this technology in similar environments.

Keywords

Asynchronous learning

Computer-mediated learning

Computer-mediated instruction

Computer-mediated communications

Distance learning

Education administration

I. INTRODUCTION

On April 9, 1997, educators from twenty-two countries met in Salzburg, Austria to attend a nine-day seminar on distance learning. The focus of the seminar was to share experiences in planning and implementing distance learning projects for teaching English as a foreign language in their countries. In Iceland, radio transmission is used to provide instruction to fishermen who spend weeks at sea. In Indonesia, television is used to provide basic language literacy to inhabitants of the hundreds of islands that make up this country. In India and Pakistan, a combination of mail, television, and the Internet is being considered to improve English language skills in villages in the remote northern mountain provinces. When considering distance learning, images of great distances or geographic obstacles are frequently invoked to provide a basic rationale for why alternate forms of instruction are required. However, this may not always be the case.

Students who lead busy lives in large metropolitan areas such as New York City are showing an interest in taking distance learning courses in their homes or places of business because of the increasing time demands of their families or jobs. At City University of New York (CUNY), the largest urban university in the United States, with more than 200,000 students in twenty colleges within the confines of 321 square miles, the first asynchronous learning course using the Internet was conducted at Hunter College in Spring 1997. This graduate course, entitled <u>Administration and Supervision of the Public Schools - The Principalship</u>, was offered in the Division of Programs in Education. Funded by the Alfred P. Sloan Foundation, it was intended to serve as a model for other courses at Hunter College and CUNY. If successful, it was anticipated that faculty and students in other CUNY colleges would consider taking advantage of this type of learning. The purpose of this study was to examine student learning experiences particularly with regard to issues of instructional design as applied to the asynchronous learning model used in this course at Hunter College.

Asynchronous learning has been used in various forms throughout the world for decades. The United Kingdom's Open University serves as one of the more successful models of this type of learning. However, the term asynchronous learning has been made popular in the United States in recent years because of the major funding provided by the Sloan Foundation program for asynchronous learning networks (ALN). It is related to the terms, computer-mediated learning, computer-mediated instruction, and computer-mediated communications, in which the computer is used as a tool for supporting instructional activities. For purposes of this study, asynchronous learning is defined as learning at anytime or in anyplace using Internet and World Wide Web software tools (e-mail, electronic bulletin boards, and Web pages) as the main vehicles for instruction.

II. REVIEW OF THE LITERATURE

It is not the intent here to undertake an extensive review of the literature on distance learning.

Excellent reviews have been provided in recent years by Schlosser and Anderson [1], Moore and Kearsley [2], and Sherry [3], However, a brief look at some of the current literature on asynchronous learning would be helpful for framing the subject of this study. More specifically, since the focus of this study was student learning experiences and issues of instructional design, research related to this aspect of asynchronous learning was reviewed.

A fundamental aspect of learning is the social and communicative interactions between student and teacher, and student and student. This is true in face-to-face as well as asynchronous learning activities [4]. The ability to ask a question, to share an opinion with a fellow student, or to disagree with the point of view in a reading assignment is critical to student learning. Several aspects of asynchronous learning require adjustments on the part of students and teachers for successful interactions to occur.

Ruberg, Taylor, and Moore [5] observed that students must adjust to the non-linear nature of asynchronous learning that is not typical in face-to-face situations which tend to be linear focusing on a single discussion thread. Asynchronous learning sessions can have multiple threads with several discussions and interactions progressing. Students can be responding to the teacher but also to other students depending on their interest and point of view. Students can initiate a new discussion as easily as the teacher. In this respect, asynchronous learning can empower students and allow them to participate on an equal basis with the teacher in establishing and pursuing discussion topics.

With this empowerment comes responsibility and an important aspect of a successful asynchronous learning activity is whether or not students adjust to this new role [6]. Teachers find they have to allow students to exercise and develop this responsibility. A teacher becomes a facilitator of instruction and assists students in pursuing threads within a discussion that the students determine are important. Lippman [7] and Anderson [8] refer to this as creating a "community of inquiry" wherein all participants are equal and able to initiate or pursue topics as they wish.

Developing this community of inquiry is not without potential problems. Students in this environment need to understand their responsibility for being active contributors to instruction. They cannot assume that others, either teachers or students, will simply carry the instructional load. This favors a more mature student who is self-directed and willing to take on responsibility for learning. To a degree, this supports findings that mature, motivated students are typically better suited for asynchronous and distance learning activities [2].

In addition to accepting responsibility, students also need to have the experience and knowledge base to sift the discussion for misinformation. Sproull and Kiesler [9] caution about discussions that continue based on misinformation because in asynchronous mode an instructor cannot immediately correct or clarify a comment. This may be dismissed as not a serious issue but with the amount of information being provided, this can be more troublesome than it appears. In asynchronous learning, the amount of student participation can increase, and the number of comments can easily lead to what Mackay [10] described as information overload. Furthermore, comments in on-line discussions tend to be longer than in face-to-face situations. With more information from many sources, students need to be more attentive to both the who and what of a discussion. Herbert Simon, economist and Nobel Prize laureate, succinctly cautions that "a wealth of information can create a poverty of attention," ([11], p. 200).

Another aspect of interaction and communication that can be problematic in an asynchronous environment is the loss of visual clues during a discussion. Body language is important in a face-to-face classroom discussion. A smile on a student's face is interpreted by the teacher as a sign of understanding; a student nervously looking at his wristwatch is interpreted as boredom or lack of patience. On the other hand, a teacher motivates or provides emphasis with inflection or hand movement. However, Sproull and Kiesler [9] point out that while these visual signs may be helpful, if misinterpreted, they may also be detrimental. Regardless, they exist and duplicating visual clues in an on-line discussion is not that simple. Other clues may be identifiable by closely reading wording or the turn of a phrase in an e-mail message or posting.

Technical issues associated with student participation in asynchronous discussions cannot be minimized particularly if access takes place in homes or in places of business. It is difficult to control these environments and the students again must assume a certain responsibility for assuring their access to technology. Teachers likewise need to become familiar with the technology so as to be able to use it routinely but also to assist students having technical problems. Sherry [3] emphasizes that instructional needs of students and not the technology must be the focus of learning. Situations wherein students or teachers are having technical difficulties distract from the major learning objectives. On the other hand, technology may initially be perceived as chic with a bit of wonder. Students willingly participate because of the novelty or "fun" of using technology. Trentin [12] observed that network-based learning can quickly fall into a "rut" if activities are not well-organized and structured to last for the duration of the learning cycle or period. Well-presented content in the final analysis is as important as the technology.

In summary, a good deal of research has been conducted on distance learning. However, as technology advances and changes, so do the issues associated with the design of instructional models. While researchers can draw from the past for insight, new situations using new technology require continual study and evaluation. As the Internet and other network-based technologies advance, opportunities arise for developing new approaches to instruction such as asynchronous learning networks. As educators attempt to develop and implement these approaches, on-going evaluation and study particularly from the student perspective will be necessary.

III. METHODOLOGY

A. The Course - ADSUP 702

The Education Administration and Supervision Program at Hunter College is a thirty-credit graduate program leading to New York State certification as a school administrator. New York State requires a minimum of eighteen graduate credits plus an internship. The program at Hunter requires twenty-four credits (eight courses) plus six credits for an internship.

The course offered in an asynchronous learning mode entitled, Administration and Supervision (ADSUP) 702 - <u>Organization and Administration of the Public Schools - The Principalship</u>, is a required course. This course is designed as an introduction to the issues of school organization and administration. These include leadership, school finance, curriculum, and dealing with various building-level constituents. The course examines the principal as both the instructional and administrative leader in the teaching/learning environment. It was considered to be appropriate for asynchronous delivery because it requires a good deal of self-directed reading and study on the part of students as is appropriate for advanced graduate studies. Faculty teaching this course guide students as they pursue topics as well as formally teach subject matter.

B. The Students

To enroll in the graduate program in Education Administration and Supervision at Hunter College, all students must have at least five years of teaching experience and earned master's degrees. More than 80% are women. Approximately 25% are students from minority groupings. Almost all of them pay their own tuition which for some is a financial burden. Some students have made the decision to attend classes rather than take on a second job as coaches, tutors, or other after-school positions. Approximately 80% percent of these students work in New York City public schools while the remaining 20% work in private schools or in public schools outside of New York City. For the past ten years, the program has maintained an enrollment of 100 to 125 students, almost all of whom are part-time. Because of funding and a desire to ensure academic quality, the enrollment in the program has been limited.

All of the students are education professionals already certified as teachers by New York State. They are dedicated to their profession and are expending enormous energy in improving their skills and abilities in order to become school administrators (principals, assistant principals, directors of programs). New York State, like most states, requires a graduate program for individuals to become certified as school administrators. These students represent a group of self-starters who are conscientious and view their studies as vehicles for professional growth and advancement. They recognize the importance of technology and approximately 40% of the program's enrollees have access to computer and Internet technology either in their homes or in their schools. Many of these students are professionally curious about an alternative pedagogical experience such as asynchronous learning using the Internet and other current technological tools.

All of the students are commuters who balance full-time jobs, families, parenthood, and higher education in a carefully planned day which includes rushing for subways and buses to meet the next commitment. They are a mature group who organize their daily lives around lesson plans, making sure their children get to the babysitter or day care center, maintaining a home, and when time permits, completing homework assignments. Offering a course to them that can be taken at anytime or in anyplace would surely have a good deal of appeal. They would be able to fit their graduate studies into their busy lives and eliminate the need to travel several times per week to the College. For the purposes of experimenting with a distance learning model, these students typify the mature, self-directed, and busy "students" who could take advantage of and benefit from this form of instruction.

From the group described above, seventeen (N=17) students enrolled in ADSUP 702 for Spring 1997. Their average age was thirty-six years. Thirteen were female and four were male. The ethnic composition was as follows: two were African-American; two were Latino, and thirteen were White/Caucasian. All of these students volunteered to take this course. Thirteen of the students accessed the Internet at home, two had access in their schools, and two had access at home and school.

C. Instructional Components

The model for delivering this course asynchronously was designed to utilize the Internet, World

Wide Web, LISTSERV, and e-mail facilities. Prior to Spring 1997, the instructor had been using World Wide Web software and e-mail to enhance courses taught in traditional settings. Students had been able to access syllabi, assignments, and lecture notes via Web pages in these courses. Students had also been able to make one-to-one inquiries of the instructor using e-mail. However, actually teaching using any of the above technologies had not been attempted at Hunter College until Spring 1997. To deliver instruction and to provide the basic interactive components, LISTSERV software was used to conduct on-line group discussions. Students used e-mail software to connect to a LISTSERV that was set up specifically for the course. The instructor conducting the course was responsible for establishing and administering the LIST.

The course was organized according to themes and weekly topics. The Web site (see URL: http://discovery.hunter.cuny.edu/~tpiccian/ad702297.html) for the course contained twenty-four Web pages that included a syllabus, reading assignments, weekly discussion topics and questions, supplementary reading material, and related links. These materials were always available and served as the organizational anchors for the course. Each topic was organized for discussion on the LISTSERV during a specific week and based on assigned readings and case studies. Four students were selected each week along with the instructor to be the co-discussion leaders. The use of students as co-discussion leaders was designed to encourage them to be contributors to and not simply receivers of learning activities. Once the discussion of a topic commenced on Monday morning, any student could contribute to the discussion, ask a question of another student or the instructor. At the end of a week's discussion, the instructor summarized the topic, added additional notes and comments, and posted these to the Web site for access by the entire class.

To connect to the LISTSERV, students used any commercial or other Internet and e-mail provider such as America On-line, Compuserve, or Prodigy. While utilization of a communications software package such as Lotus Notes was considered, it was determined that it would be too cumbersome to require all the students to acquire and load this software on their computer systems at home or in their schools.

To provide students with a "comfort level" in using asynchronous technology for instruction, monthly evaluation sessions were held in which students met with the instructor as a group. Individual meetings with the instructor were also available during regularly scheduled conference times. While all students participated in the monthly sessions, very few students met privately with the instructor for a conference and instead used e-mail extensively for one-to-one inquiries and discussions with the instructor.

D. Evaluation Techniques

As stated earlier, the major purpose of this study was to examine the student learning experiences in taking an asynchronous course. To accomplish this, a combination of quantitative and qualitative data was collected. Students were asked to keep logs of their weekly activities for certain periods which they turned in to the instructor. Students completed satisfaction surveys at the fifth week and again at the end of the course (fourteenth week). At the end of the course, students were also asked to write an evaluation of their experiences with the course addressing specific questions such as:

1. Do you feel that this course was successful for you?
2. Do you feel that your overall learning was less than, about the same, or greater than in a traditional course?
3. If successful, what aspects of the course contributed to its success?
4. If unsuccessful, what aspects of the course proved problematic for you?
5. What suggestions do you have for improving this course?
6. Would you take another asynchronous learning course if offered here at Hunter College?
7. Would you recommend that other students in the Administration and Supervision Program take an asynchronous learning course?

8. Provide any other comments that you think would be helpful for this evaluation.

No attempt was made to gather specific student performance data for this study. Performance data may be incorporated into a future study Grading for the course was based on writing assignments, class participation especially as discussion leaders, and a term project. Students had the option of submitting their assignments via e-mail or through the regular mail.

IV. RESULTS

A. Student Participation

Critical to an instructional activity is the level of participation which was measured by monitoring weekly on-line postings to the LISTSERV. Data was maintained by both students and the instructor during the length (fourteen weeks) of the course. On average, students made 30.66 postings per week on the LISTSERV ranging from 17 to 46 postings per week, or almost two (1.81) postings per student per week. The lowest number of postings (17) occurred during Week 1. The instructor made on average 4.5 postings per week. The number of individual students posting on the LISTSERV averaged 15.08 students per week with a range of 12 to 17 students. This represents an 88.7% average weekly participation on the part of students. This compares favorably if not exceeds many traditional, face-to-face classes. Students accepted the responsibilities of their roles as active participants in teaching and learning. In discussing their participation, students commented that the technique of using them as co-discussion leaders contributed to their active participation. Students were not only responding to the instructor but also to comments and questions raised by several of their colleagues. This technique worked well and is highly recommended to others considering developing asynchronous learning models.

In addition to the number of postings, students were asked to maintain time-logs for several weeks during the course. These time-logs recorded any course-related on-line activity whether reading a fellow student's posting, entering one's own posting, e-mailing the instructor, or accessing the course's Web site. They were not to reflect time spent doing reading or writing assignments. The traditional face-to-face class time for this course is 100 minutes (2 fifty-minute sessions) plus optional conference time with the instructor. For one sample week, students logged on an average of 5.64 times and averaged 147 minutes of on-line activity with a range of 125 minutes to 180 minutes. This provides an overview of "class" time and indicates that many students were engaged almost daily and for longer periods than would normally occur in a traditional face-to-face course. However, these figures should be interpreted carefully because student efficiency in using LISTSERV and e-mail facilities varied. For example, some students composed e-mail messages and postings while logged on while others composed messages off-line on word processors and then simply "copied and pasted" them while on-line.

Overall, students spent more time directly in "class" in the asynchronous course than they would have in a traditional course. Postings to the LISTSERV were frequently two or three paragraphs and required the students to read carefully their colleagues' comments. Likewise, in developing their own postings, students tended to reflect and think through their comments. In this respect, the asynchronous course seemed to provide more opportunity for reflective practice than spontaneous reaction as is typical in a traditional class.

B. Student Satisfaction Survey

Data on student satisfaction with their learning experiences were measured using a student satisfaction survey administered at the fifth week and at again at the fourteenth week of the semester. The survey, designed specifically for this course, asked a series of questions regarding student experiences in taking this course in comparison to traditional face-to-face courses. The survey was administered twice to determine if there was any change in student satisfaction during the length of the course. In the data provided in Table 1, responses were based on a five-point Likert scale with 1= decreased, 2 = somewhat decreased, 3 = no change, 4 = somewhat increased, and 5 = increased. A sample question was: "In comparison to a traditional class, in

this course the quantity (or quality) of interaction decreased -> increased?"
The means of the student responses to the items are summarized in Table 1.

Survey Item	5th Week	14th Week	Total
Amount of interaction with other students decreased/ increased	4.12	3.88	4.00
Quality of interaction with other students decreased/ increased	4.29	4.29	4.29
Amount of interaction with the instructor decreased/ increased	3.82	4.06	3.94
Quality of interaction with the instructor decreased/ increased	4.06	4.41	4.23
Quantity of your learning experience decreased/ increased	4.06*	4.64*	4.35
Quality of your learning experience decreased/ increased	4.41	4.53	4.47
Motivation to participate in class activities decreased/ increased	4.35	4.47	4.41
Overall Experience poor/excellent	4.41	4.70	4.56

Mean Responses (N=17) *Statistically Significant Difference at the .05 Level

Table 1. Student Satisfaction with the Course

The data in Table 1 indicates that a high level of student satisfaction with their learning experiences was present at both intervals (fifth and fourteenth weeks). With the exception of the "quantity of your learning experiences" students were consistent in their responses on all questions.

The "quantity of your learning experiences" was the only question that had a statistically significant difference in Week 5 compared to Week 14. One interpretation of this difference was that after fourteen weeks, the students were exposed to significantly more material than after five weeks and hence the "quantity of learning experiences" increased.

This was the first time that any of these students had taken an asynchronous course. While all had access to the Internet, they were not necessarily highly experienced computer users. Most of them considered themselves intermediate computer users. In designing the technological components of the course, a significant effort was made to keep them simple and less intrusive into the instructional process and to minimize student frustration with the technology. A series of questions was asked of the students with regard to their experiences with using technology for this course. Responses were based on a four-point scale with 1= not a problem, 2 = minor problem, 3 = moderate problem, and 4 = major problem. The means of the student responses to these items are summarized in Table 2.

Survey Item	5th Week	14th Week	Total
My familiarity with technology was not a problem/major problem	1.18	1.18	1.18
Ability to get on-line was not a problem/major problem because of time constraints	1.53	1.59	1.56
Ability to get on-line was not a problem/major problem because of technical difficulties	1.35	1.35	1.35
Use of the computer took more time than it was worth was not a problem/major problem	1.06	1.06	1.06
Using technology in this course was easy/difficult	1.29	1.35	1.32

Mean Responses (N=17)

Table 2. Experiences with the Use of Technology in the Course

The results in Table 2 indicate that the technology in general was easy to use and did not pose any significant problem in allowing students to participate in class activities. In discussing the survey results with the students, the only major comment with regard to using the technology was with the difficulty especially in February and March, of logging on to the America On-Line service. It was during this period that America On-line experienced significant congestion due to oversubscribing its service. Most students, however, quickly learned that logging on at non-peak hours (early morning/late night) enhanced their ability to connect to the service.

C. Selected Student Evaluation Comments

Students were asked to write an evaluation of the course and to respond to specific questions enumerated in the methodology above. Generally, the student evaluations were three to five pages in length. Below is a small sample of some of their comments, chosen to provide insights into issues of success and concern in participating in this course. These comments are organized according to themes that were repeated by several students.

1. Posting to a LISTSERV vs. Speaking up in a Traditional Class

"I was very hesitant to write my first comment. I guess I felt exposed. Writing a comment allows for more scrutiny. Participating in [a traditional] class is easier. You say a brief comment and it is considered briefly".----Rochelle

"It was interesting to see how everyone interpreted the question, and then responded to each other. In a regular class, many people would not have contributed because they either felt uncomfortable speaking or feared repeating another person's comments."----Todd

"In a [traditional] classroom setting, not everyone is comfortable speaking. In a fast-paced class, individuals who need more time to process information before speaking, may not get the opportunity to be involved in the discussion."----Sonya

2. Time Commitment to an Asynchronous Course

"I will never fall behind on discussions again. It was awful trying to catch up on everyone's comments....I find the discussion more in-depth than a traditional course."----Bonnie

"I am enjoying reading the comments of my peers, but it is sometimes overwhelming to read all of the replies"----Lori

"They [asynchronous classes] are good learning opportunities if one is committed to the time it takes."----Joanna

3. Student/Instructor Roles

"Seems like we're all becoming more comfortable--much more interchange.... Dr. P's comments help center the discussion and move it forward."----Shelley

"Learning is very much alive! I can't wait to see where the discussion is going. There is always time for that extra comment or question. The bell never rings, and the class is never over....E-mates are always prepared."----Sonya

"I found it intriguing that I felt like I was in a classroom even though I was in front of a computer."----Paulette

"The system is relatively easy to use. Advice and assistance from the instructor were frequent and effective."----Dan

"It seems we [students] have more of a voice in the discussion."----Rochelle

"It is a totally different way of learning and sharing."----Judy

"This course requires students to read and prepare in order to participate and respond. It provides a good opportunity for learning."----Lori

"Increased reflection and intelligent discussion on my part and others in class."----Shelley

4. Convenience of Taking an Asynchronous Course

"As graduate students, most of us work. It is hard to travel from point A to point

B...Asynchronous classes are a solution to our high-paced, hectic lives."----Rick

"It is a more flexible form of class and allows one to participate around one's personal life."----Devorah

"The fact that I can log on at my convenience and as often as I want...I can work at my own pace."----Mirza

"[While] it reduces travel time, saves money, and people can work in the privacy of their homes, as a full-time working mother and student, it has been difficult to find the time every night to participate. In [a traditional] class, there are not disturbances from members of the family."---Teresa

D. Interpreting the Selected Student Evaluation Comments

The student evaluations provided good insight into some of the dynamics of asynchronous learning. It is interesting to note that even with this experienced group of teachers, concern about speaking up in a class exists. The asynchronous learning approach does not remove this aspect of a class but reshapes the concern from speaking up for a moment in a traditional class to opening oneself up to "more scrutiny" by having to write more extensive comments which become available for continual review. The students' evaluation comments indicate that while some students prefer speaking up in class, others do not. On the other hand, some students preferred having the time to develop their thoughts before expressing themselves which is not always possible in a traditional class because the discussion moves on. In designing asynchronous learning models, expanding the time provided for reflective activity is highly desirable. However, a balance in terms of time allocated for discussing a topic and student time commitments should be struck so that the discussion topic does not seem to "go on and on" without closure.

Asynchronous learning in this class took more time than would have been necessary in a traditional class. Reading and writing substantive LISTERV postings took more time than the normal exchanges in a traditional class. To a degree, students had to get used to this type of interaction. At the beginning of the course, their postings tended to be several paragraphs in length. This was the subject of one of the early monthly evaluation sessions, and the point was well made by the students themselves that while not wanting to inhibit anyone from expressing themselves, succinctness in posting LIST-SERV messages would be appreciated.

Student and instructor roles were changed in the asynchronous course. The students had more of a voice in the discussions. As mentioned earlier, the students on average made 30.66 postings per week while the instructor made 4.5 postings per week. Clearly, students were reading a good deal more of each other's comments/questions than those of the instructor. In addition, students were able to establish new threads that became the foci of a substantial part of some weeks' discussion.

The students in this class accepted this empowerment and responsibility. In conducting an asynchronous learning course, instructors should be prepared to share some of their traditional centeredness with the students. However, this does not mean that the instructor takes a laissez-faire approach; to the contrary, the instructor may have to be more involved as a facilitator of learning. It will also require additional time for the faculty member to adjust his or her teaching style to asynchronous activities.

A major reason for experimenting with asynchronous learning in a large urban university was to provide a convenience for students. While most students commented that this was indeed the case, ironically some cited distractions and disturbances at home that they would not have had in class at the college. While at home or work, the students remained available to their family or others as opposed to a traditional class, where the students are primarily available to the instructor and fellow students. This supports Anderson's observation that for many students, the demands of profession, family, and community provide little extra time at any hour, and that the physical relocation that normally occurs during face-to-face classes provides a spatial separation from day-to-day pressures and commitments. "This separation can provide the face-to-face participant with increased amounts of available time" ([1], p. 133), a provocative caveat with which to conclude this discussion.

V. CONCLUSION

This study evaluated the student learning experiences with the instructional design components of an asynchronous course at a large urban university. The model developed for this course is considered appropriate for other faculty considering offering courses in an asynchronous mode. In considering the model, faculty should carefully assess the maturity and academic preparedness of their students as well as the subject matter of the course. Some adjustments and modifications will likely be necessary.

Lastly, it bears repeating that networking technology is changing rapidly. A few years ago, only a small percentage of academics in the United States and Western Europe, mostly in engineering and the sciences, were using computer networks for instruction on a regular basis. Today, the Internet and the Web are being used more frequently by educators at all levels, in all disciplines, and in all parts of the world. For those considering using networks as integral components of instruction as in asynchronous learning, on-going evaluation and study is highly recommended to determine if the techniques used meet the instructional needs of the students.

ACKNOWLEDGEMENTS

T his paper was made possible with the assistance of the Alfred P. Sloan Foundation, Dr. Frank Mayadas, Program Officer; the Hunter College Distance Learning Award Program, Dr. David Caputo, President; and the City University Open Systems Center, Dr. Michael Ribaudo, University Dean and Colette Wagner, Director. The author is grateful for their support.

REFERENCES

1. **Schlosser, C.A., & Anderson, M.L.** *Distance Education: Review of the Literature.*, DC: Association for Educational Communications and Technology, 1994.

2. **Moore, M.G. & Kearsley, G.** *Distance Education: A Systems View.* Belmont, CA: Publishing, 1996.

3. **Sherry, L.** "Issues in Distance Learning." *International Journal of Distance Education*, 1 (4), 337365, 1996.

4. **Ruberg, L. F., Taylor, C.D., & Moore, D.M.** "Student Participation and Interaction On-line: A Case Study of Two College Classes -- Freshman Writing and Plant Science Lab. "*International Journal of Educational Telecommunications*, 2 (1), 69-92, 1996.

5. **Newman, D.** "Cognitive and Technical Issues in the Design of Educational Computer Networking." In L.M. Harasim (Ed.), *On-line Education: Perspectives on a New Environment* (pp. 99-116). New York Praeger, 1990.

6. **Lippman, M.** *Thinking in Education.* Cambridge: Cambridge University Press, 1991.

7. **Anderson, T. D.** "The Virtual Conference: Extending Professional Education in Cyberspace. *International Journal of Educational Telecommunications*, 2(2/3), 121-135, 1996.

8. **Sproull, L.S. & Kiesler, S.** *Connections: New Ways of Working in the Networked Organization.* Cambridge, MA: MIT, 1991.

9. **Mackay, W.E.** "Diversity in the Use of Electronic Mail: A Preliminary Inquiry." *Transactions on Office Information Systems*, 6(4), 380-397, 1989.

10. **Varian, H.** "The Information Economy." *Scientific American,* 273(3), 200-202, 1995.

11. **Trentin, G.** "Internet: Does it Really Bring Added Value to Education". *International Journal of Educational Telecommunications,* 2(2/3), 97-106, 1996.

12. **Stubbs, M.** *Language, Schools, and Classrooms.* London: Methuen, 1976.

ABOUT THE AUTHOR
(FOR THIS ARTICLE)

Anthony G. Picciano has twenty-seven years of administrative and teaching experience specializing in the areas of education administration and educational technology. He has managed and been a director of several large-scale technology projects in the City University and State University of New York and has held several major administrative positions including dean at the College of Staten Island and vice president at Hunter College. He has served as a consultant for a variety of public and private organizations including the New York City Board of Education, the New York State Department of Education, the U.S Coast Guard, and CITICORP.

Dr. Picciano completed his PhD at Fordham University in 1985 and is currently a professor in the

Education Administration and Supervision Program in the Department of Curriculum and Teaching at Hunter College. His teaching specializations include educational technology, organization theory, and research methods. He also has been a faculty fellow since 1994 at the City University Open Systems Laboratory, a facility dedicated to experimenting with advanced uses of instructional technology and to providing staff development programs for organizations including public schools, colleges, and private businesses. As part of his work with this Laboratory, he has made numerous presentations and conducts workshops and seminars for a variety of professional groups throughout the Northeast.

He has been involved with a number of major grants from the National Science Foundation, the U.S. Department of Education, IBM, and the Alfred P. Sloan Foundation. He is presently a project coordinator for the New York City Collaborative for Excellence in Teacher Preparation, an NSF-funded program designed to improve the teaching of science, mathematics, and technology in New York City schools.

His major research activity during the past five years has been in designing multimedia teaching and learning models. He has collaborated with The American Social History Project and Center for Media and Learning at CUNY on a number of projects dealing with subjects such as Irish immigration in the 1850s, women's rights and labor issues at the turn of the century, and school integration in the 1950s.

One of these programs, *The Five Points: A Multimedia Experience in Social History*, was selected to be part of a New Learning Technologies Exhibit, held in San Diego in 1992. His present research interests are centered on distance learning technologies including asynchronous learning using Internet tools and media distribution systems.

Dr. Picciano has written a number of articles for professional journals and publications such as the

Journal of Educational Multimedia and Hypermedia, Computers in the Schools, The Urban Review, Equity and Choice, and *EDUCOM Review*. His most recent book, *Educational Leadership and Planning for Technology* (1998, Simon & Schuster) is a revision of his previous work, *Computers in the Schools: A Guide to Planning and Administration* (1994, Macmillan Publishing).

APPENDIX B

Five Pillars of Quality Online Education

In 1997, Frank Mayadas, affirmed that any learner who engages in online education should have, at a minimum, an education that represents the quality of the provider's overall institutional quality. Any institution, he maintained, demonstrates its quality in five inter-related areas - learning effectiveness, access, scale (capacity enrollment achieved through cost-effectiveness and institutional commitment), faculty satisfaction, and student satisfaction. These five have become Sloan-C's **Five Pillars of Quality Online Education**, the building blocks which provide the support for successful online learning.

The **LEARNING EFFECTIVENESS** pillar is concerned with ensuring that online students are provided with a high-quality education. This means that online students' learning should at least be equivalent to that of traditional students. This does not necessarily mean that online learning experiences should duplicate those in traditional classrooms. Rather it means that instructors and course developers should take advantage of the unique characteristics of online environments to provide learning experiences that represent the distinctive quality of the institution offering them.

SCALE is the principle that enables institutions to offer their best educational value to learners and to achieve capacity enrollment. Institutional commitment to quality and finite resources require continuous improvement policies for developing and assessing cost-effectiveness measures and practices. The goal is to control costs so that tuition is affordable yet sufficient to meet development and maintenance costs -- and to provide a return on investment in startup and infrastructure. Metrics may compare the costs and benefits of delivery modes by discipline and educational level; faculty salary and workload; capital, physical plant and maintenance investments; equipment and communications technology costs; scalability options; and/or various learning processes and outcomes, such as satisfaction levels and retention rates. These types of comparison enable institutions to develop better strategic plans for market demand and capture; achieve capacity enrollment; develop brand recognition; and secure long-term loyalty among current and prospective constituents. Practices for scale help to leverage key educational resources while offering new online learning opportunities to students and faculty. Practices for scale help to leverage key educational resources while offering new online learning opportunities to students and faculty.

ACCESS provides the means for all qualified, motivated students to complete courses, degrees, or programs in their disciplines of choice. The goal is to provide meaningful and effective access throughout the entire student's life cycle. Access starts with enabling prospective learners to become aware of available opportunities through effective marketing, branding, and basic program information. It continues with providing program access (for example, quantity and variety of available program options, clear program information), seamless access to courses (for example, readiness assessment, intuitive navigability), and appropriate learning resources. Access includes three areas of support: academic (such as tutoring, advising, and library);

administrative (such as financial aid, and disability support); and technical (such as hardware reliability and uptime, and help desk). Effective practices for measuring increasing accessibility may analyze and apply the results student and provider surveys, narrative or case study description, focus groups, or other means of measuring access. Larger-scale access implementation may also result from mission-based strategic planning in a variety of institutional areas.

FACULTY SATISFACTION means that instructors find the online teaching experience personally rewarding and professionally beneficial. Personal factors contributing to faculty satisfaction with the online experience include opportunities to extend interactive learning communities to new populations of students and to conduct and publish research related to online teaching and learning. Institutional factors related to faculty satisfaction include three categories: support, rewards, and institutional study/research. Faculty satisfaction is enhanced when the institution supports faculty members with a robust and well-maintained technical infrastructure, training in online instructional skills, and ongoing technical and administrative assistance. Faculty members also expect to be included in the governance and quality assurance of online programs, especially as these relate to curricular decisions and development of policies of particular importance to the online environment (such as intellectual property, copyright, royalties, collaborative design and delivery). Faculty satisfaction is closely related to an institutional reward system that recognizes the rigor and value of online teaching. Satisfaction increases when workload assignments/assessments reflect the greater time commitment in developing and teaching online courses and when online teaching is valued on par with face-to-face teaching in promotion and tenure decisions. A final institutional factor -- crucial to recruiting, retaining, and expanding a dedicated online faculty -- is commitment to ongoing study of and enhancement of the online faculty experience.

STUDENT SATISFACTION reflects the effectiveness of all aspects of the educational experience. The goal is that all students who complete a course express satisfaction with course rigor and fairness, with professor and peer interaction, and with support services. Online students put a primary value on appropriate, constructive, and substantive interaction with faculty and other students. Effective professors help students achieve learning outcomes that match course and learner objectives by using current information and communications technologies to support active, individualized, engaged, and constructive learning. As consumers, students are satisfied when provider services-learning resources, academic and administrative services, technology and infrastructure support -- are responsive, timely, and personalized. Effective practices may analyze and apply the results of student and alumni surveys, referrals, testimonials or other means of measuring perceived satisfaction with learning communities. Student satisfaction is the most important key to continuing learning.

Retrieved from: https://cole2.uconline.edu/courses/209413/pages/five-pillars-of-quality-online-education Accessed: March 24, 2021

APPENDIX C

Selected List of Publications and Scholarship

Books

Picciano, A.G., Dziuban, C., Graham, C. & Moskal, P. (in press). *Blended learning: Research Perspectives, Volume 3.* New York: Routledge/Taylor & Francis, Publishers.

Jordan, C. & Picciano, A.G. (2020). *The community college in the post-recession reform era: Aims and outcomes of a decade of experimentation.* New York: Routledge/Taylor & Francis, Publishers.

Picciano, A.G. (2019). *Online Education: Foundations, Planning, and Pedagogy* (1ˢᵗ Ed). New York: Routledge/Taylor & Francis, Publishers.

Picciano, A.G. & Jordan, C. (2018). *CUNY's first fifty years: Triumphs and ordeals of a people's university.* New York: Routledge/Taylor & Francis, Publishers.

Dziuban, C.D., Graham, C.R., Ko, S. Moskal, P., Pacansky-Brock, M., Picciano, A.G., Rossen, S., Stein, J., and Ubell, R. (2018). *Online & Blended Learning: The Complete Volumes.* New York: Routledge/Taylor and Francis. This is an anthology of books on online learning.

Picciano, A.G. (2017). *Online education policy and practice: The past, present, and future of the digital university.* New York: Routledge/Taylor & Francis, Publishers.

Dziuban, C., Picciano, A.G., Graham, C. & Moskal, P. (2016). *Conducting research in online and blended learning environments: New pedagogical frontiers.* New York: Routledge/Taylor & Francis, Publishers.

Picciano, A.G., Dziuban, C., & Graham, C. (Eds.) (2014). *Blended Learning: Research Perspectives, Volume 2.* New York: Routledge/Taylor & Francis, Publishers.

Picciano, A.G. & Spring, J. (2013). *The Great American Education-Industrial Complex: Ideology, Technology and Profits.* New York: Routledge/Taylor & Francis, Publishers.

Picciano, A.G. (2011). *Educational Leadership and Planning for Technology (5th Ed.).* Boston: Pearson Education.

Picciano, A.G. and Dzuiban, C. (Eds.) (2007). *Blended Learning: Research Perspectives.* Needham, MA: The Sloan Consortium.

Picciano, A.G. (2006). *Data-Driven Decision Making for Effective School Leadership.* Columbus, OH: Pearson Education.

Picciano, A.G. (2006). *Educational Leadership and Planning for Technology (4th Ed.).* Upper Saddle River, NJ: Pearson/Merrill/Prentice-Hall.

Picciano, A.G. (2004). *Educational Research Primer.* London: Continuum Press.

Picciano, A.G. (2002). *Educational Leadership and Planning for Technology (3rd Ed.).* New York: Simon & Schuster/Prentice-Hall.

Picciano, A.G. (2001). *Distance Learning: Making Connections across Virtual Space and Time.* New York: Simon & Schuster/Prentice-Hall.

Picciano, A.G. (1998). *Educational Leadership and Planning for Technology (2nd Ed.).* New York: Simon & Schuster/Prentice-Hall.

Picciano, A.G. (1994). *Computers in the Schools: A Guide to Planning and Administration.* New York: Macmillan.

Editor of Special Issues/Editions

Picciano, A.G., Buban, J., Dringus, L, Moskal, P. (Ed.) (2018) Special Edition of the *Online Learning Journal* featuring articles that were considered the best papers delivered at the 2017-2018 Online Learning Consortium Conferences. Vol. 24(3). Needham, MA: The Online Learning Consortium.

Picciano, A.G., Buban, J., Dringus, L, Moskal, P. (Ed.) (2017). Special Edition of the *Online Learning Journal* featuring articles that were considered the best papers delivered at the 2016-20`7 Online Learning Consortium Conferences. Vol. 23(3). Needham, MA: The Online Learning Consortium.

McDonald, P., Moskal, P. & Picciano, A.G. (Ed.) (2016). Special Edition of the *Online Learning Journal* featuring articles that were considered the best papers delivered at the 2015-16 Online Learning Consortium Conferences. Vol. 20(3). Needham, MA: The Online Learning Consortium.

Picciano, A.G. (2015). Editor for a Special Issue of *Education Sciences* on the theme *Blended Learning: A Global Perspective. http://www. mdpi.com/journal/education/special_issues/blended-learning*

McDonald, P. & Picciano, A.G. (Eds.) (November, 2014). Special Edition of *Online Learning* (formerly the *Journal of Asynchronous Learning Networks*) on the theme *Blended Learning in the Health Sciences: Four Investigations from George Washington University.* Vol. 18(4). Needham. MA: The Online Learning Consortium.

Dringus, L., Fidalgo, H., Picciano, A. & Vignare, K. (Eds.) (February, 2014). Special Edition of the *Journal of Asynchronous Learning Networks* on the theme *A Universe of Possibilities.* Vol. 17(4). Needham, MA: The Sloan Consortium.

Dringus, L. & Picciano, A.G. (Ed.) (2012). Special Edition of the *Journal of Asynchronous Learning Networks* featuring articles that were considered the best papers delivered at the 17th Annual International Sloan-C Conference on Online Learning. Vol. 16 (5). Needham, MA: The Sloan Consortium.

Banerjee, G. & Picciano, A.G. (Ed.) (2011). Special Edition of the *Journal of Asynchronous Learning Networks* featuring articles on blended learning specifically the theme *Transitioning to Blended Learning.* Vol. 15 (1). Needham, MA: The Sloan Consortium.

Picciano, A.G. (Ed.) (2009). Special Edition of the *Journal of Asynchronous Learning Networks* featuring articles on blended learning specifically the theme *Blending with Purpose*. Vol. 13 (1). Needham, MA: The Sloan Consortium.

Picciano, A.G. (Ed.) (2007). Special Edition of the *Journal of Asynchronous Learning Networks* featuring research on Online Learning in K-12 Schools and Teacher Education. Vol. 11 (3). Needham, MA: The Sloan Consortium.

Articles/Chapters/Reviews (Sample)

Picciano, A.G. (in press). Online learning, COVID-19, and the future of the academy: Implications for faculty governance and collective bargaining. *Journal of Collective Bargaining in the Academy*, Vol. 12.

Picciano, A.G. (September 2019). Artificial intelligence and the academy's loss of purpose!

Online Learning, 23(3). https://olj.onlinelearningconsortium. org/index.php/olj/article/view/2023

Picciano, A.G. (September 2017). Theories and frameworks for online education: Seeking an integrated model. *Online Learning, 21*(3). https:// olj.onlinelearningconsortium.org/index.php/olj/article/view/1225

Ciabocchi, E., Ginzberg, A., & Picciano, A.G. (September, 2016). A study of faculty governance leaders' perceptions of online and blended learning. *Online Learning, 20 (3)*.

Picciano, A.G. (December 2015). Planning for online education: A systems model. *Online Learning* (formerly the *Journal of Asynchronous Learning Networks*), *19(5)*. https://olj. onlinelearningconsortium.org/index.php/olj/issue/view/47

Dziuban, C. & Picciano, A.G. (June 16, 2015). The evolution continues: Considerations for the future of research in online and blended learning. EDUCAUSE Center for Analysis and Research (ECAR) Bulletin http://www.educause.edu/library/resources/evolution-continues-considerations-future-research-online-and-blended-learning

Picciano, A.G. (2014). A critical reflection of the current research in online and blended learning. *Lifelong Learning in Europe (LLinE), 4.* http://www.lline.fi/en/article/research/442014/a-critical-reflection-of-the-current-research-in-online-and-blended-learning

McDonald, P. & Picciano, A.G. (November, 2014). Introduction to the Special Edition of *Online Learning* (formerly the *Journal of Asynchronous Learning Networks*) on the theme *Blended Learning in the Health Sciences: Four Investigations from The George Washington University.* Needham. MA: The Online Learning Consortium.

Picciano, A.G. (September 2014). Big data and learning analytics in blended learning environments: Benefits and concerns. *Interactive Journal of Artificial Intelligence and Interactive Multimedia. 2(7).* pp. 35-43.

http://www.ijimai.org/journal/sites/default/files/journals/IJIMAI20142_7.pdf

Picciano, A.G., Seaman, J., & Day, S. (2014). Online learning in Illinois high schools: The voices of principals. In *Exploring the Effectiveness of Online Education in K-12 Environments* (Heafner T.L., Hartshorne, R., & Petty, T., Editors). Oakland: Idea Group, U.S.A.

Picciano, A.G. (February 2014). Introduction to the Special Edition of the *Journal of Asynchronous Learning Networks: A Universe of Possibilities.* 17(4). Needham, MA: The Sloan Consortium.

Picciano, A.G. February 2014). MOOCS: The hype, the backlash, and the future. University Outlook. Pp. 6-9. http://universityoutlook.uberflip.com/i/260407/2

Picciano, A.G. (2014). Review of Social foundations of education, 3rd Edition by Castelli, P.A. & Castelli, V. L. Durhan, NC: Carolina Academic Press. *Teachers College Record, January 17, 2014.*

http://www.tcrecord.org/Content.asp?ContentID=17385

Graham, C., Picciano, A.G., Kaufman, T., Popham, J.A., & Wiley, D. (2013). Data-driven decision making in the K-12 classrooms, In the *Handbook of Research on Educational Communications and*

Technology (Spector, J.M., Merrill, M.D., Ellen, J. & Bishop,M.J., Editors). New York: Springer.

Picciano, A.G. (June 2012). The evolution of big data and learning analytics in American higher education. *Journal of Asynchronous Learning Networks, 16*(3). http://sloanconsortium.org/jaln/v16n3/evolution-big-data-and-learning-analytics-american-higher-education

Picciano, A.G., Seaman, J., Shea, P. & Swan, K. (Summer 2011) Examining the extent and nature of online learning in American K-12 education: The research initiatives of the Alfred P. Sloan Foundation. *The Internet and Higher Education.*

Picciano, A.G., Seaman, J., & Allen, I.E. (2010). Educational transformation through online learning: To be or not to be. *Journal of Asynchronous Learning Networks*, 14, (4).

http://sloanconsortium.org/sites/default/files/2_jaln14-4_picciano.pdf

Picciano, A.G. & Seaman, J. (2010). *Class Connections: High School Reform and the Role of Online Learning.* Boston: Babson College Survey Research Group.

http://www3.babson.edu/Newsroom/Releases/online-high-school-learning.cfm

Picciano, A.G. & Seaman, J. (2009). *K–12 Online Learning: A 2008 Follow-Up of the Survey of U.S. School District Administrators.* Needham, MA: The Sloan Consortium.

http://www.sloan-c.org/publications/survey/pdf/k-12_online_learning_2008.pdf

Picciano, A.G. (2009). Blending with purpose: The multimodal model. *Journal of the Research Center for Educational Technology*, 5(1). Kent, OH: Kent State University.

http://www.rcetj.org/index.php/rcetj/article/view/11

Picciano, A.G. (2009). Blending with purpose: The multimodal model. Journal of Asynchronous Learning Networks, 13 (1). Needham, MA: The Sloan Consortium. pp. 7-18.

Picciano, A.G. (2009). Developing and nurturing resources for effective data-driven decision making practice. In *Handbook of Data-Based Decision Making in Education* (Kowalski, T.J. & Lasley, T. J., Editors). Mahwah, NJ: Lawrence Erlbaum Associates, A Division of Routledge Publishing.

Picciano, A.G. & Steiner, R. (2008). Bringing the real world of science to children: A partnership of the American Museum of Natural History and the City University of New York. *Journal of Asynchronous Learning Networks*, 12(1). Needham, MA: The Sloan Consortium. This article was also selected to be part of a website dedicated to the United Nations commemorating 2008 as the "Year of the Child". http://www.distanceandaccesstoeducation.org/Results.aspx?searchMode=3&criteria=en

Picciano, A.G. (2007). Interview with Chris Dede. *Journal of Asynchronous Learning Networks*, 11(3). Needham, MA: The Sloan Consortium.

http://www.sloan-c.org/publications/jaln/v11n3/v11n3_2dedeinterview_member.asp

Picciano, A.G. & Seaman, J. (2007). K-12 online learning: A survey of U.S. school district administrators. Journal of Asynchronous Learning Networks, 11(3). Needham, MA: The Sloan Consortium.

http://www.sloan-c.org/publications/jaln/v11n3/v11n3_3piccianoseaman_member.asp

Mayadas, A.F. & Picciano, A.G. (2007). Blended learning and localness: The means and the end. Journal of Asynchronous Learning Networks, 11,1). http://www.sloan-c.org/publications/jaln/v11n1/v11n1_1mayadaspicciano_member.asp

Picciano, A.G. (2006). Online learning: Implications for higher education pedagogy and policy. *Journal of Thought, 41* (1), pp. 75-94.

Picciano, A.G. (2006). Blended learning: Implications for growth and access. *Journal of Asynchronous Learning Networks, 10,*(3). http://www.sloan-c.org/publications/jaln/v10n3/index_member.asp

Dziuban, C., Hartman, J., Niemic, M., Oakley, B., Otte, G. Picciano, A.G., and Schroeder, R. (Spring 2006). Report on the first Sloan-C workshop on blended learning in higher education. In J. C. Moore (ed.) *Elements of Quality Online Education: Engaging Communities, Wisdom from the Sloan Consortium, Volume 6*. Needham, MA: The Sloan Consortium.

Picciano, A.G. (2004). Assessment, online learning, and a faculty perspective: A course case study. In *Elements of Quality Online Education: Into the Mainstream, Volume 5* by Bourne, J. and Moore, J.C. The Sloan Consortium. pp. 215-226.

Picciano, A.G. (2004). Assessment, challenges, and opportunities for online learning. In *Elements of Quality Online Education: Into the Mainstream, Volume 5* by Bourne, J. and Moore, J.C. The Sloan Consortium. pp. 177-184.

Picciano, A.G. (2004). The Internet: Social issues and the young. In *Smart School Leaders: Leading with Emotional Intelligence* Patti, J. and Tobin, J. (editors). Dubuque, Iowa: Kendall Hunt, Publishers. pp. 356-361.

Picciano, A.G. (September, 2003). Digital diploma mills and accreditation. Editorial in *Sloan-C View: Perspectives in Quality Online Education, 2*(6).

http://www.sloan-c.org/publications/view/v2n5/coverv2n6.htm

Picciano, A.G. (2002). Review of Increasing Student Learning Through Multimedia Projects by Simkins, M., Cole, K., Tavalin, F., & Means,

B. Alexandria, VA: ASCD. *Teachers College Record, 105*(4), pp. 691-693. http://www.tcrecord.org/Content.asp?ContentID=11056

This was selected as one of the top three book reviews for 2002 by the Teachers College Record.

Picciano, A.G. (2002). Beyond student perceptions: Issues of interaction, presence, and performance in an online course. *Journal of Asynchronous Learning Networks, 6*(1). http://www.aln.org/alnweb/journal/jaln-vol6issue1.htm

Picciano, A.G. (2002). Developing a Web-based course model at an urban university. *Berufs und Wirschaftspadagogik – Online* ISSN 1618-8543l, (June 2002). http://www.bwpat.de/

Bourne, J., Oakley, B., & Picciano, A.G. (2001). Executive Summary of the *Proceedings of the 2000 Sloan Summer Workshop on Asynchronous Learning Networks.* Center for Asynchronous Learning Networks.

Picciano, A.G. (2000). Computer learning. *In Encyclopedia of Psychology,* A.E. Kazin (Ed). American Psychological Association and Oxford University Press.

Picciano, A.G. (2000). Discussion of The University of Wisconsin-Stout Asynchronous Learning Network case study in *On-Line Education: Learning Effectiveness and Faculty Satisfaction.* Center for Asynchronous Learning Networks, 99-100.

Picciano, A.G. (1998). Developing an asynchronous course model for a large, urban university. *Journal of Asynchronous Learning Networks, 2*(1), pp. 3-19.

http://www.aln.org/publications/jaln/v2n1/v2n1_picciano.asp

Picciano, A.G. (1996). Collaboration, constructivism, and computing: Integrating pedagogical approaches to create active learning environments. CUE Newsletter, Summer 1996, pp. 4-5.

Picciano, A.G. (1994).Technology and the evolving educational-industrial complex, *Computers in the Schools, 11*(2), pp. 85101.

Picciano, A.G. (1994). The Lincoln School and the General Education Board. *Rockefeller Archive Center Newsletter,* Fall 1994, pp. 35.

Picciano, A.G. (1994). The Development and evaluation of a multimedia model for teaching social history. Technology and Teacher Education Annual, Vol. 4, pp. 478481.

Picciano, A.G. (1994). Computers, decision making and college administration. *Computers in the Schools, 9*(4), pp. 95106.

Picciano, A.G. (1993). The Five Points: The design of a multimedia program on social history. Journal of Educational Multimedia and Hypermedia, 2(2), pp. 129147.

Wagner, C. and Picciano, A.G. (1993). The View from within: A multimedia courseware development project at a large university Central Office and faculty perspectives. *EDUCOM Review, 28*(1), pp. 3035.

Gonzalez, G. and Picciano, A.G. (1993). QUEST: Developing competence, commitment, and an understanding of a community in a fieldbased, urban teacher education program. *Equity and Choice, 9*(2), pp. 3843.

Picciano, A.G. (1993). Using multimedia to teach social foundations in an urban teacher education program. Technology and Teacher Education Annual, Vol. 3, pp. 3640.

Picciano, A.G. (1992). Teaching technology in a field-based, undergraduate education program. *Technology and Teacher Education Annual, Vol.2,* pp. 350-353.

Picciano, A.G. (1991). Computers, city and suburb: A study of New York City and Westchester County public schools. *The Urban Review, 23*(3), pp. 191-206.

Picciano, A.G. and Kinsler, K. (1991). Hunter College's QUEST Program, computers and urban education. *Computers in the Schools*, 6(1-3), pp. 175-177.

Reports/Monographs (Sample):

Dabbagh, N., Bass, R., Bishop, M., Costelloe, S., Cummings, K., Freeman, B., Frye, M., Picciano, A. G., Porowski, A., Sparrow, J., & Wilson, S. J. (2019). Using technology to support postsecondary student learning: A practice guide for college and university administrators, advisors, and faculty. Washington, DC: Institute of Education Sciences, What Works Clearinghouse. (WWC 20090001) Washington, DC: National Center for Education Evaluation and Regional Assistance (NCEE), Institute of Education Sciences, U.S. Department of Education. https://whatworks.ed.gov.

Picciano, Anthony G. (2013). *Pioneering Higher Education's Digital Future: An Evaluation of the Alfred P. Sloan Foundation's Anytime, Anyplace Learning Program (1992-2012).*

https://aalp-sloan-report.gc.cuny.edu/resources/

Picciano, A.G. & Seaman, J. (2010). *Class Connections: High School Reform and the Role of Online Learning.* Boston: Babson College Survey Research Group.

https://www.onlinelearningsurvey.com/reports/class-connections.pdf

Picciano, A.G. & Seaman, J. (2009). *K–12 Online Learning: A 2008 Follow-Up of the Survey of U.S. School District Administrators.* Needham, MA: The Sloan Consor*Survey of U.S. School District Administrators.* Needham, MA: The Sloan Consortium.

http://www.sloan-c.org/publications/survey/ pdf/K-12_Online_Learning.pdf

Picciano, A.G. & Seaman, J. (2007). *K–12 Online Learning: A Survey of U.S. School District Administrators* Needham, MA: The Sloan Consortium. Needham, MA: The Sloan Consortium.

https://www.onlinelearningsurvey.com/reports/k-12-online-learning.pdf

In the 1980s, as part of my responsibilities at the College of Staten Island and in conjunction with work I was doing for the Middle States Association of Colleges and Universities, I conducted a series of studies on student outcomes including:

Student Attrition/Retention Study at The College of Staten Island

Office of Institutional Research (74 pps.) ERIC Identifier: ED192647

Study of Recent Alumni at The College of Staten Island

Office of Institutional Research (131 pps.) ERIC Identifier: ED212229

Student Satisfaction at The College of Staten Island

Office of Institutional Research (104 pps.) ERIC Identifier: ED197701

These studies served as models for institutional research offices throughout CUNY. I also was commended by the Middle States Association for my work on the above.

Creative Works:

Picciano, A.G. (2013). *Pioneering Higher Education's Digital Future: Twenty Years (1992-2012) of the Alfred P. Sloan Foundation's Anytime, Anyplace Learning Program.* This website documents the Alfred P. Sloan Foundation's grant program. It contains a plethora of material including an evaluation report and video commentary. http://aalp-sloan-report.gc.cuny.edu/

Picciano, A.G. (2010). "Reflections". Video documenting the reflections and perceptions of major grant recipients of the Alfred P. Sloan Foundation's *Anytime, Anyplace Learning Program, 1992-2010.*

Picciano, A.G. (1996). "Central High." A multimedia program incorporating video from Blackside Inc. *Eyes on the Prize* with other video, images, and text to teach the issues involved with Brown v. Board of Education and the integration of Little Rock Central High School in 1957.

Brier, S., Brown, J., Vasquez, A. and Picciano, A.G. (1994). "Heaven Will Protect the Working Girl." A multimedia program incorporating video from The American Social History Project's *Who Built America?* series with other video, images, and text to teach about immigrant women working in the garment industry ("sweatshops") of New York City in the early 1900s.

Brier, S., Brown, J., Eynon, B., and Picciano, A.G. (1991). "The Five Points." A multimedia program incorporating video from the American Social History Project's *Who Built America?* series with other video, images, and text to teach about Irish immigrant life in New York City in the 1850s. This program was selected to be part of several exhibits including a national exhibit entitled "New Learning Technologies" held in San Diego, California and sponsored by IBM in June, 1992.

Name Index

Moskal, Patsy	7,8
Mulkeen, Tom	4
Murdoch, Bill	1
Murphy, Joe	4,5
Naples, Bruce	6
Nasaw, David	4
Nelson, Joseph	8
Nesbitt, Michael	5
Ng, Andrew	8
Nie, Norman	1,3
Niemiec, Mary	7
Niman, John	6
Norvid, Peter	8
Nwosu, Naomi	8
Oakley, Burks	7
O'Reilly, Patrick	8
Ortiz, Mary	5
Otte, George	7
Panero, Nell	9
Papert, Seymour	6
Pappas, Liza	8
Paradise, Ed	4
Patti, Janet	7,9
Penna, Terri	4
Petersen, Brian	7
Petrides, Mike	4
Petrone, Grace	4
Phillip, Manfred	7
Plyter, Norm	3
Polesinelli, Maryann	8
Polishook, Irwin	7
Porowski, Allan	9
Priestrer, Lorraine	4
Proshansky, Harold	5